A Journey Beyond

What They Say about G. Ross Freeman

"Ross served as my mentor and teacher about the church and how we could best use media effectively in the church. His vision and help were invaluable to me in the development of GNTV. . . ."
—Donald R. Wood

"Nothing means more to us than to claim Ross and Bess as dear friends of long standing. They have honored us several times by staying in our home. We admire them very much. . . ."
—Isaac and Nona Bunce

"Ross Freeman has been a blessing to me as long as I have known him. . . ."
—Leonard Grace

"Thanks a lot for doing this for Ross. I am glad to be a part of the plan. . . ."
—Will Peterson

"I appreciate the opportunity of being a part of such a deserving project in honor of G. Ross Freeman."
—John Sherer

"Ross can get the best out of you and never criticize the bad in you. . . ."
—Roy Lifsey

"Ross is a consummate communicator with an interest in every possible communication tool that can help spread the gospel message. He has personally utilized these tools in his work for the kingdom throughout his active ministry and now in retirement. . . ."
—Alice Smith

"We knew he was a worker, always reaching out for new ideas and helping us to reach out so that we could do more than we realized in our country church. . . ."
—Joyce Youmans

"Laity appreciated him for strong leadership in empowering them for ministry. . . ."
—Dean Milford

"I have never known a more energetic minister. I doubt that there is anyone in the church who has been as creative; who knows it better; or who can articulate its needs, its history and its future as well as Ross Freeman. He has proven himself wise with common sense and practical understanding. Throughout his career, he has been resolute, uncompromising with courage to support sometimes unpopular causes. . . ."
—Bishop Richard C. Looney

A Journey Beyond

The Autobiography of
G. Ross Freeman

PROVIDENCE HOUSE PUBLISHERS
Franklin, Tennessee

Copyright 2001 by G. Ross Freeman

All rights reserved. Written permission must be secured from the publisher to use or reproduce any part of this book, except for brief quotations in critical reviews or articles.

Printed in the United States of America

05 04 03 02 01   1 2 3 4 5

Library of Congress Catalog Card Number: 2001087929

ISBN: 1–57736–211–X

Cover design by Gary Bozeman

PROVIDENCE HOUSE PUBLISHERS
238 Seaboard Lane Franklin, Tennessee 37067
800-321-5692
www.providencehouse.com

To Bess

whose habit of happiness,
generosity of spirit,
and unselfish love
has made this
journey a constant surprise
and our home
a delight.

Contents

PREFACE AND ACKNOWLEDGMENTS	ix
PROLOGUE: THE PARTY	xiii
1. ENTERING THE STREAM	3
2. TRAVELING RURAL CIRCUITS	19
3. EXTENDING HORIZONS	41
4. ENABLING PASTORS	61
5. INSPIRING LAITY	81
6. RELISHING MINISTRY	103
7. ENCOURAGING MEN	129
8. ENJOYING THE LARGER CHURCH	147
9. UNDERSTANDING THE JURISDICTION	173
10. COOPERATING WITH LEADERS	195
11. DREAMING FOR THE FUTURE	215
12. MAKING THE STORY PUBLIC	233
EPILOGUE: BEYOND THE PARTY	251
ABOUT THE AUTHOR	266

Members of the Southeastern Jurisdiction Association of Conference Presidents of United Methodist Men taken at Lake Junaluska during the November 2000 meeting. These were the men who insisted that this book be written.

Preface and Acknowledgments

This story would never have been written had it not been for the Southeastern Jurisdiction Association of Conference Presidents of United Methodist Men. President Denver King from Kingsport, Tennessee, recognized Roy Lifsey from South Georgia and approached him with an idea.

Always ready with an innovative proposal to advance United Methodist Men, Roy suggested that the association authorize a project that might rally the men.

Questions were raised immediately. What kind of project? How would the group get money for it? Who would head it up?

Roy had their attention.

"Since Ross Freeman has meant so much to the men, let's do something for the jurisdiction to honor him," he continued.

They were interested.

Roy pushed it.

"Why don't we sponsor the publication of his biography, sell the books and use the proceeds to raise money for what ever project we select?"

The association liked the idea in principle. They authorized Roy and Walter Johnson to investigate the writing and publication of a book. All of this was to be kept secret until information could be collected and reported back to see if such a project was feasible. The Association received the facts and voted for the next steps.

Suddenly they ran into a dilemma. How could such a project be undertaken without getting the information from me and my files? Roy and Walter Johnson consulted my son George.

"He has to know. It can't be done as a surprise," George advised them.

I rebelled at the idea. "It's unthinkable. There's not enough to write about. Nobody is interested."

They insisted that the men wanted to do it. How could I deny my friends the privilege? Plans were already underway. I would have to allow it, they insisted.

Several authors were suggested, including Gregg Lewis who has become famous for writing the life stories of people including several books on Promise Keepers. Gregg's father was a professor at Asbury Theological Seminary. Gregg's father-in-law and mother-in-law were both members of the North Georgia Conference. Gregg and his family were active members of the Trinity United Methodist Church in Rome. My son George was their pastor. Gregg knew me and was interested in my story. He would be ideal.

Unfortunately he was completely contracted for three or more years in the future and couldn't touch it.

In the meantime I had started collecting memories and material. I even drafted a possible outline for organizing the files. Several members of the committee saw it. Roy Lifsey showed it to Jim Snead. Jim discussed it with Andrew Miller, of Providence House Publishers in Franklin, Tennessee. Andrew is the son of a United Methodist minister. Jim and Roy talked to him about an author who might undertake the story.

After seeing the notes I prepared and knowing something of my background, he suggested that I write an autobiography.

So the committee followed his counsel. They reasoned that since my career ended as an editor and they remembered other things I had written, they would persuade me to write it. I finally yielded, and gave myself to it.

These pages have been written from my perspective, from my little corner of the universe. This is my view of what

Preface and Acknowledgments

happened in my life. Seen from any other angle, especially God's, the picture will be quite different. It is therefore not to be taken as gospel. Nor is its historical accuracy guaranteed. I have not willfully said anything untrue, but memory can embellish facts when they are recalled at this stage of the journey.

It is my autobiographical story—movements and experiences in which I have been involved—seen in retrospect. Recognize that I didn't do any of this alone. I was only a small participant in a much larger picture. I make no pretense of telling the whole story.

As Ernie Pyle said in writing about the foot soldiers in World War II, "These men and women saw the war in terms of what was happening within ten feet on each side of them." Others could report the grand sweep of battles and what was happening to nations and civilization. He wrote what the lonely soldier felt in the foxhole. It is in that same sense that I am telling what happened to me along this journey.

The title envokes two images. I have always felt that I was on "a journey," with no permanent abiding place, always traveling. Somewhere there is Scripture for that. We are pilgrims, citizens of another country, only passing through this life.

The other image is that "beyond" the present situation there is something more. From my earliest years, I have considered myself under appointment. Bishop Arthur J. Moore drilled the idea into me when I was very young. In those years when he read the appointments, he closed with, "As a Methodist preacher, you are to go where sent, and to stay away from where you have been." His word for me was the authority of the church.

When I was assigned a new job, I learned all I could about it, gave it everything I had, and did my best to make a difference while I was there. I followed three rules: (1) Never criticize my predecessor; (2) Never second-guess my successor; and (3) Never envy what is done for those who follow me.

Whether it was good or bad, I tried to follow those rules. I felt that way about the churches I served, my years at Emory, my time on the Macon District, my tenure with the Jurisdictional Council and Junaluska, and those weekly deadlines with the *Wesleyan Christian Advocate*. I had my day in each place. When I moved on, I never looked back. Each new adventure consumed me. I went running to it eagerly, and, in the spirit of Paul, "Forgetting those things which are behind, I press forward . . . ," responding to the demands of what lay ahead.

Memories linger of special friends who have enriched my life. You know my special debt to you. Some ties have continued many years and held strong across many miles regardless of my official appointments.

So the story begins.

Thanks to these wonderful people and others who made this story and encouraged its publication:

Charles and Millie Adams
William F. Appleby
Briarcliff United Methodist Men
H. Reginald Broxton
Larry Bryant
Isaac and Nona Bunce
Lee and Martha Cain
Charles Cason
Correll Cowart
Herschel Darsey
Ed and Kathy Deen
John Dickerson
John Dowell
Joe Giddens
Leonard Grace
Myles Greene
Carlos Greenway
Joe Hamilton
Chick Harvey
Guy K. Hutcherson
Norman P. Johnson
Walter L. Johnson
Joe Kilpatrick
Denver King
Roy and Jean Lifsey
Liberty UMC United Methodist Men
Richard C. Looney
Harold and JoeAnn Lumley
Leland McKeown
Donnie and Jane Morris
Montene Morris
North Georgia Conference United Methodist Men
Norman Paschall
Will Peterson
J. Taylor Phillips
Princeton UMC United Methodist Men
Gene Rankin
Marlene King Richards
Paul Shell
John Sherrer
Alice Smith
James H. Snead
B. R. Snooks
Statesboro First United Methodist Church
Charles Steele
Benham Stewart
Thomasville District United Methodist Men
Mrs. Willard Taylor
Eddie Ray and Gwen Upchurch
Larry Walden
Joseph V. White
Charles Williamson Jr.
Wytheville District (VA) United Methodist Men
Harry Woodson
Elmo and Elaine Wright

Prologue: The Party

"Tonight we pay tribute to one of the best enablers and motivators of laypeople I have ever known as he retires from the South Georgia Conference," Judge J. Taylor Phillips began the program after dinner.

It was hard for me to realize that he, and the others who followed him, were talking about me. Was the boy from the "other" side of the tracks in the small town of Tennille, Georgia, in the wrong place?

I was not prepared for the crowd, or the individuals who came at some sacrifice to be present, when I walked into the banquet hall of Mulberry Street United Methodist Church that night in 1993.

I knew the *Advocate* board had planned something. I thought it would be a small dinner for members of the board and staff of the *Wesleyan Christian Advocate* with maybe a gift to bid us farewell. After all I was completing seven years as editor. Tradition dictated something be done in recognition of my retirement.

Our children had wanted to plan a party for us marking fifty-two years under appointment, but we refused to allow it. Then one day in the late spring, Don Kea called to tell me to reserve June 3, 1993, for something they were planning. I couldn't refuse what my board instructed me to do. I didn't want to be fired before I retired.

So the Board of Directors of the *Advocate* and the Georgia United Methodist Communications Council arranged the affair. They chose a steering committee, issued invitations, and proceeded. I just knew that they expected me to show up. The committee and those who were invited kept the details secret.

Members from every appointment I served during my career, save two, were present. Some of us had worked together back in the beginning of my ministry when I was city missionary in Macon. They had come from my days in Appling County, at Emory University, in Statesboro, in the Macon District, and in the conferences of the Southeastern Jurisdiction with their twenty-four jurisdictional associations. Others had labored together in causes like the soil and water conservation effort, the rural church program, the lay witness movement, Discover God's Call. Several were there from days with the conference lay leaders, and especially leaders representing United Methodist Men.

Active and retired ministers, district superintendents and lay officials from both conferences took time to drive to Macon for the occasion. Pastors of the churches where our families held membership, the *Wesleyan Christian Advocate* board of directors and staff, the Georgia United Methodist Communications Council, and friends from the United Methodist Center where I had made my work-home for seventeen years were there.

Many had driven hours across the state and beyond to be present for the occasion. My children and grandchildren and great-grandchildren were there. My first daughter and her husband came from California. Most of my extended family, within reach, set aside time to attend. Blood relatives, in-laws, church members, friends, colleagues, plus other well-wishers had traveled to Macon for the party.

Five bishops reserved one of their precious evenings to be present: Retired Bishop and Mrs. Mack B. Stokes, Bishop and Mrs. C. W. Hancock, and Bishop William R. Cannon. Bishop L. Scott Allen had expected to come, but his plan was interrupted. The two active Georgia Bishops were on the program:

Prologue: The Party

Five Bishops and their wives honored us with their presence at the Retirement Party planned by the Wesleyan Christian Advocate Board and the Georgia United Methodist Communications Council at Mulberry Street Church in Macon June 3, 1993. Standing with us, left to right: Bishop C. W. Hancock, Bishop William R. Cannon, Bishop Richard C. Looney, and Bishop Lloyd Knox. Bishop and Mrs. Mack B. Stokes were also there. Bishop and Mrs. L. Scott Allen had arranged to attend, but their situation changed.

Bishop and Mrs. J. Lloyd Knox of the Atlanta area and Bishop and Mrs. Richard C. Looney of the South Georgia area.

Each face provoked memories of events and places where we had been together and things we had done. I was in a daze by such an extravagant outpouring of affection. I could not fully grasp the moment nor digest what was being said.

My practical mind sought relief by computing the hours the crowd drove to get there and how late they would be returning home, or if indeed they would have to spend the night.

Judge Phillips, president of the Georgia Communications Council, guided the affair and presented Don Kea, Bishop Looney, Bishop Cannon, and others to speak.

Dr. Donald R. Wood of Good News TV and Eddie Ray Upchurch of WUBI-TV in Baxley planned and produced the surprise video.

Don Wood and the staff of Good News Television, assisted by WUBI-TV in Baxley, had prepared a video about aspects of my life. Comments were recorded on video from Bishop Mack B. Stokes, Dean Milford, Donald R. Wood, my son George R. Freeman Jr., Joyce Youmans, Montene Morris, Donnie Morris, Jane Morris, Eddie Ray Upchurch, and Gwen Upchurch. Personal data had been gleaned surreptitiously from family albums and the memories of my friends.

Phrases danced in and out of my awareness as one after another appeared on the television screen to say nice things. It was unreal. They seemed to be talking about somebody else.

"Ross has an unbelievable variety of gifts and skills; he has been a good administrator, a good thinker, a good preacher, blessed with an uncanny ability to communicate with people . . ."

Prologue: The Party

"We knew he was a worker, always reaching out for new ideas and helping us to reach out so that we could do more than we realized in our country church . . ."

"They came into our lives in 1947 and have been a great inspiration to our family ever since . . ."

"The Freeman household was always open to relatives, friends, strangers, or anybody in need. When we were growing up, there was always somebody else living with us. We children counted twenty-three different people who lived with us from a month to three years: students, family members of long-term patients in the Emory Hospital, older people who needed a haven until arrangements could be made, young girls who were pregnant and needed a safe place for a while . . ."

"Ross gave the church tremendous leadership in his capacity as executive director of the Southeastern Jurisdictional Council on Ministries . . ."

"He never imposed or demanded but was always willing to share from the depth of his heart and experience. He had the capacity to hear what others were saying . . ."

"Laity appreciated him for strong leadership in empowering them for ministry . . ."

"When Bishop Joel McDavid created a Blue Ribbon Committee to develop a comprehensive plan of communication for Georgia, we turned to Ross for guidance as chairman. This plan, like so many others, bears the imprint of Ross Freeman's genius . . ."

"His love for people and the church was evident in all his appointments. See what he accomplished among the poor as Macon city missionary; in churches of the Darien circuit, the Baxley circuit, the Woodstock circuit, Statesboro First; through the connectional ministry at Candler School of Theology; Macon District Superintendent; executive director of the Southeastern Jurisdictional Council on Ministries; as editor of the *Wesleyan Christian Advocate*; as spokesman for the small church movement, the United Methodist Rural Fellowship, the Hinton Rural Life Center; the Protestant Radio and Television Center, the Good News TV, the Southeastern Jurisdiction TV Network; and in countless General Church assignments for studying the ministry and planning for the future."

A Journey Beyond

My admiration for Mack B. Stokes began in 1953 when he welcomed me as a co-laborer fifteen years ago at the Candler School of Theology. After Dean Stokes was elected Bishop and assigned to the Jackson, Mississippi, area and retired to Atlanta, the friendship continued. Bishop Stokes reflected on the video: "It makes me sad to realize that he is no longer going to be editor of the *Wesleyan Christian Advocate*. He's done a marvelous job as editor. Under his leadership it became one of the best journals in the whole church. He deserves a great deal of credit."

The video left me wondering and dizzy.

Before I could absorb it, the formal statements began.

These excerpts from statements by Bishop Cannon, Bishop Looney, and Dr. Kea indicate reasons for my blushing embarrassment.

BISHOP WILLIAM R. CANNON

"He was only twenty-nine when I invited him to join my administration," Bishop Cannon said in recalling how our years started at the Candler School of Theology.

"When he came for the interview, his calm, his graciousness, his self-confidence, and his brilliant mind impressed me. As soon as I stated a case, he immediately comprehended it. When I outlined a problem, he had a solution. We worked side by side for fourteen years at Emory. We proved to be kindred souls. He relieved me of a lot of burdens, took on difficult situations with students, and knew how to manage things.

"When I came back to Georgia as bishop, he was superintendent of the Macon District. He was always thoroughly prepared, always conscientious, and never took advantage of our friendship to get favors for himself or his friends. He was a wonderful superintendent. Whatever he did, he did in an unassuming, self-effacing way.

"He proved to be one of the statesmen of the church. He said what needed to be said, he took a stand on issues, and he would not compromise his convictions for anything. We deprived the church of so much in not having him in the Council of Bishops. No one could have adorned the office more nor done things which we needed to have done in the church than he."

Prologue: The Party

BISHOP RICHARD C. LOONEY

"I first met Ross Freeman when I was a student at the Candler School of Theology," Bishop Looney said in speaking at the retirement banquet.

"We have all followed his illustrious career with gratitude for the way not only South Georgia but the whole church has been served.

"I have never known a more energetic minister. I doubt that there is anyone in the church who has been as creative; who knows it better; or who can articulate its needs, its history and its future as well as Ross Freeman. He has proven himself wise with common sense and practical understanding. Throughout his career, he has been resolute, uncompromising with courage to support sometimes unpopular causes.

"When I came to the South Georgia area as Bishop seventeen years later, evidence of his leadership as superintendent of the Macon District remained. I often wonder what he could have done with an Annual Conference or an Area. One of the tragedies of the church in our time may have been that he was not turned loose to be a bishop."

DR. DON KEA

"We honor tonight one who has demonstrated gifts as a pastor, an authority in the rural church, and a leader of the United Methodist Church. He served with distinction as an administrator of our leading seminary, as a district superintendent, and as a denominational executive of the nine southeastern states," Dr. Don Kea, chairperson of the board of directors of the *Wesleyan Christian Advocate*, commented at the retirement party.

"In every situation, he has proven to be one of the very finest visionaries that the South Georgia Conference has produced. Not only is he a dreamer; he is a doer who gets things done. Though his record in each assignment has been enviable, his greatest legacy will probably stand as his seven years as editor of the *Wesleyan Christian Advocate*. He was the right person at the right place at the right time.

A Journey Beyond

"He came to the post at a critical time in the long, long history of the *Advocate*. Winds of change were sweeping through the newspaper world. Fewer and fewer people were reading. Postage and printing costs were spiraling upward. Subscriptions were eroding. Technology was making time-proven methods obsolete. New looks, new formats, new writing styles emphasizing visual attractiveness were demanded. Publications that did not adapt to these changes were fading out of existence. The board followed the lead of the editor and plunged into the computer age. Efficiency and productivity of the staff responded. Quiet shifts in the format made the paper more attractive and readable. An aggressive search for newsworthy material, and a telegraphic style which appealed to a television oriented generation, appealed to church people. The new provocative editorial policy sometimes created controversy. Hot letters were mailed to the chairman and other members of the board. Even the bishops caught their share of criticism for something the editor said or wrote.

"But he caused us all to think. The financial picture began to change. Red ink losses were gradually converted to black ink surpluses. Treasurer Martha Berry presented a glowing financial picture at the board meeting a few weeks ago.

"At that meeting Dr. Freeman reported to the board that during his watch as editor, the staff had produced 350 weekly editions of the *Advocate* with a total of 4,550 pages. These pages translated into column inches equaled 2,835,000 inches of copy. This was enough to produce 945 books of 300 pages during his seven years at the *Advocate*.

"He confided to the board a secret which he and Bess had not shared with anybody else, not even their children. I am presuming to break their confidence tonight. He always has been, as you know, in demand as a preacher, teacher, and retreat leader. He and Bess decided, when they accepted the position as editor, to accept such invitations as they could schedule without jeopardizing any work of the editor. They agreed, after deducting travel and other expenses, to divide any honoraria between special needs of the *Advocate* and gifts to ministerial students."

Prologue: The Party

A FLASH BACK

While these plaudits were embarrassing me, my mind flashed back to a scene more than fifty years earlier. We gathered around a light bulb in the backyard of the Holloway family in one of the crowded communities in South Macon. Curious neighbors had come for a revival.

In those days I was a student at Mercer University and served as city missionary in Macon. My assignment was to *be* the church with people in the three neediest slum areas of Macon.

Visiting in the homes one day, I asked if we could have a revival in that neighborhood. They said, "Of course not; we don't even have a church." I suggested that we ask several people to let us have a service in their homes. We might get four or five who would be willing. If so we could ask other people to gather in.

They got excited about the possibility. Their neighbors came. Before the week was over, we had more people than could fit in the small rooms. So Mr. Holloway invited us to move into his backyard and continue. He put up some rough, sawmill slab benches in the small yard, and hung an electric bulb in a tree. We had what was known then as "the backyard revival."

Services ran for two weeks. Fifty-four people were converted and requested baptism.

Not too long ago I received a letter from a woman in Columbus. She and her sister had been watching one of our television programs on GNTV in Macon, and they wanted to know if I was the same Ross Freeman who was in Macon in 1942 or 1943. If so, she had a picture of me with her daddy standing in their backyard in the south side of Macon. I was. She sent me a copy of the picture.

Other voices on that June 3, 1993, evening at Mulberry dimmed as the sounds and memories of that experience long ago came back to life.

The retirement party was drawing to a close.

Judge Taylor Phillips read a proclamation from the mayor of Macon designating "June 3, 1993 as G. Ross Freeman Day . . ."

in honor of the occasion, gave Bess and me matching watches in the tradition of retirement parties, and presented us a generous check.

Eddie Ray and Gwen Upchurch shocked us with the keys to a new car with the observation, "After driving the 1976 Volvo 250,000 miles up and down Georgia roads pursuing stories for the *Advocate*, we thought it best for you to drive into retirement with a new vehicle."

We didn't sleep much that night. We didn't even recall the menu, but memories were stirred. . . .

A Journey Beyond

CHAPTER ONE

Entering the Stream

My earthly pilgrimage began traumatically in Stillmore, a small village of Emanuel County, in southeast Georgia.

I was born in the front bedroom of Mr. and Mrs. George Glover—Uncle George and Aunt Leila, or "Sister." She was my mother's oldest sister. We called her Sister. That's what Mama called her.

I can only attest to what I was told about it later.

Much later.

It was part of the family legend that nobody talked about. Mama told me the story just before she died.

Mama and Daddy, and my older brother, Lester Monroe, moved to Stillmore from Toomsboro to be with Sister and her husband in 1923.

Mama had lived in Stillmore before. Her father, Andrew Ross, whom she called Poppa, was a section foreman on the railroad. He died in Norristown, September 1, 1917, and is buried in Stillmore. Mama, whose seventeenth birthday was fifteen days later, and her mother, Catherine Ross, moved to Toomsboro, Georgia, to live with her grandmother's youngest son, Olan Sanford Ross.

A JOURNEY BEYOND

In Toomsboro, Ollie Ross was attracted to Lester Freeman. He lived with his widowed mother, Ida Stephens Freeman. Ollie Ross and Lester Freeman were married seventeen months later on February 19, 1919.

She was a little over eighteen. He was twenty-three and seven months. Their first child, Lester Monroe, was born December 11, 1919. The parents of both Lester and Ollie were dead. She was pregnant. Daddy needed a job.

So Mama and Daddy moved to Stillmore in 1923 to work with Uncle George in his mercantile business. They sold groceries, fresh meat, dry goods, farm supplies, and provisions for sawmill people around the countryside.

Uncle George killed himself July 6, 1923.

The next morning Daddy went with "Sister" to Swainsboro to arrange with the undertaker for the funeral.

While they were gone, at that most inopportune time, I chose to make my appearance. I was born, July 7, 1923, in the same house where Uncle George had killed himself.

I was named for Uncle George. My middle name, Ross, was my mother's maiden surname. So I began the journey as George Ross Freeman.

Whether the tensions and traumas of that hot, hard summer warped my psyche and colored my general outlook on life, I don't know. If it is true, as the poet says, that we are a part of all that we have met, then it is quite likely that the highly charged emotional and tragic events into which I was born shaped my life in some measure.

FROM THESE ROOTS

Through the scholarly diligence of our brother Ramus in collecting genealogical data, we are just now learning, at the turn of the twenty-first century, some of the history of the two families that reach beyond the memories of our grandparents.

Our Ross family tree boasts strong Scotch-Irish roots. This branch of our forebears descended from the Ross clan from Scotland. Adventurous members migrated to England and Ireland and eventually to America. They were sturdy farmers with an abiding kinship with the soil. Some of the men

Entering the Stream

formed a part of the labor pool that built the railroads across the frontier.

Mama's grandfather, Thomas Ross, was a red-bearded Irishman born in Richmond County, Georgia. His son, Andrew Ross—a pure Scotch name—and Catherine Matilda Powell were married March 16, 1876, in Richmond County, Georgia. He was twenty-three; she was twenty. At one period he was overseer of a large plantation in Washington County near Augusta before he went to work for the railroad as a section foreman.

As a section foreman his responsibility was to ride the rails, clearing the right of way, replacing cross ties and rails for an assigned number of miles. His crew of three or four strong, hardworking laborers kept the railroad tracks in repair and safe.

Mama, Ollie Adel Ross, was the baby of eleven children, born when her mother was forty-four years old and her daddy was forty-six. When Poppa, as Mama called her father, died in 1917, she and her mother had to move out of the company-owned house in Norristown, Georgia. They moved to Toomsboro in Wilkinson County Georgia, and lived with Mama's youngest brother Olan, who was the Central of Georgia railroad agent there. Grandmother Ross died at age sixty-four, December 21, 1920, twenty-three months after Mama and Daddy married.

Somewhere the Ross ancestors met the Methodists. Strong religious convictions and godly righteousness can be traced through succeeding generations.

Our sources have not been able to prove one link in the Freeman generational chain because the census report did not name the children in a family at one period but recorded only the sex. Still we have evidence to support the claim that our Freeman ancestry is traced back through North Carolina, Virginia, and Massachusetts to John Freeman who was born in Sussex, England, about 1541. There are some fascinating characters among them, some scoundrels, and some influential leaders of church and state.

Daddy's mother, Ida Stephens, was a beautiful young woman according to her pictures and reputation. Her first husband died leaving her with two small sons when she was twenty-one. She married Bartley Henry Freeman, September 17, 1891, and they had two children, my father, Lester, and his sister, Willie Pearl. Daddy was sixteen years old when his daddy, Bartly Henry Freeman, died, too young for the responsibility of the household.

Daddy's mother died eight years later, just a few months after Daddy and Mama married. Grandmother married her third husband, J. B. Folds, a short time before she died, but she did live to see me.

Daddy was bereft. His parental anchors were gone.

Mama was only nineteen.

Twenty months after the wedding, her mother died. Both my parents lost their mothers in a matter of weeks.

Somewhere in his early years, there might have been a tragic flaw. Daddy lost the business, farm, and home. Maybe it was his youth. Maybe it was losing his father when he was sixteen. Maybe it was so much grief in so short a time. Maybe it was the times. Maybe it was the release from tension after World War I, and the world depression that sent America's economy skidding into disaster. Something impacted his life. For whatever reason, life in our family was especially difficult when I was growing up during the Great Depression.

There is a clear line in the American psyche between the way people think who grew up during the depression and the way people think who grew up after the depression. After the crash of 1929, many people lost everything and the incidence of suicide was alarming. Banks failed. Industries closed. There was no money. Families lost their homes and farms. Bread lines were long. Jobless men walked the roads or rode the rails as hoboes. Women and children suffered. Those who survived were forever marked.

Several principles, taught by repetition, anecdote, and example, became a way of life for children who grew up in the depression:

- Do without.
- Make do with what you have.
- Don't go into debt.
- Produce your own food.
- Buy it cheaper if possible.

Entering the Stream

- Never throw anything away.
- Put a little something back for hard times.
- Learn to enjoy simple pleasures.
- Always make room for family in your house.
- Share with your neighbors.

Daddy was fascinated by cars. So far as I recall, he never bought a new one or even a used one from a dealer. He was a good mechanic, a stickler for clean, orderly tools, and maintained his own vehicles. He liked working on them and delighted in trading with his friends.

My parents lived in tough times. Life was never easy for them. They experienced the privations of the Great War, the Great Depression, and World War II. Still they gave to the world six children, seventeen grandchildren, thirty-six great-grandchildren, and seventeen great-great-grandchildren. There are seventy-six descendants, so far, in their direct bloodline. After her own children grew up, Mama opened her heart and home to thirty-one foster babies on whom she lavished love and tenderness until they were adopted.

We always had a vegetable garden, a chicken yard, fresh eggs, and sometimes a cow for milk. Daddy provided meat by hunting and fishing and butchering cows and hogs. He was usually able to find work as a butcher or grocer; if not, he started a business.

Daddy had an uncanny way of starting over, of winning friends, of beginning businesses. During one of the happier times he operated the commissary for the Tennille Manufacturing Company. The cotton mill, along with the company store, closed. It was the Great Depression.

Daddy helped many people, we have now learned, who were down on their luck. Often, without any of the family knowing it, he furnished groceries, paid utility bills, and caught up rent in arrears for families in distress. When he had money, he was generous.

I was the second of six children—five boys before they finally had a daughter—born to Lester (no middle name) Freeman and Ollie Adel Ross Freeman. My oldest brother was Lester Monroe. After me came Ramus Guy, William Maynard, and Oran Sanford. Our only sister, Catherine Ida, was named for her two grandmothers.

All the children lived.

Daddy died in the Emory University Hospital February 20, 1969, at age seventy-four, one day after their golden wedding anniversary. It was a long, hard trip to Atlanta for Mama, but she came on their anniversary. She returned home after watching by his bed through the long hours of his last day. I wondered what memories were going through her mind and what she was thinking as she traveled the lonely miles that night.

In more than a hundred years only four members of this family died—Mama and Daddy, their oldest son, and one infant great grandson.

Mama was a widow twenty-five years; she died June 23, 1994.

GROWING UP

We were known as the "Freeman children" in the small town. As we were growing up, I thought we were the only Freemans in the country. No Freeman relatives lived nearby. Across the Oconee River in Toomsboro, where Daddy grew up, there were several families of Freemans.

Like so many children of the depression, we created our own entertainment with simple games and homemade toys. A block of wood in our imagination became an automobile or truck. A tin can was our football; tightly wound rags and string substituted for baseballs; broken tree limbs became bats.

Sports intrigued me. Daddy pitched for the community baseball team. I wanted to be athletic and box, play baseball and football. I tried them all. But I started to school in September the year I was five in July, and it was hard to compete with the "big boys" in my class. I "went out" for football my first year in high school. They didn't have a uniform to fit me. I didn't even have a helmet. I was too small. I only weighed eighty-five pounds when I was finally permitted to play. They pieced together a uniform, and I become a regular substitute. Too few boys were in our school, so they had to use me. As I gained some weight, I played guard and center and tackle for three years.

Entering the Stream

"The Freeman children" growing up during the Depression in Tennille, Georgia. Lester Monroe, George Ross (me), Ramus Guy, William Maynard, Oran Sanford, and Catherine Ida.

I also wanted to play and sing country music. A guitar was fashioned out of a wooden cigar box. I carved a neck with a knife and pulled wire out of a window or door screen to substitute for strings. There was no music in it, but it kindled imaginations.

I wanted a real guitar and saved money to buy one when I began to earn money. It cost five dollars with a case. Mama found a way to pay the music teacher at school for lessons. I learned the rudiments but did not become proficient. It was only when I made friends with a traveling guitar player who was locked up in the county jail that I began to learn to make music. He taught me what he knew of chords and rhythm and runs in exchange for cigarettes and such money as I could scrounge. What I learned, I taught my brother Ramus. He in turn taught Oran and several other boys in town. We had regular practice. Some of them, including Ramus and Oran, became quite good.

Even though I could not excel in sports, the guitar provided admission to various social circles. I learned that it was possible, with a guitar, to attract an audience and be accepted. From this venture I gained a measure of self-confidence. So I carried my guitar when I visited from town to town. Sometimes I would even sing on the street and collect a few pennies from passersby. Occasionally I got invitations to provide music at school or country dances or other social occasions. As my interests shifted, I laid the guitar down.

An older woman in town collected some children to give lessons in art and oil painting. Reflecting now, I suspect that she was one of the writers and artists paid by the WPA (Works Progress Administration) under President Franklin D. Roosevelt. She found some skill in me to encourage, but not much. I collected some brushes and tubes of paint during the experiment. She guided me in painting my Daddy's favorite bird dogs and several other pieces that are still in the family.

I discovered a talent for lettering. Daddy encouraged me in it. The skill could be used for signs and displays in the store. While I was in high school, I made spending money as an untutored but enterprising sign painter. I learned by watching others who were professionals. Several of the outdoor signs painted with enduring white lead (no longer permitted because of the health hazard) and lampblack still can be read on buildings in Tennille and Wrightsville after sixty years. I doubt that any of those painted in Sandersville or Milledgeville or other places still exist.

Our constant relocation stopped when we got to Tennille, a small town built around the railroad, a cotton mill, and agriculture in Washington County. There the family settled down, established a successful business, bought a home, and reared their children.

I worked in the grocery store and market as a clerk and delivery boy. Those were the days when people who bought anything from the store expected it to be delivered to their home. My older brother (until he left home at fifteen to join the Navy) and I took groceries to people around town; at first on foot, then on a bicycle, and then by car as we got old enough to drive.

Entering the Stream

When I was ten or eleven years old I worked all summer picking cotton, carrying daily papers, and working in the store to save enough for a new bicycle. I was proud of the elegant, new means of transportation. It promised to make my life easier. In less than a month, somebody stole it from our front porch. I never recovered it or got over it. I've never had another bicycle.

In addition to growing up in a small town store business, I delivered the *Augusta Chronicle* to subscribers in the town. When I was nine I bought my first life insurance policy with earnings from the paper route. From that time I made my own spending money, paid for my own clothes, and took care of my own expenses except for room and board.

Before I graduated from high school at fifteen, I operated two greasy-spoon lunch counters, had a sign painting shop and started a rolling store business—a phenomenon of the depression. People in the countryside had little or poor transportation. It was difficult for them to get to the store in town. Besides, they had no money. I would buy staples, load them into my vehicle, and drive to the scattered houses where people would barter what they had for what I had. They had eggs, sometimes chickens, often country butter, and in-season vegetables from their gardens. These they exchanged for sugar, coffee, canned goods, blocks of ice, snuff, tobacco, and other provisions from town. We kept our supplies in a storeroom at home, loaded up every morning for the daily route, and returned at evening. We could find a ready market for fresh yard eggs, frying-size chickens, hens, and fresh produce.

When I left home shortly after graduating from high school, Daddy took over the profitable barter and delivery business and outfitted a large panel truck. Since I had some skill as a sign painter, I painted the panels of the van with a sign that identified it as "Freeman's Rolling Store." I still have a picture of it. Daddy could buy wholesale, get all the family involved and operate a profitable grocery and meat market in addition to the rolling store. He butchered hogs and cows, bought from the farmers, and sold the pork and beef in the market. There were no federal regulations at that time. Only the customers had to be pleased.

A Journey Beyond

FINDING THE CHURCH

Mama was a Methodist who sometimes played the piano for Sunday school and church as a girl. My sister Catherine found a leaflet among Mama's keepsakes for "The Official Program of the South Georgia Conference of the Methodist Episcopal Church, South, for Go to Sunday School Day, February 10, 1918." It was an interesting relic from another day. I treasure it.

Daddy never joined the church. Where he lived, attending church was not the thing to do. Reverend C. C. Boland, a young Methodist preacher who was serving as pastor of the Toomsboro Church, married Mama and Daddy. Reverend Boland was a member of the South Georgia Conference who died in 1942 at age fifty-six. Neither of my parents were active while we were growing up. They were beaten down by the depression. After we settled in Tennille, we were within walking distance of the Methodist church, and the children attended Sunday school regularly and "preaching" spasmodically.

Several deeply moving experiences during my childhood and early youth were formative. They still linger in my memory.

My brother Maynard became ill with scarlet fever. The entire family had to be quarantined for three months. Only Daddy was allowed to leave the house, and he had to take precautions. All of us were worried, and bored.

Mama's oldest sister, in whose house I was born, now lived in Jacksonville, Florida. She realized our plight and sent us a beautiful Bible storybook. Mama would collect the children on the kitchen floor and read these stories to us.

The story of the Crucifixion was read so vividly that it moved me to tears. I could see the chains, the whip lashes, the crown of thorns, the nails, the darkness, the cries from the cross. So far as I remember that was the first time I had heard the story. Later, when Mrs. George Daniels, our Sunday school teacher, asked me to play Judas in an Easter pageant, I refused. It was not only that I was too timid. But I remembered that Judas betrayed Jesus. And I didn't want anybody to think that I would betray Jesus. Mrs. Daniels reminded me of that story a few years before she died.

Entering the Stream

One night I was in a service at the church. A youth choir was providing special music. They were singing, "Tell me the story of Jesus, write on my heart every word; tell me the story most precious, sweetest that ever was heard." Their voices blended. The girls were radiant. I don't know whether it was the music, the words, or the pretty girls that created a reverent sense of the holy; but I was conscious of God.

Late one afternoon I was returning from my route in the rolling store. I was tired and still had miles to go. A shady place under a tree was so inviting. I decided to stop and rest awhile.

An older friend had presented me with a gift from the Pocket Testament League not long before. I was impressed, and agreed to keep it in my pocket. That was the promise. They didn't ask that the recipient promise to read it. So I kept it in my hip pocket, out of sight to prevent embarrassment.

When I rested against the tree on the hillside that late summer afternoon, the book in my pocket was uncomfortable. I removed it. I thumbed the pages drowsily. It stopped on the first chapter of the Revelation. I began to read indifferently. Then I read faster. The images gripped me. All at once I was so absorbed that I sat up straight. I read all the way through. Then I said aloud, "What if all this is so?" I turned over on my face and prayed. I didn't know how, but I asked God to have mercy and save me.

The next Sunday morning I was in church. Our pastor was a young Methodist preacher, Reverend S. Larry King. I didn't know what to do, but I listened. At the conclusion of the sermon, the pastor invited anybody who wanted to live for God to come forward. I didn't even stand up. During the third verse, I was lifted out of the pew and propelled to the altar. That day, Brother King, as I grew to call him, guided me to baptism and membership in the church.

The next day, on the rolling store route, I told everybody I saw about joining the church and my determination to lead a Christian life.

My conversion meant a new focus, a new direction for my life. I began to read the Bible, to take personal prayer seriously, and to look for churches to attend every night.

The grown-up Freeman children with our mother, Ollie Ross Freeman.

Even my dates with Bess meant finding a prayer meeting or revival service or Sunday night activities at church. I sought mature Christians to guide me. I just couldn't get enough of church and fellowship with the people of God.

I think Daddy was proud of me, but he never said so. He was a very private person with many scars. I never knew what he thought of my call to preach or whether he kept up with my career. I lived in a world that he knew little about, though there are distinguished clergy among our Freeman ancestors. He heard me preach only five or six times when I came for revival services at Piney Mount or Tennille. He never visited any of my churches or saw places where I worked.

As I said earlier, Daddy died in the Emory University Hospital during my last year in academic administration and supervised ministry at the Emory University School of Theology. I had been working at Emory for fifteen years. He never saw my office or the School of Theology. We got closer and shared more during those long vigils before his death. We,

Entering the Stream

of course, carried him back to Tennille for the funeral. He would have been very quietly proud of the crowd who came to the service and of the things that were said. He had no idea that so many people thought so highly of him. After his death, I often remembered something he told me or laughed at some joke he told. In many ways we were closer after his death than when he was alive.

CALL TO PREACH

I became a boy evangelist, witnessing as I had opportunity, and making occasions to preach in abandoned churches.

Lucian Dixon, an older man who knew my parents when they all were young in Toomsboro, ran a country crossroad store near Oconee in Washington County. I worked for him part-time while I was in school. In his earlier years he had lived in Atlanta, was active in evangelical churches, and often led singing in revivals around the city. Near the country store where he worked, there was an abandoned Primitive Baptist Church called Rutherford. Mr. Dixon and the Reverend Larry King, local Methodist pastor, decided to get permission from the two or three members that they could find to have a community revival in the old church. They did, and spread the word about the services through the country store into the community. Volunteers were recruited to clean the place and scrounge up some kerosene lamps to provide light. I was deeply involved in the cleanup and plans.

On the second night, Brother King announced that he had to make a trip to Douglas, Georgia, to check on his wife's father who was sick. Then he told the little congregation that the following night I would preach. It surprised everybody and shocked me. I was only sixteen, but I decided to give my testimony. It went well. Kind people bragged on me. They insisted that I speak again the next night.

We organized a community Sunday school at Old Rutherford after the revival and continued preaching services. Years later they started a cemetery behind the church. Mr. Dixon is buried there.

My career as a boy evangelist was launched. Mr. Dixon served as front man and made arrangements for services to be held in abandoned churches within a radius of fifty miles. He led the singing and conducted the services. He taught me about church music and other things during the course of our travels. I spoke with more enthusiasm than knowledge, but people responded. This went on for several months.

Brother King, a graduate of the Candler School of Theology, guided my preparation for the examination by the District Committee for a license to preach. I had just turned seventeen. He drove me to Macon to meet the august and somewhat frightening committee in the Mulberry Street Methodist Church. Though I was intimidated, I evidently gave a good account of my studies.

They voted that day for me to be given a license to preach.

In the same building fifty-two years later my friends gave me a retirement party.

MACON CITY MISSIONARY

Larry King moved from Bay Springs, Piney Mount, and Tennille to the church in East Macon in November of 1941. He urged me to enroll in Mercer University and arranged for me to work with him in East Macon. I began college in the winter quarter of 1942, already behind those who began in September.

Dr. Silas Johnson, the district superintendent, used me as Macon City missionary to help finance my education. I was assigned to work with the children in the slum communities near the East Macon Church, the Second Street Church, and the Cherokee Heights Church. I had two predecessors, but they left few leads for me to follow.

The district paid me twenty-five dollars a month, not even enough to pay tuition. After a year they increased my stipend to fifty dollars a month. I walked from my room in East Macon to Mercer and back because I didn't have enough money for the five cent bus fare each way. I usually drank a nickel Coke and ate a five-cent package of cheese or peanut butter crackers for lunch. I had little money for books or supplies and none for extras.

Entering the Stream

Mrs. B. M. "Aunt Willie" Thomas in the East Macon Church, a widow raising a grandson, gave me a free room and sometimes meals. At that period, my family could not help me financially. They needed every dime for my younger brothers and sister. I was on my own. Occasionally Mama would slip a dollar bill into one of her infrequent letters to me. Aunt Annie Freeman from Toomsboro, a distant relative, drove up to Macon and bought me a white cord suit so that I could be properly dressed for church. Others were kind to me during the struggles of those years.

Mercer was good to me. They gave me the same ministerial scholarship they provided Baptist ministerial students. Still, I had a hard time each quarter. The president, Dr. Spright Dowell, saw my distress at registration time because I had not been able to pay fees the preceding quarter. He volunteered to sign my tuition note so that I could continue in school. Mercer and Macon expanded my horizons to see beyond the limitations of Tennille.

In one of the flashbacks during my retirement party, I told about the "backyard revival" in south Macon. This whetted my desire to preach. Working weekly with the kids from that community, in a slum area near Cherokee Heights and in East Macon, gave me an opportunity to visit in their homes and teach what I was learning about the Christian life.

Sarah Elizabeth (Bess) Bennett from Oconee, about fifteen miles from Tennille, had been my sweetheart since 1939. She was the second of five girls and one son born to Henry Frank Bennett and Sarah Pearl Womack Bennett. Bess was born in Macon, grew up in Oconee, and worked for a while in Baltimore after graduating from high school to help support her family. She was a student at Toccoa Bible College while I was at Mercer.

The war was on. Families were separated.

We decided that we could help support one another if we were married.

So we began our journey together June 15, 1942, continued our studies at Mercer and our ministry as city missionaries.

CHAPTER TWO

Traveling Rural Circuits

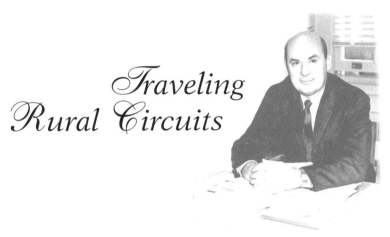

Everybody was feeling the strain of World War II. At the front, thousands of our soldiers were being killed. Many people at home were working double shifts in support of the war effort. Rationing and shortages of all kind were harsh. Clergy, though not drafted, were volunteering as chaplains and marching off to war. There was a serious shortage of ministerial leadership in the South Georgia Conference. Many churches were losing their pastors. Bishops and cabinets were having a difficult time finding bodies to supply the churches. This is why I wound up as pastor of nine churches on the coast of Georgia.

Macon District Superintendent Dr. George E. Clary Sr., who had succeeded my benefactor Dr. Silas Johnson, called me to his home to meet on his front porch with Bishop Arthur J. Moore and a small neat man whom he called James.

In simple eloquence, the bishop described the situation on the coast in the spring of 1943 and talked about churches in which his ministry began. He told of people in the six churches on the Darien Charge that stretched from Mt. Pleasant near Jesup in Wayne County through Everett City in Glynn County, and up the coast through McIntosh County reaching to Midway in Liberty County. They were without a pastor, and he didn't have one to send. It turned out that the other man was Dr. James W. Hitch, district superintendent of the Waycross District. Dr. Hitch was a missionary to Korea. For some time he had been a Japanese prisoner of war. When he was finally released, Bishop Moore brought him home and assigned him to the Waycross District in one of his strategic moves. This amazing story of heroism and courage moved me to admiration. When these two, with Dr. Clary's approval, asked me to leave college and accept the assignment, I did not refuse.

DARIEN AND THE COAST

Who could withstand such a plea? Bishop Moore was himself serving all of South Georgia, North Georgia, Florida, Cuba, all the Methodist Churches in the Far East, Europe, and North Africa. There was no question about my going, even though it meant interrupting my education and perhaps reducing my opportunities for appointments in the future. My bride of a year and I moved in June, though Annual Conference met then in November, full of trepidation and hope. We stopped in the Midway Church and prayed at the altar on the way to Darien.

A few months later the pastor from Ludowici left for the chaplaincy, and I was asked to add the Townsend and Cox churches as well. In less than a year, another pastor left for military service, and Fleming was added to my responsibility.

For a while I served nine churches scattered for more than eighty miles. In addition to the heavy driving with gas rationing and thin tires, I preached five times one Sunday and seven times the next.

My salary when we went there was the same as it was in Macon, fifty dollars a month. In addition we had to buy a car, keep it up for the long, rough roads, buy fuel when we had ration stamps, and patch tires that should have been discarded. Many nights on the narrow, busy U.S. Highway 17, we had to drive home on a rim with the wheel off the pavement as murderous traffic zoomed around us.

Traveling Rural Circuits

Early on we decided that we would spend the night at which ever end of the charge we concluded the day. The next day we visited the people in that community before returning to Darien. Spending the night at Midway was a problem. Our horrendous schedule meant that we wound up the day at Midway. After we had greeted the worshippers, they all drove away to their homes. We had no place to stay. Fort Stewart was up the road in Hinesville, crowded with military personnel and their families trying to spend precious time before shipping out. There was no motel in Midway, even if we had money to pay what seemed to us the exorbitant rates. We didn't. We didn't have enough gas stamps to return to Darien and come back the next day for pastoral visitation in the homes. So we slept in our single seated Plymouth, just off the highway at a flowing artesian well. It was a dangerous thing to do. We were young and on fire for the Lord, so we didn't see any danger. The next morning, we freshened up at the well, ate what food we had, and then drove through the community visiting our parishioners.

Of course they had no idea what we were doing, and we were too proud to tell them. After several months, the wonderful Roger Youmans family found out about it. They owned Yellow Bluff, a fishing camp on the coast, with cottages and rooms and a dining room. I had attended the men's retreat at Yellow Bluff with the fellows from Macon. As soon as the Youmans discovered our secret, they very generously made Yellow Bluff our home for many happy visits.

Wilbur Fulton was the chief layperson at South New Port. He had played the piano for the services while Arthur J. Moore served in the region. He and his family were a strong support for us.

God prospered the work. Attendance in all the churches increased. Vacation Bible Schools attracted children, and they in turn brought their parents. Finances improved. Instead of the pastor receiving the offerings each time, keeping the records and paying the bills, we designated a charge treasurer who received the money from the local churches. Our operation became more efficient and more businesslike. We refurbished the beautiful historic Darien Church, renamed and restored the Mt. Pleasant Church, and painted Morgan's Chapel for the first time.

A Journey Beyond

One Sunday afternoon I suggested to the Morgan's Chapel people that it would be nice to have the building painted. Their homes were not. They saw no reason to paint the church. The community, a little isolated pocket of poverty that had been bypassed by civilization, was populated by families who had married and intermarried so much that there was very little ambition or hope even among the young people. We felt compelled to do something to help if we could. The suggestion that we paint the church was a tiny effort in that direction.

I had learned that a hardware store in Darien was having a paint sale. I suggested that we could probably buy enough paint for twenty dollars to do the job if we painted it ourselves. A little interest stirred. I told them that someone had handed me a five dollar bill that could be used on it. Reluctantly, one after another of the men pulled out a dollar and sometimes three. In a very few minutes we had enough to start. We decided to meet the next Saturday to talk about how to do it. The women also came. They said that if the men would work during the day, the women would prepare a meal each night. Somebody else thought that since the benches would have to be removed, we could line them up in the yard, and after supper have a preaching service. We did. It worked. The little building was painted inside and out. It was not a professional job. Paint was splattered. But the job got done in a week.

True to their promise, the good women served food at the close of the day. One evening during the revival service, I asked if anybody wanted to say anything. To everybody's amazement "Miss Nettie" Wallace stood up. Her husband was called "Gummy"—it may have been short for Montgomery. I never knew. He made his living catching shrimp in a throw net that he held with his teeth. The problem was that he had only two teeth. Fortunately the two teeth met and so enabled him to hold the net when he cast. "Miss Nettie" called herself a "yankee." She came from somewhere north of Atlanta we discovered. She had buried three husbands. Occasionally she would interrupt the preacher in church with a loud question or comment.

When she stood up that night, none of us knew what to expect. Her first words surprised us.

Traveling Rural Circuits

"I used to be a great sinner," she began in a subdued voice. "I said to myself one day, 'Nettie Wallace, you know you can live for Jesus for one day.' So I decided to try. And I did.

"The next day I said to myself, 'Nettie Wallace, you lived for Jesus yesterday, and I know you can do it another day.'

"And I did. This went on for a week, one day at a time. Then I said to myself, 'Nettie Wallace, you have lived for Jesus a whole week. I believe you can do it another week.'

"And I did. I've been faithful for a month, and I am determed [sic] to go on living for Jesus."

Not a snicker. Not a whisper. Then a sob from her daughter. A holy sense of God silenced us all.

Not long after, I visited her at home. She had ordered some wallpaper from Sears Roebuck and tacked it on the walls over the rough, unpainted walls. She had planted some flowers in the yard, and she had "Gummy" cleaning up trash from around the house.

One after another, people started improving their houses. That was a long time ago, more than half a century. Just a few years ago, I went back there for a homecoming. A couple eagerly reminded me that I had married them fifty years ago that spring. The new church, beautifully designed and attractively furnished, stood as a beacon in the community of beautiful homes with well-kept lawns and well-dressed people.

A new district superintendent, Reverend J. C. G. Brooks, persuaded Jake Lackey, who was graduating from the Candler School of Theology in December, to begin his ministry in the Waycross District rather than South Carolina where he grew up. The nine churches were then arranged into two pastoral charges. I was given Darien, Everett City, and Mt. Pleasant which by then had been restored and named Akin Memorial.

Budget for the pastor's salary increased from the six hundred dollars a year it had been when we came to thirty-six hundred dollars for the two pastors when we divided. My salary was increased to three thousand dollars the following year because of the increased activity made possible by the division.

Two of our children were born while we were in Darien, Benita Joye and George Ross Freeman Jr. The third one, Merrie Louellen, had to wait until we got to Baxley.

A Journey Beyond

A LARGER VISION IN BAXLEY

One great benefit from my years in Darien (1943–46) was the privilege of getting to know a young Episcopal priest, the Reverend Archie Torrey III. His congregation worshiped in the beautiful church across the park from the Methodist Church. We were neighbors and talked often. I stood in awe of his broad experience and knowledge.

Archie was the grandson of the famous professor from Moody Bible Institute and world evangelist, Dr. R. A. Torrey. Archie grew up in China where his father, Dr. R. A. Torrey Jr., was a Presbyterian missionary until he was driven out by the communists. He broadened my perspective.

When I moved from Darien to the six churches of the Baxley Circuit in Appling County (1946–51), Archie gave me a book of poems by Don West, *Clods of Southern Earth* as a going away present. I still have it, though it is dog-eared and falling apart. It remains in a favorite section of my library among books that have influenced my life. Many of the poems are tagged for quick reference. I have read selections from it for many audiences because of the poignant and vivid and earthy pictures of share-croppers, tenants, sawmill hands and families beaten down by poverty. These poems got into my soul. I could identify with their hopelessness and despair and pain. They helped to shape my outlook on life and to awaken my sympathy for those whose life is hard and raw. I became concerned about the plight of the helpless and hopeless poor in society.

I still cry when I see a poor mother with several small children searching expectantly through the stores at Christmas trying to find something for the kids, but everything is so expensive.

Though I had grown up among the poor, my work among the farmers and turpentine workers of Appling County took on a different intensity because of the influence Archie Torrey had on my life through the poems of Don West. Here I began to speak to farmers, and to work for the improvement of rural communities. I became convinced that the way to build rural communities was by building rural churches. My commitment to Christ which had been primarily viewed as evangelism until now, became a passion for making the institutions of rural communities forces for transforming life for the people.

I began working with the county agricultural and home demonstration agents, with the Rural Electric Administration (REA), programs to provide telephones in rural communities, the Farm Bureau, the county health program to eradicate hookworms from the children of the county. We organized, and had programs to encourage people to take advantage of special opportunities. We organized countywide Rural Life Conferences to feature health, education, economic, religious, music, and cultural activities. The purpose was to provide information and involvement and action in the institutions of the community. We were able to obtain the cooperation of most of the denominations in these efforts.

The soil and water conservation efforts across America, started by President Theodore Roosevelt, received an enormous boost when the rural churches began to teach that farmers had a stewardship responsibility to protect and enrich the good earth. This was one of the programs that led me to understand that rural churches had an obligation to serve the total community. This insight broadened my understanding of ministry beyond evangelism to include social action. I came to understand what John Wesley meant about the gospel embracing both personal holiness and social holiness.

Our experience in community organization led us to see the advantages of organizing the churches. At that time there were ten Methodist churches in Appling County. They joined, with the blessing of the district superintendent and Annual Conference, in the organization of the Altamaha Larger Parish. Denominational leaders at the national level encouraged the same vision. Help was provided through ideas, material, and resources.

The Women's Division of the Board of Global Ministries (Board of Missions as it was called then) developed a program to provide trained church and community leaders to pilot areas to see what could be done. The first church and community worker in the South Georgia Conference, Armine Davis (who later married Buddy Dimon of Columbus), was assigned to work

Class of 1944 admitted into in the South Georgia Annual Conference by Bishop Arthur J. Moore at Mulberry Street Church in Macon. I am the second from left.

with us in the Altamaha Larger Parish. Remarkable results followed. What started as a pilot project became a full-grown movement by the women of the Board of Missions. Resources and skills that Armine brought expanded and enriched the vision for Methodism in Appling County. We had a combined budget to which all the churches contributed, trained and utilized a group of lay speakers who made it possible to provided services of worship in every church every Sunday, and had monthly countywide meetings of young people and laity.

The Women's Division of the Board of Missions promoted annual Schools of Mission in every conference and church. Along about this time, one of the courses was about the relation of the rural church to the community. The textbook, *Rural Prospect*, was written by Mark Rich. I was invited to teach the course in the Conference School of Mission. This led

Traveling Rural Circuits

to invitations to teach in schools of mission all over the state. All at once I was an "expert" because I was doing what others were writing about. I could describe firsthand our experiences in Appling County. For a number of years I taught in the conference Schools of Missions in North and South Georgia.

ADDING ANOTHER DIRECTION

In the mid-1940s, the Candler School of Theology in cooperation with the Southeastern Jurisdictional Council began offering continuing education workshops for country pastors. I was offered a scholarship. At the first one I met Dr. Earl D. C. Brewer and Dr. James W. Sells who became lifelong mentors. They opened doors, enlarged my view of the church, and became two of the pivotal influences of my career.

A long and fruitful relationship with James W. Sells—one of the most imaginative, creative men the church has produced in modern times—began during that time. His genius was in finding people of potential, encouraging them, and opening doors for them. Leaders he found and mentored to bless the church are spread throughout the southeast. He certainly did this for me. He invited me to be "his helper" at every Jurisdictional Conference from 1948 until I was elected a delegate in 1960.

Dr. Sells taught a course in Creative Rural Writing in the first Rural Pastor's School at Emory in 1946. I took the course. As a result, Dr. Sells asked if I would attend a national conference the following year, capture the essence of the lectures and workshops and write them up for him. So I participated in the first National Rural Church Conference the Methodist Church ever organized in July of 1947 at Lincoln, Nebraska.

I was able to see the inner working of a national gathering of the church. The idea grew out of Dr. Sells's experience as director of the Rural Life Commission appointed by Governor Bailey in Mississippi. His was the creativity and imagination that persuaded the denomination to call such a conference. It made an impact on the Methodist Church.

While I was there I learned that a few visionary persons had organized the Methodist Rural Fellowship in the famous

"Woodshed Meeting" at the General Conference meeting in Atlantic City in 1940.

These rugged individualists felt that the rural church was not getting a fair shake by the General Conference delegates. The new movement provided a vehicle for people to express their concern and plan ways to strengthen small membership churches. They could in turn work to improve the quality of life in rural communities. I believed in what they were doing. I joined. Several other clergy and laypeople attending the National Rural Life Conference from South Georgia also joined. In an impromptu meeting we agreed to have a luncheon at annual conference in Columbus and organize. They elected me president, and I took the responsibility seriously.

Thus began my leadership roles in the conference. There were not many of us at first, but we had the largest constituency in the conference. Most of the churches in South Georgia were small. They felt in some ways disenfranchised. Unwittingly I became a voice, a symbol, because of the progress made among the churches of Appling County and my willingness to take a stand.

As president of the Conference Methodist Rural Fellowship, I wrote Bishop Arthur J. Moore to see if he would permit me a few minutes on the floor of the conference to speak in the interest of the rural church. I told him we would also like to have space to present a display and distribute material for the small churches of the conference. He agreed very graciously and encouragingly. It was written into the agenda of the 1948 Annual Conference meeting in Cordele. In those days there was room in our larger churches to accommodate the conference. I spoke to an Annual Conference for the very first time at this Cordele session.

The emphasis was continued in 1949 during the Annual Conference at St. Luke in Columbus. Again the Bishop consented for me to address the conference and to permit the Methodist Rural Fellowship and Town and Country Commission together to prepare a display.

Bishop Moore, with a keen historical perspective, led the conferences in preparation for an observation of "Methodism at the Mid-Century."

Traveling Rural Circuits

He invited leaders from both the North and South Georgia Annual Conferences to serve on a special team to plan work into the future. To my amazement, he invited me to be part of this leadership team because of my vision for the rural church. He called the group to the newly established Epworth By The Sea to consider this assignment.

He commissioned Dr. Alfred M. Pierce to write a book to commemorate the observance. The purpose was to bring the classic *History of Georgia Methodism, 1735–1866* by the Reverend George Gilman Smith D.D. up to date. The Pierce book was called *Lest Faith Forget* and was designed to tell the story from 1866 to 1950. Dr. Pierce asked me to draft a paper with suggestions about the impact of the rural church in South Georgia.

The Annual Conference at the Mid-Century was in Savannah. It was an extravaganza designed to celebrate our history in the magnificent Wesley Monumental Methodist Church.

Again Bishop Moore was generous in allowing opportunities for the Methodist Rural Fellowship and the Town and Country Commission. He permitted us to hang a huge banner about the significance of the country church, to have space for an attractive display, and to arrange for Dr. A. H. Rapking to speak to the conference. Dr. Rapking was the first executive of the National Town and Country Commission of the Methodist Board of Missions and the foremost authority on the rural church in Methodism. We also scheduled him to address the Town and Country Banquet as well.

Without any financial assistance from the conference to underwrite such an ambitious program, we had to find a way. One of the members of the Asbury Church on the Baxley Circuit was the generous and farsighted J. P. Morris. When he learned what we were trying to do to magnify the country church, he offered to pay for the banner and the cost of the banquet. We wanted the bishop and district superintendents along with other leaders of the conference to be guests. It worked. They came.

Bishop Moore, president of the Southeastern Jurisdictional Council at the time, wanted to have a jurisdictional celebration of Methodism at the Mid-Century. He persuaded the other bishops and members of the council to have it in Savannah at the Wesley Monumental Church. This event brought hundreds of influential Methodists from the conferences of the southeast.

Dr. James W. Sells, one of the council executives, worked with rural churches. His enthusiasm convinced the program committee to use one of the dramatic programs he had written as rural church editor of *The Progressive Farmer* to highlight one of the night programs.

When it was firmly fixed in the program, Dr. Sells invited me to use members from the Asbury Church of the Baxley Circuit and produce the program. It was something for the country church of two hundred members to lead that august Jurisdictional Convocation in worship at the mid-century. Church people from the city joined the Jurisdictional Convocation to fill the impressive sanctuary. Attention was being called to the rural church.

The committee Bishop Moore appointed to be in charge of planning observances of Georgia Methodism at the mid-century was determined to pay tribute to the contribution rural churches had made, boost the morale of those who labor in small churches, and tell the stories of what they are doing.

The next year the South Georgia Conference Methodist Rural Fellowship and the Town and Country Commission started a project to recognize pastors and congregations who were doing a good job in small places. We planned a rural church banquet during conference to honor pastors and members who were doing solid work but who were never recognized for it.

In preparation, a committee of the Town and Country Commission was assigned to select a "Circuit of the Year" from each district. For the first five years, I edited a booklet, *Meet the Circuits*, to tell their stories. Later others assumed responsibility for it. That banquet became one of the best attended extracurricular activities at Annual Conference. Since that time, until very recently, there has been a banquet at Annual Conference to recognize the achievements of small churches and their leaders.

Traveling Rural Circuits

SHAPING A VISION

Once when he wanted to enlarge my horizons, Dr. Sells outlined a trip for me to visit places where outstanding work was being done in rural ministry around the Southeastern Jurisdiction. On this trip I met several pastors doing outstanding work in small churches; later they became leaders of the denomination. What I saw, what I learned, and what I experienced fired my imagination for work in Appling County.

During these years on the Baxley Circuit I wrote two series of articles on the rural church for the *Wesleyan Christian Advocate*. The first series described the trip Dr. Sells had arranged for me. I was young, with nothing to commend me to the editor, but I was inspired by what could happen in rural churches of Georgia. Apparently my brash enthusiasm appealed to him. He published the articles.

Emboldened by his willingness to print my material, I wrote another series in which I proceeded to tell the Methodist leadership in Georgia what should be done to save the small membership churches. Unbelievable. Brash. Out of line. Arrogant.

In one of them I made an impassioned plea for the conference to do something to lessen the gap between the salaries of pastors of large churches and circuits. My proposal was to equalize pastoral salaries like they do for missionaries and in British Methodism. I received a flood of mail. Most laypeople and small church pastors who wrote applauded the idea. Pastors of large churches blistered me as having communist ideas. Some of those letters still smolder in my files.

The articles caused a stir. Several rural church pastors, fired with fresh courage, decided to act. Justice and fairness demanded it. One of those concerned about the small membership church was H. W. "Speed" Scoates, chairman of the South Georgia Conference Commission on Town and Country Work. His report in 1949 included a resolution calling for the conference to establish a minimum salary for its pastors. The resolution was referred to the Conference Board of Missions and Church Extension for study. They were

South Georgia Cabinet pausing for a picture during Annual Conference at Porterfield United Methodist Church in Albany. Bishop John Owen Smith, seated at center with (left to right), Alvis A. Waite Jr., Vernard E. Robertson, C. E. "Ned" Steele, Edward H. Carruth; and standing (left to right), Guy K. Hutcherson, Eugene Cariker, Cardy C. Edmundson, H. W. "Speed" Scoates, and myself.

to propose a plan the following year when conference met at Wesley Monumental in Savannah.

At that point in the history of the conference, the Board of Missions administered the Mission Supplement Fund which allocated grants to struggling churches upon the recommendation of the district superintendents. Albert Trulock was president of the Board of Missions and Church Extension. As an afterthought when he presented his report, Trulock said, "The Board has not had time to study the problem of providing a minimum salary program for the conference."

The small church boys were disappointed. After a year to study, no relief was being proposed. Cardy Edmundson had found a line item in the report of the Commission on World

Service and Finance calling for an increase in the salaries of district superintendents. That night some of the small church pastors met to commiserate with one another. A plan was born out of their desperation.

The strategy was to offer a motion to amend the budget recommended by the Commission on World Service and Finance at the point where the salaries of the district superintendents where given for the next year. The motion called for the conference to delay action on the proposed salary increases for the superintendents until a plan was devised to provide a minimum salary for pastors at the bottom of the scale.

Cardy Edmundson agreed to risk offering the motion. He had seen an article on salaries being paid new college graduates that illustrated how poorly some of our most deserving pastors were being paid. He got the floor. Excited by this article and how unfairly the church was treating its pastors, he began his argument. He noted that in two days the Commission on World Service and Finance had recommended a raise for the district superintendents, but the Board of Missions and Church Extension had not "had time to even study the plight of the pastors in small churches." Edmundson made his motion that "action on this item be delayed until a minimum was established for the conference." Several persons were prepared in advance to speak in support of the motion.

Bishop Moore was in the chair. The motion shocked him and stunned the conference. The Bishop ruled Edmundson out of order because he spoke to the issue before offering the motion. I was sitting nearby and rushed to the floor to make the motion. "Speed" Scoates, one of the strategy team, immediately seconded the motion. This time it was in order. The Bishop hesitated, waiting for some parliamentary help or speech from the floor. None came. Leaders thought the action so absurd that the conference would overwhelmingly defeat it and squelch the radical young men. The Bishop had to put the motion before the group even though he was obviously surprised and displeased. When the vote was taken, to the consternation of the leaders in the conference, the motion was overwhelmingly approved. No increases were given the district superintendents that year!

A JOURNEY BEYOND

The following year, delegates approved a minimum salary program to support those pastors appointed to small churches. Equitable salary is now the law of the church. Each church contributes to the fund to guarantee a minimum for any pastor assigned to serve by the Bishop.

Wider doors were opening. I continued to preach in revivals, but new horizons were beckoning. An inner conflict arose between my early commitment to evangelism and my increasing view of the church as the transforming agency in society.

MISSION TO CUBA

In the meantime, Jim Sells, as executive secretary of the Jurisdictional Council with responsibility for the Methodist work in Cuba had scheduled himself to teach in a Pastor's School on the rural church. It developed that he couldn't go. I had two weeks relatively free, so he assigned me to take his place. My wife and three children used the days to visit our families in Washington County, Georgia.

I took an overnight train from Atlanta to Miami, flew to Matanzas, Cuba, and was driven eastward to our Methodist agricultural mission station in the foothills of the mountains. This was before the Castro revolution. He and his communist revolutionaries were preparing to take over the country just a few miles east of the mission station in the mountains.

Here I met the Richard Milk family, agricultural missionaries from Wisconsin. What a wonderful family they were with three young white-headed children. He taught the Cuban peasants to grow peanuts and make peanut butter to enrich their diets with protein. He taught them to raise chickens for meat instead of roosters for fighting. Later, while we were in Woodstock, the Milk family visited us on furlough.

We met John Stroud, his wife, and two sons who had been in China as missionaries. The Communists drove them out. The Board of Missions relocated them in Cuba. Not long after we were there, the Communists drove them out of Cuba. A part of his genius was in building inexpensive chapels in isolated rural communities. He could do it at that time for

Traveling Rural Circuits

$150 American dollars. One of the first things we did after moving to Woodstock was to receive an offering and send him money to build a rustic chapel.

The Pastor's School was a good experience. I taught them what I could about the work of small churches, especially in rural communities. At night, laypeople joined us for camp meeting. I was a curiosity to them. When I was introduced, they were told that I was "deaf and dumb"—I could neither speak nor understand Spanish. Those wonderful, happy Cuban Methodists laughed with me, smiled with understanding as I taught and preached through an interpreter. It was my first time to try speaking through an interpreter.

One of the participants, Segundo Pedro, whose mother had chosen a biblical name for him, decided that I needed a haircut. He insisted. He had learned to barber in prison. His manual clippers were old and dull; so were his scissors. The water was cold. I sat on an uncomfortable stool. It was the most painful and worst haircut I ever got. But he had a great time doing it and teasing me.

He had been converted during Bible study in prison. When he was released, he married the teacher. She had brought him to the Pastor's School and camp meeting. He was a happy, gregarious, outgoing personality. I liked him a lot. He organized a dramatic group that week, and they improvised the story of his life. He told them the story segment by segment. Actors would improvise the dialogue. It was, the people told me, impressive. When Castro took over, Segundo fell from grace, turned informer against the Christian community and caused terrible suffering. It was sad.

I also met a very talented young man, named Lopez, who created religious sculpture. He saw the bust of John Wesley on the front cover of *World Outlook*, a magazine published by the Board of Missions. He duplicated it. I was very moved that he gave me one of them. I still have it in my study.

Some time was given to touring Methodist schools and churches on the island before I had to return to give a full report to Dr. Sells and the Jurisdictional Council. The days gave me insight into the primitive, unfair conditions under which most of Cuba lived. I have loved the Cuban people since.

A Journey Beyond

A DIFFERENT VIEW IN WOODSTOCK

Jim Sells kept encouraging me. He wanted me to attend Emory. He spoke to the Atlanta-Marietta district superintendent, Dr. Lester Rumble. Dr. Rumble was a leader in the North Georgia Conference. He had heard me speak on several occasions about the rural church. More than that, his brother Woodbridge Rumble was superintendent of the school in Darien and chairman of the board while I was pastor there. So Dr. Rumble, somewhat familiar with my work, listened as Jim Sells asked him about arranging a student appointment for me near enough to attend Emory. We had three small children, and I needed to be within daily commuting distance.

We had traveled a little in the mountains. The rolling hills of middle Georgia, we knew. The flatlands of the coastal plains, we knew. The stretches of unending pine forests and the mysterious marsh lands of the South Georgia coast, we knew.

But mountains we did not know. They were awesome. Something wonderful happened the first time we drove through North Georgia mountains and came upon Tallulah Gorge. We were transfixed in fascinated wonder as vistas stretched endlessly from the overlook. We watched their enchanting glory. We stood in reverence and awe.

Mountains still release in Bess and me feelings of majesty whether we are in the Smokies, the Blue Ridge, the Adirondacks, the Rockies, the Alps, or wherever.

No matter how often or how long we gaze at their splendor, they are never the same. Each season is different. Indeed no two hours are the same. Minute by minute, shifting lights and shadows reveal new mysteries.

I've watched the lengthening shadow of one mountain climbing the western slope of another. Hollows and ridges, etched more sharply through the stark winter nakedness, are more clearly visible. In the waning daylight, they change from ash gray to light brown, and become black against the night sky. During the fall spectacular, the massed autumn golds and oranges and reds and browns are even more brilliant against the dark evergreens. They've been like this for millennia—ever changing.

Traveling Rural Circuits

Bess and I just as we were leaving the Altamaha Larger Parish in Baxley for Woodstock with the three children: Joye on the right, George on the left, and Merrie in between.

That's what happened to a boy from the flatlands of South Georgia when he saw mountains reaching over mountains for the first time. Even more happened when my horizons were enlarged by other turning points in my life.

As God arranges things, the Woodstock Charge was open that conference. Woodstock had not been a student appointment. Dr. Rumble persuaded the pastor-parish committee that I was "an experienced" pastor with proven strengths. They agreed to receive me (1951–53).

During those years, Bishop Moore who had responsibility for North and South Georgia, always finalized the appointments the week before Annual Conference. So after he had finished with the South Georgia Conference, he moved the following week to complete the appointments before opening conference in North Georgia. That meant there was a week between the two conferences.

Moving date for pastors changing appointments was a week later. We had to vacate the parsonage at Baxley and wait two weeks before we could move into the Woodstock parsonage. This enabled me to go to Cuba in between.

We did, however, move into Woodstock a week late. Dr. Sells took my place the first Sunday. He not only preached a good sermon, but he paved the way for me to get off to a good start. I had obtained a list of the officials and families in the three churches before I left, and on the train to Miami, I wrote them a letter explaining my absence the first Sunday and expressing my pleasure at being appointed to serve them.

Smith L. Johnston Sr. was the leader of the charge. He had been a member of the Uniting Conference in 1939, several other General and Jurisdictional Conferences, North Georgia Conference lay leader and a wonderful man. He became my staunch supporter and opened many doors for me. He helped to finance my education, bought my first George Muse's suit, and championed anything I felt the church ought to do. Unfortunately he died suddenly during my second year, and having his funeral was hard for me.

There were three churches on the charge, each unlike the others, but together they were strong with solid and committed leaders.

Woodstock was a sophisticated and educated congregation. They were the strongest financially and had services every other Sunday when I arrived.

Bascomb was comprised of farmers and teachers and young adults who worked in Marietta and Atlanta. They were old fashioned, presided over by a patriarch who kept the church at work and faithful. They still celebrated Children's Day the first Sunday in June every year with a program by the children and recognizing their value to the church.

Little River had more people than either of the others. They had strong traditions, but they were also willing to try new things. The revival tradition was important to them. The church grew out out a camp meeting. Annual encampments were held for many years. With this tradition in mind, we planned a Mission Revival, an Education Revival, a Stewardship Revival, and Evangelistic Revival. These efforts were successful and greatly enriched the understanding of the congregation.

Traveling Rural Circuits

Attendance grew. Finances were no problem. A wholesome spirit prevailed. We enjoyed the people.

The second year we arranged for Fletcher Anderson to join the staff. He had transferred from the Asbury Theological Seminary to the Candler School of Theology as a senior. He was brilliant, but with limited motor skills. I tried for a year to teach him to drive. I finally gave up. But what a brain.

His skills and willingness enabled us to make some sociological studies of the communities, double the preaching services in all three churches, and prepare the churches for the division of the charge that came later so that all three churches could be station churches to accommodate the growing population.

When Fletcher graduated the following year, he applied to the Board of Missions for an assignment as a short-term missionary. He was sent to Argentina, and married a wonderful local woman in Argentina after a couple of years. Their marriage meant they could not continue their service, according to the rules of the Board, in her country. So they asked to be transferred to Peru. Later they applied for admission to the Annual Conference as a pastor in Argentina. They were accepted and became pastor of the multicultural congregation with services every Sunday in five languages at the heart of Buenos Aires.

When his father became ill in Miami, Fletcher asked to be transferred to the Florida Conference. He was assigned to supervise Spanish-speaking churches in Miami in order for him to be near his father in his last years. After his father died, still with the heart of a missionary, he was given an assignment in Mexico. He and Mrs. Anderson, now retired, are living in Florida.

The wonderful people at Bascomb, Little River, and Woodstock, with their openness and flexibility, gave me another view of ministry.

My work with Fletcher, my growing involvement at Emory and the Religious Research Center with Dr. Earl Brewer expanded my vision so that I could see a much larger church than I had ever known. I was still committed to the rural church and evangelism, but now I could see much more.

CHAPTER THREE

Extending Horizons

As my exposure to larger horizons grew, the more I realized that I needed knowledge. Against the advice of my district superintendent and many older friends in the conference, I broke away from my comfort zone after five happy years in Baxley to return to school.

I applied for admission to the Emory University Graduate School. I wanted to study the interaction between church and society. Dr. Earl Brewer agreed to guide my program. The closer we worked together the greater became my admiration for him, and the more he saw of my work the more confidence he had in me. It was a great honor when he invited me to be his assistant in the Religious Research Center to help with his research and to work with seminary students in learning the techniques of studying their parishes. I learned more from him than from the formal classes. Imagine the changes that this door opened.

MEET THE CIRCUITS

A part of the commitment to the rural church that I brought to Emory was expressed in writing and publishing the booklet on *Meet the Circuits* for the South Georgia Conference from 1951 to 1955. Though lip service was being paid to the importance of the small membership church, not much was being done to help them. The Town and Country Commission and the United Methodist Rural Fellowship agreed to make the conference aware of what was being achieved in many of these congregations. We agreed, as we reported in chapter two, to write the stories and honor these circuits at annual conference.

The plan was to have district committees, including the district superintendent, to study reports from all the circuits and select one to be recognized each year from each district. I agreed to collect the information, write the material and see to the publication of the booklets for the first four years. The responsibility then was given to others, but the pattern had been established.

We wanted to publicize the successful activities, encourage others to be creative, and make the entire conference aware of what was being done. The subtitle for the first booklet was "Georgia Methodism in the Mid-Century Recognizes Nine Rural Circuits in the South Georgia Conference—1951." Each had a lesson to teach and inspiration to share:

- Go Thou and Do Likewise
- Cooperation is Responsible
- He Calls Them by First Names
- Put People to Work
- Build Ye the Church
- Unity Through Organization
- The Drama of Development
- Emphasizing the Word of God
- In His Own Country

Meet the Circuits for 1953 was special. It was being prepared at the time when Dr. Herbert E. Stott, national president of the Methodist Rural Fellowship was serving as a visiting professor at the Candler School of Theology. He wrote a singularly valuable chapter on "Methodism's Rural

Extending Horizons

Movement." Information of this caliber and on this subject from one of the major leaders of the rural church movement could not be duplicated.

The second chapter, "The Place of the Rural Church," contains material written about the importance of the rural church by Bishop Arthur J. Moore, Mrs. J. Wallace Daniels (President of the Woman's Society of Christian Service), Reverend Anthony Hearn (Chairman of the Conference Board of Evangelism), Reverend Roy J. Bond (executive secretary of the Conference Board of Education), Reverend G. N. Rainey (Conference missionary secretary), and Dr. Albert S. Trulock (pastor of Valdosta First).

Chapter three highlights ways in which country churches are making progress, and chapter four gives the report of each of the circuits.

The Commission on Town and Country Work, under the leadership of H. W. "Speed" Scoates, chairman, and Reginald Edenfield, secretary, attempted an ambitious project to expand what we had been doing in *Meet the Circuits*. The commission persuaded the Commission on Finance and Administrative to underwrite a statistical survey and write a report on *Methodism in South Georgia*.

"This study is a cooperative venture between various boards and commissions of the conference (especially the Methodist Expansion Committee), the Town and Country Commission and the Candler School of Theology. Credit for compiling the data and preparing the tables goes to Charles Culbreth as a part of his senior project at Candler. G. Ross Freeman guided his work and wrote the analysis and interpretation of the survey. Dr. Earl Brewer assisted in outlining the study, developing the procedures, and pointing out significant facts and trends."

The book included the 1954 version of information and achievements by the churches chosen for the annual *Meet the Circuits* report so that the chain would not be broken. Though nothing of such far-reaching importance has been done since, each year the banquet and recognition program has resulted in a booklet until 1996.

A Journey Beyond

CHURCH AND COMMUNITY WORKSHOP

Dr. Brewer, who was already known nationwide as one of the foremost authorities in the rural church, worked out an exchange term with Dr. Herbert C. Stott at Illiff School of Theology in Denver. Brewer and his family went there to teach as a visiting professor; Stott and his family came to Candler.

It was a lucky break for me. I became the guide and on-the-site champion of Dr. Stott. I took his courses, worked under his direction in the Religious Research Center, and grew by leaps and bounds during the long conversation times we spent together. He broadened my view of the church. Our friendship continued after he left Illiff to become full professor at the Boston University School of Theology through our common interests and associations at the general church level.

With Dr. Brewer away, I became the resident authority on his methods of scientific sociological research and acting director of the Church and Community Workshop.

We continued to provide ministers with information about agricultural and industrial developments, insight in the problems of labor and management, sociological and population analysis skills, and other non-ecclesiastical matters. Such a purpose attracted supporters. Invaluable help came from the University of Georgia. The College of Agriculture, Agricultural Extension Service and Soil Conservation Service became valued allies. They gladly contributed leadership. The Farm Foundation in Chicago provided money each year to pay the salary of a sociologist or agricultural economist. Several denominational executives gave financial assistance for their pastors to come. Emory University invested heavily in the event. Both Dean Trimble and Dean Cannon gave generous interest and time.

Year after year brilliant speeches and lectures fired searching discussion groups. Those responsible for planning the workshop were convinced that the amount of material participants carried away in notebooks was not as important as what happened to them in the two-week process. Annual reports of participants, sponsors, leaders, and a summary of

Extending Horizons

the subject matter and discussions were distributed to the participants, the denominational executives, and the hundred or so individuals and companies who supported the enterprise. This spread the word about the innovative approach being made in continuing education. Interest continued for twenty-three years in the project.

PUBLISHED REPORTS

Another publishing venture grew out of the Church and Community Workshop. Since we raised the money basically from corporations, we felt obligated to write an annual report and send them to the contributors and participants. One day it occurred to us that since the work was being done anyway we might enlarge the reports and distribute them broadly as a way to spread valuable information. Such a publication would provide another way to publicize the astounding work of the rural ministers of the year.

Our committee planned the fifteenth Church and Community Workshop for July of 1959. The remarkable Robert West Howard—who edited *This is the South*—was invited to the staff that year for a series of presentations. The opening panel was pivotal. It was designed to provide the participants some insight into the background of the South, the explosive developments since World War II, and the impact that these changes had made upon the people, institutions, and communities. The panel was made up of key leaders who were a part of the Wonderview retreat who dreamed up *This is the South*. Just to throw these persons together for a little while generated flashing insights. Ideas sparkled. But to put them around a table in front of a hundred or more ministers with the express assignment of helping these pastors understand something about the thrilling saga of the South was to guarantee an exciting time. Since we were still enthralled by the vision and book, the same ideas naturally surfaced. Jim Sells mentioned the term "benchmark." A benchmark, it was explained, is a point of measurement established by the Geodetic Survey. Surveyors make legal land measurements from it.

Ivy Duggan said, "We all have benchmarks. We measure everything else by our benchmark. Who we are? Where we came from? What is important to us. We use them to reestablish our bearings when we get off course. They are the permanent reference points of our lives."

The opening panel of the 1959 Church and Community Workshop under the inspiration of Bob Howard provided the theme of *The Bench Mark*—a 138-page book of the wit and wisdom from participants. He thought that the quality of the lectures and workshops had enough meat to capture for a book. Every participant became a reporter. Stories told were written down. Experiences shared were recorded. Sessions were kept on audiotape for later transfer to the written page. Typists volunteered to transcribe handwritten notes. Bob Howard, who knew how to put a book together, edited the material during the two-week period and prepared it for a publisher. We turned a corner and produced a book instead of a report. For several years we did the same thing. My brother Ramus edited the next two. Others continued the tradition until the workshops were discontinued after I left Emory. The total collection of reports has a remarkable record of participants including the rural ministers of the year, lecturers and workshop leaders, sponsors who made it all possible, and resources for the period.

When Dr. Brewer returned to Candler after the year at Illiff, he wanted to be relieved of responsibility for the Church and Community Workshop to pursue expanded interests. Other opportunities were clamoring for his attention. He recommended that I become the director and agreed to be related to it as senior professor to give it status and credibility and to award academic credit for those pursuing degrees.

All at once responsibility for managing the program, enlisting workshop leaders, recruiting the interdenominational participants from the seventeen states, and working with the finance committee of business and foundation leaders to raise money to finance the costs and scholarships overwhelmed me. For fifteen years I continued in this capacity along with my other duties at Emory, refocusing and enlarging the ministry of more than fifteen hundred pastors.

Extending Horizons

Rural Ministers of the Year for 1953. Alexander Nunn (far left), editor of The Progressive Farmer, *presenting the certificates at Emory University. I am the third from the left.*

It was an extension of my commitment to the rural churches, but hearing the lectures, listening to the pastors from the field, meeting with the leadership teams and working with the planning and finance committees enlarged my horizons and expanded my world.

Primarily because of my work on the Baxley Circuit and other leadership, I was designated "Rural Minister of the Year for Georgia" in 1953 by *The Progressive Farmer* and Emory University. This program was started at the instigation of Dr. James W. Sells. As rural church editor of *The Progressive Farmer*, he proposed it to Dr. Clarence Poe, Dr. Alexander Nunn, and the other editors. Simultaneously he outlined the possibility to Dr. H. B. Trimble, dean of the Candler School of

Dr. James W. Sells, Rural Church Editor of The Progressive Farmer *and Executive Secretary of the Southeastern Jurisdictional Council, chatting with three of the Rural Ministers of the Year from the Class of 1953: Me, Georgia, seated; Father Paul Brinkler, Catholic, Kentucky; Dr. Sells; Rev. Charles P. Hamilton, Episcopalian, Mississippi. This ecumenical program continued for fifteen years.*

Theology, and Dr. Brewer as a way to bring recognition to pastors who serve in small and hard places. It was an unlikely marriage. Dr. Sells was persuasive enough to get both the family-oriented farm magazine and the prestigious university seminary to approve such an effort for country preachers.

This highly acclaimed program continued for twenty-one years until 1969 with enormous media attention across the

Extending Horizons

South for the individuals who were honored and the institutions sponsoring the program. For more than a dozen of those years, I directed this popular enterprise along with the Church and Community Workshop and my other duties at Emory.

CHURCH DEVELOPMENT PROGRAM

A new development emerged in the early 1950s from this conglomerate of academic, publishing, business, philanthropic foundations, religious and judicatory forward-thinking leadership concerned about rural community life. Seeing the benefits growing out of the Rural Minister of the Year program, the fertile brain of Dr. James W. Sells wondered what would happen if we announced a Rural Church of the Year recognition.

The idea was broached with the finance committee of the Church and Community Workshop. Among them were such noted leaders as D. W. Brooks, founder and general manager of the farmers' cooperative international, Cotton Producers Association, now Goldkist; J. C. Haynes of the Sears Roebuck Foundation; Don Hastings of Hastings Seed Company; Cully Cobb of Ruralist Press; Ivy Duggan of Trust Company of Georgia Atlanta and the State Department in Washington; Hill Hosch, Farm-Industry Trust Company of Georgia; John Liles, vice president, Federal Reserve Bank; William H. Wilkerson, Auto-Soler, Atlanta; Dean H. B. Trimble, and later Dean William R. Cannon, of the Candler School of Theology; and others who had a personal or professional interest in the health of rural communities in the south. What a remarkable collection of big, public-spirited men.

The idea took root in the imagination of Sears Roebuck Foundation Regional Director J. C. Haynes. A meeting was arranged with some of his top foundation officials, Dr. Sells, Dean Cannon, Dr. Brewer, and me to explore what such a program would look like.

After several sessions, Dr. Brewer emerged as the chief architect of the plan that won the approval of the Sears Roebuck Foundation and Emory University. The Church and Community Development Program was created with a central committee and state committees to direct it.

A JOURNEY BEYOND

The plan was to develop guidelines for local churches to use in developing a better church, a better community, and a better world. A catalog of suggestions to help church committees in each of the three categories was printed along with the rules for keeping records and preparing a scrapbook type of report. The program was to be open to all churches regardless of denomination or race. It was a teaching effort as well as a contest to encourage participation.

Dr. Brewer guided in designing and writing the material for the local churches. Mr. Haynes and the team from the Sears Roebuck Foundation wanted Dr. Brewer to direct it. He refused. Other interests clamored for his attention and consumed his time. The Emory Graduate School at the time was developing a doctoral program in religion with Dr. Mack B. Stokes, associate dean of Candler, chairing the committee. Most of the faculty had to come from the School of Theology. Dr. Brewer was a chief player in that academic development. There was no way he could be released to work on the Church and Community Development Program. He proposed me as director.

I was serving the Woodstock charge as a student pastor while I was attending graduate school. I had every intention of returning to the South Georgia Conference to serve as a pastor when I finished my educational venture. We had been happy with churches to serve and people to love. This would be an entirely different world, moving away from the local church. My involvement in the project was as Dr. Brewer's assistant. Now a different situation had arisen. It meant a major shift in the direction of my life.

After agonizing several weeks, with fear and trepidation, we moved from the world I knew to a larger world. The decision opened other doors. I was responsible for recruiting members for the central committee and the state committees. All the prospects were giants in my eyes. They were professors in state colleges of agriculture, denomination executives, bankers, business, and professional leaders. They were known leaders. And I was asking them to serve with me, an unknown, in a project sponsored jointly by The Sears Roebuck Foundation and Emory University?

Extending Horizons

This meant learning key people in the colleges of agriculture around the south. It meant studying the history and ways of working with leaders in at least seventeen different denominations in as many states. Without their cooperation and endorsement, their churches would not participate. It was necessary to interpret the program and win their understanding of the goals so that they would not see this as an intrusion or as a conflict with what they were trying to do. More than that I had to be sensitive to the racial situation so that African-American churches would cooperate and not be alienated. We wanted to help, to encourage good work, to broaden understanding, to enlarge the vision for local churches.

Recognition at an Emory University banquet and region-wide publicity along with a small prize was the incentive. But the major reward came from the cooperative work in their local communities and in the growth of their churches.

CONSERVATION

While I was serving in Appling County, I became convinced that saving the soil and water resources of this land was imperative. The more I read about *The Holy Earth* by Liberty Hyde Bailey, the more certain I became that soil and water conservation is a religious obligation. "The earth is the Lord's," Scripture tells us. That means it is sacred. It also means that God holds us responsible for protecting, enriching, and passing it on to the next generation better than we found it. I continue to study and speak about it.

My involvement with the colleges of agriculture, the Extension Service and the Soil Conservation Service increased my conviction that we are stewards of God's good earth. The words of an unnamed tenant farmer quoted to me years ago sums it up, "We are tenants of the Almighty, entrusted with a portion of his good earth, to dress and keep, and pass it on to the next generation."

At the annual meeting in 1961, I was named Georgia state chaplain of the Soil and Water Conservation District Supervisors. Many of the supervisors of the program were devout church families. The session had almost the religious revival atmosphere of a country church. Technicians and volunteers alike were serious about what they were doing. I marveled at their commitment.

My major responsibility was to attend the sessions, lead vesper services, offer formal prayers, and occasionally deliver a major address on the religious implications of saving the soil. In addition I worked with a special committee to design and distribute materials for churches around the state to use during Soil Stewardship Week each year. A lot of energy was used in creating the concepts, writing and distributing news stories, and radio and television spots. We included ideas for local churches to use in both urban and rural services, scripts for sermons, or talks for civic clubs. We even had school children writing papers on soil and water conservation. Those selected by the schools were printed in local newspapers.

Among my keepsakes are a silver bowl inscribed from the Soil and Water District Supervisors, a certificate naming me a member of the Soil Conservation Society of Georgia, and a resolution read by my good friend Joe K. Hawkins. In a part of it, he read:

> Dr. G. Ross Freeman has been closely associated with soil and water conservation for many years. He has actively participated in numerous ministers' conferences over the state in promoting soil stewardship.
>
> In 1961 Dr. Freeman was appointed state chaplain of the Soil and Water Conservation District Supervisors and has rendered outstanding services for ten years in this position.
>
> Through his enthusiastic leadership and able guidance, Georgia became the first state in the nation to have chaplains of individual soil and water districts. He planned and conducted conferences of these chaplains to set the stage for the most widespread and most effective observations of Soil Stewardship Week in history.
>
> Through his untiring efforts, Dr. Freeman has given inspiration to district supervisors, professional conservationists,

Extending Horizons

ministers and laypeople in all walks of life to be better stewards of our God given natural resources. He has made literally hundreds of talks to religious and civic groups, presented many radio and television programs, and written scores of articles for newspapers on soil stewardship. He has prepared and published sermons, Scripture references, illustrations and other material on soil stewardship for use of ministers of all denominations throughout the state.

In order to obtain widest use of material from the Soil Stewardship Week national office, as well as that produced by our Georgia committee, the district supervisors agreed to name district chaplains. The district supervisors and the district chaplains teamed up to call meetings of ministers in their districts, talk about the plans and urge each pastor to observe Soil Stewardship Week in their churches. They proved valuable in promoting participation through the state.

For ten years I was honored to serve in this capacity. The 1960s was a decade of unrest across the nation. This positive emphasis brought people together.

Also hanging in a treasured spot in my study for more than thirty years is another plaque with a golden seal. Across the top is the inscription, "Soil Conservation Society of America." The Soil Conservation Society of America is made up of professional conservation and scientific technicians. Few clergy have ever received one. This makes it special to me because of the friends who proposed me for it. Written on the legend are these words:

> The Grade of Honorary Membership is granted to G. Ross Freeman, he having made outstanding contributions and demonstrated his worthiness to the field of soil and water conservation. August 25, 1965. Signed: Minott Silliman, Jr, President and H. Wayne Pritchard, Secretary.

HINTON RURAL LIFE CENTER

Jim Sells was always looking for some way to expand the influence of the church. His initial work with the Southeastern Jurisdictional Council was as extension secretary. The title came from the Methodist Episcopal Church,

South, and included responsibility for Sunday Schools and rural churches. His work rapidly expanded to include radio, missions, stewardship, and developing lay leadership. His response to this was to create organizations and institutions. His antennae were tuned constantly to fresh opportunities which had not occurred to others.

His method was to travel the roads and byways of the Southeast by automobile. In this way he felt more in touch with people and what was going on in the region. He was curious about everything he saw and asked probing questions of any who had interesting information. Getting close to people and keeping in touch with those who knew things enabled him to gain insights far beyond those who stayed close to church circles.

One Sunday he went to church in Hayesville, North Carolina, just across the Georgia line from Hiwassee and Young Harris. That Sunday he met Walter and Velma Moore. His interest was so sincere and his questions so revealing that they invited him to their mountaintop retreat, Wonderview, at the head of Lake Chatuge.

Some years before, the Moores bought the "mountaintop" from Mr. Harold Hinton, head of the West Point Manufacturing Company in the Chattahoochee Valley. He dreamed of a hunting lodge in this beautiful spot. The lodge was started. Then his health broke. He never had a chance to finish it. When the Moore's bought the property they planned cottages to rent during the tourist season.

While they shared their hopes with the probing Jim Sells, another dream was being born. Never one to deny a dream, Jim nourished and cultivated it. Jim could see the unfinished lodge completed and used by the church as a rural retreat center for research and teaching. The Moores were likewise visionaries. Mrs. Moore, a retired home economics teacher, could see vast possibilities in such a center for enriching rural life and strengthening the rural church and community.

They would like for the mountaintop to be used for such purposes, but they were not in position to bring the plan to fruition. So a partnership was born.

Extending Horizons

Jim Sells approached Mr. Hinton's widow about being a part of completing the lodge. She agreed to help if it could be named for her and her husband. Jim Sells approached Wilson Nesbitt of the Duke Endowment Rural Church Fund with a request for assistance in furnishing and staffing such a center. Jim Sells approached Earl Brewer and me about ways the Candler School of Theology could be involved as a research and teaching facility. Jim Sells approached the Town and Country Department of the Methodist Board of Missions (now the General Board of Global Ministries) to see if they would assign a church and community worker to the center and use the facility for training purposes. With his unique gift of persuasion, Jim Sells obtained agreement from these diverse constituencies, engineered approval from the Jurisdictional Council, created a board of directors and proceeded.

Earl Brewer had a graduate student from the Memphis Conference working on a doctoral program at Emory, Harold McSwain, whom he recommended to serve as the first part-time director while he completed his degree. What a genius of an idea. Gladys Campbell was assigned as a church and community worker to the Hinton Rural Life Center. The two of them served Hinton well. He went on later to develop a prestigious program in Ohio combining the resources of United Theological Seminary and the United Methodist Theological School of Ohio to enrich the rural institutions and communities of the state. He became in many ways the guru giving credibility and leadership to the United Methodist Rural Fellowship. Gladys Campbell moved from Hinton to New York as director of Church and Communities Ministries for the Board of Global Ministries. Others followed them, but they stamped the pattern for the future.

Doyce Gunter came from a very successful term as director of the Sand Mountain Larger Parish in North Alabama to study for a doctorate with Dr. Brewer. Near the end of his studies, he was chosen to succeed Dr. McSwain. During that period I was president of the Hinton Rural Center, fashioning dreams and giving practical guidance to the staff

A Journey Beyond

as its future began to unfold. After Dr. Gunter completed his tenure, he moved to the North Mississippi Conference as creator of a larger parish. From there he was elected president of Wood College to continue imaginative work in providing leaders for rural churches and communities.

In the next change of directors, the search committee selected Rene Bideau, originally from North Carolina but then serving in New England. He gave such creative and exciting leadership that the attention of the General Board of Global Ministries was attracted to him. He was elected from Hinton to be the associate director of the General Board of Global Ministries as chief executive of the National Division. Here he worked again with Gladys Campbell. The two of them encouraged and provided financial support for the expanding influence of Hinton Rural Life Center into a national center for research and training.

When Rene Bideau moved from Hinton to New York, I was executive director of the Southeastern Jurisdictional Council on Ministries. I assumed the responsibilities of interim director for nearly a year and carried those duties along with my other work until the search committee could complete its task. The ultimate choice to succeed Bideau was unfortunate, overly influenced by persons beyond the board. He did not succeed.

The present director, Reverend Clay Smith, however, was the right person. He has pushed the horizons of the original dream far beyond those envisioned by Jim Sells and the Walter Moores. With that one brief exception, all the directors brought solid commitment and enormous skill to this primary institution of the rural church in the south.

My involvement was total from the beginning until 1987. I have been officially related to Hinton while I was at Emory, during the years in Statesboro and the Macon District, and through the ten years while I was Executive Secretary of the Jurisdictional Council on Ministries.

I served in almost every capacity as a member of the board for more than a quarter century, until I resigned in 1986 when I became editor of the *Wesleyan Christian Advocate*. The work continues to flourish.

Extending Horizons

THE LORD'S ACRE MOVEMENT

The Lord's Acre concept was dreamed and promoted by a Presbyterian minister, Dr. Dumont Clark. Financial support for launching the program was provided by the James McClure Foundation of Asheville, North Carolina. I was in Appling County when it started, learned about it, and encouraged our people to try it. Asbury and Hopewell have both continued the emphasis though the nature of the program understandably has shifted in the half century since then. Jim Sells was a natural promoter and spread the idea through the Methodist network and *The Progressive Farmer*. He was rural church editor of *The Progressive Farmer* (today it is *Southern Living*) at the time and promoted the program interdenominationally.

As director of the Church and Community Workshop, I wanted every country preacher who attended to know about this movement. We brought Dr. Clark several times to teach or lecture in the school. Much about his initial vision and its worldwide spread caught fire. He was a saintly visionary who was able to get things done.

When Dr. Clark retired, the Lord's Acre movement directors sought a successor to continue the work around the world. They turned to a North Georgia Conference mountain preacher. Jack Waldrep became the new director. He was a unique individual. One of the people I admired most.

He had a slight speech impediment, a superior intellect, and a love for the country church. Through his leadership, the movement was spread to third-world countries and revolutionized farming as a cooperative effort between God and people.

Jack's age finally caught up with him and he was forced to give it up. He retired near Lake Junaluska and Asheville and spent his declining years in the mountains he had loved so long. He died not long ago. Before he retired, he arranged for the Hinton Rural Life Center to be the custodian of the movement and the depository of the records. The Lord's Acre program has adapted to meet changing conditions several times. A companion effort, to accommodate wage earners and urban workers, was the Lord's Hour Program. Wage earners were challenged to consider the first hour of the week as the

Worship Center of the First Lord's Acre and Harvest Festival Program in South Georgia.

Lord's Hour. Their pay for this first hour was given for missions and special causes outside the budget of the church in the same way that proceeds for the Lord's Acre were dedicated at an annual celebration. Other variations included the Lord's Pig, the Lord's Eggs, the Lord's Projects, and others.

Three things are important to keep in mind: (1) The program sanctified work and symbolized the partnership between God and his people and the Good Earth, (2) the farmer (or wage earner or whoever) decided in advance to set aside an acre (or hour or a pig from the litter or eggs laid on Sunday) for God's use. Whatever crop was planted and harvested was sold and the money was brought to the altar and dedicated to God at a Harvest Festival Service. Other things dedicated to God were also presented at that time, and (3) from the beginning the money was consider a special thanksgiving offering and used only for special over-and-beyond purposes.

MY METHOD WITH GROUPS

When I first started working with such top-drawer committees, I was clearly out of my league and so far behind of most of them that I had to learn how to function. This was fortunate. The method has served me well in harnessing the creativity of others. When there was a task to be done, or new areas to explore, I sought to:

- Bring knowledgeable and concerned people together with different points of view.
- Create an atmosphere for thoughtful discussion.
- Milk the most creative and innovative thoughts on the topic or discussion. Make notes of what was said.
- Summarize, and sometimes reshape these ideas, put them into some logical and progressive order, feed them back to enable each person to recognize his/her contribution. Participants could then own the results.
- My notes were consolidated in a "findings paper" to share with the group. Some close friends who watched me operate this way would say that the paper had been "Freemanized."

Dean Cannon, realizing my propensity to capture reliable information, asked me to serve as secretary of faculty meetings and sessions of the Academic Policy Committee. The importance of accurate and complete records for these meetings was imperative. I didn't know shorthand, but I developed my own system of jotting down key phrases, decision notes, and who made certain comments. Thus I could watch the interaction attentively and concentrate on what was important in the discussion. Immediately after the meeting, with these skimpy word-notes before me, I dictated the minutes. At that time I had almost total recall and could write full and dependable accounts of what transpired. The official record of faculty action for almost fifteen years was written in this way. I wish that I had kept my copies instead of leaving them in the files for my successors.

CHAPTER FOUR

Enabling Pastors

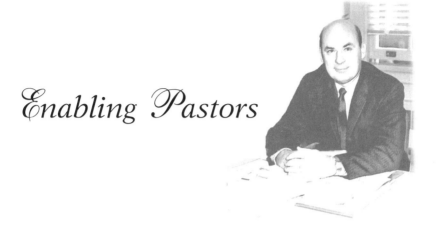

While our children were growing up in the Emory community, there was seldom a month when we did not have someone else living in the home. Friends would come from South Georgia for two or three days or longer to attend meetings or to stay with someone in the hospital.

Often our kids would come home at night to find that some friend or relative or stranger had preempted their beds. They had to find some other place to sleep. They never once complained, aloud at least, for any inconvenience or interruption of their plans it caused. They just moved over and made room.

At one time we had a student living with us for his final term at Candler. He had exhausted his resources and did not have enough to pay for his room and food. I learned that he was about to leave without completing his degree, though I had been able to provide him with a generous tuition scholarship. He did not see any way to provide money for living. At the time we had a vacant room. We invited him to use it and eat his meals with the family.

Another very special friend, whom we had known since she was a child, was finding the cost of undergraduate school

Our children—George Ross Freeman Jr., Merrie Louellen in the center, and Benita Joye on the right—sitting with their mother in 1956 as they grew up in the Emory community.

at Emory had depleted funds she had set aside for college. Our daughter, Joye, married and moved with her husband to the Marine base in California. It was a pleasure to have our friend partially fill the vacancy in our hearts by moving into Joye's room for the school year.

There were several pregnant girls we kept until they delivered and were back on their feet. Several wives whose clergy husbands were in the Emory University Hospital with long-term or terminal illnesses stayed with us for weeks at the time or as long as they needed it.

Bess and I counted fifty-five people, seventeen of whom were not related, who made their home with us for a month or longer beginning with our years as students at Mercer. They added much to our home and blessed our children with the gifts of thoughtfulness, compassion, and generosity.

Enabling Pastors

IN AWE OF EMORY

When I attended the first Rural Pastors School (later called the Church and Community Workshop) at the Candler School of Theology in 1947, I was impressed. The marble buildings and the mystique surrounding those hallowed halls stirred me as I had seldom been stirred. I was at Emory.

Growing up a poor boy in Harrison and Tennille during the depression, experiencing the interruption of my college studies during the war years, supplying small churches in South Georgia, I felt that I could never have the advantages of being a student at Emory University.

Graduates I had known from there were somehow different, a breed apart, superior in some way. They had been full-time students, studied under that storied faculty for three or more years and earned degrees.

They were smart.

They were leaders.

They were prepared to serve large churches.

Their self-assurance and knowledge intimidated me.

Now I was at Emory, if only for a two week workshop. I felt privileged just to be on the campus, to see the learned professors in person, to walk the same halls, to worship in the same chapel, and to stand in awe before the mass of knowledge

Five generations beginning with number 1, Mama, Ollie Ross Freeman, seated and holding the youngest great-great-grandchild. I'm number 2, standing to the right. Number 3 is my oldest daughter, Joye Freeman Hancock, standing to the left. Joye's daughter Laura Jones is number 4 holding her oldest, Ryan Jones, number 5, the first great-great-grandchild.

collected in the library and minds in this place. Emory was to be the focal point of my life for twenty-two years.

Two men made it possible for me to register as a student: Jim Sells, who had paved the way for many others to realize their dreams, and J. P. Morris of Baxley who gave me the courage to venture beyond what I knew by offering a series of postdated checks for fifty dollars a month to assure that I could feed my wife and three children during these student years.

Nothing but the hand of God, opening doors through friends, and directing my path in larger circles, could account for my expanding career. I certainly did not know enough to plan it. How else could this country preacher have met Arthur Moore, Earl Brewer, Dean Trimble, D. W. Brooks, top leadership at the Sears Roebuck Foundation, Alex Nunn of *The Progressive Farmer*, and the brilliant Bill Cannon. Step by step the path unfolded.

EXAMINING CANDIDATES

Only once in my life can I recall specifically asking for a particular assignment. I wrote to Bishop Arthur J. Moore in spring of 1959 to tell him reasons why I would make a good member of the South Georgia Board of Ministerial Training and Qualifications. I pointed out that because of my relation to students from South Georgia attending the Candler School of Theology, I could furnish information and insight to the Conference Board. I asked to be considered for the board. He saw the value of the request and honored it. When membership of the newly constituted boards was announced, I was there. To my amazement I was elected chairman and served for eight years.

Members of the board were qualified and conscientious. They took the responsibility seriously and served the conference well. H. W. "Speed" Scoates was registrar for the first four-year term and W. Guy Parrish was registrar the second. They dealt with the candidates efficiently and with compassion. We examined and directed and encouraged those who were offering themselves for the ministry as they made their

Enabling Pastors

Academic administration at the Emory University Candler School of Theology.

ways through the tedious process of qualifying for ordination and appointment. We began the practice of robing the candidates and presenting stoles to the new elders in South Georgia. When our committee discussed the possibility of adding dignity to the ordination ceremonies in this fashion with Bishop John Owen Smith, he applauded the idea and purchased the stoles himself for the first classes. North Georgia followed our lead in this matter. Both conferences have continued the tradition. The board added other innovative ideas during these years.

A huge part of my life has been concerned with providing and preparing pastors for churches including the fifteen years at the Candler School of Theology in academic administration and directing the program of supervised ministry.

A Journey Beyond

These experiences came to focus directly in the five and a half years I served as a member of the Bishop's Cabinet and superintendent of the Macon District.

It is not an exaggeration to say that for almost a quarter of a century most of my waking attention was invested in thinking about and planning for competent pastors to serve the church.

SKILLS DEVELOPED AT CANDLER

The position as assistant to Earl Brewer, the skills I learned in the Religious Research Center, was the result of being a student. Doors opened for me to direct the Church and Community Workshop and the expanding continuing education program at Candler. The opportunity of directing the seventeen-state, interdenominational and interracial church development program grew out of my being there. These responsibilities were preparing the way to the future. At each new step, I had to appear before the entire faculty to give an account of what I was doing and to win their approval.

Dean H. B. Trimble was retiring as dean in 1953 and moving to the Development Office to raise money through the One Percent Plan and the Committee of One Hundred for the School of Theology. Dr. William R. Cannon, professor of church history and historical theology, was chosen by the trustees to succeed Dr. Trimble. Some of the faculty resented his selection. Others, older, wanted it themselves. They fomented a small rebellion that resulted in five professors leaving when their schemes did not succeed in either blocking or unseating the new dean. One of those who left was the administrative officer and assistant to the dean. A replacement was needed immediately.

As was his custom, the new dean moved quickly. He had been impressed by what he had seen and heard of my work in the Religious Research Center, the Church and Community Workshop and the Southwide Church Development Program. He checked with several who had been closer to my work and decided that I could handle the responsibilities. He offered me the opportunity of working with him as assistant to the dean

Enabling Pastors

and director of field work. From the beginning, my responsibilities included the following:

- arranging the course schedule each quarter,
- editing the catalog and other publications of the school,
- guiding the academic program of the students to see that they fulfilled the requirements for graduation on schedule,
- awarding scholarships and finding additional financial resources to assist students in need of money in order to stay in school,
- working with faculty and student committees,
- working with pastors and being in charge of student assignments to churches,
- consulting with the bishops and district superintendents about the appointments of one hundred or so student pastors each year,
- and anything else that came up.

I was twenty-nine at the time. The salary was at the level of an assistant professor, less than I was making as a student pastor—and I had to provide my own housing. Never has salary been a determining factor in any appointment I received. The size of the job, not the salary, attracted me. Only once in my whole career did I move at an increase.

When I had time to think about it and realized that I would be working with the august faculty members of the Candler School of Theology, looking after the welfare of students and their families and guiding the studies of prospective candidates for the ministry, I was terrified.

There was much to learn. I set about mastering the requirements of the job. Of course, Dean Cannon and Associate Dean Mack B. Stokes were always available for wise counsel and patient guidance. Fortunately I had access to and a good working relationship with the administrative offices of the university. Faculty committees were designated to guide various phases of the responsibility. I was named secretary of the faculty and secretary of the Academic Policy Committee—

the two most influential bodies in the school—to keep minutes of all the proceedings. Supervision of the academic records office, the student aid office, the supervised ministry office, and the faculty secretaries were my responsibility. It was also my task to keep up with the day-to-day budgets of the school, making certain that expenditures did not exceed budgeted amounts.

The dean, associate dean, and I visited annual conferences and colleges to recruit students and garner support. We functioned in public relations and development for the school of theology. Constant cultivation of the churches and colleges was a prerequisite of success. Often the load off campus was heavier than the duties on campus.

There was never a job description. I ascertained my duties as I went along. One of Dean Cannon's methods, when things came up in faculty meetings, was to refer the matter to me for action. He was proud of his "clean desk" policy, handling everything immediately. He kept his desk clean by transferring mountains of work to mine. This practice continued when I was a district superintendent in his cabinet. I presume he did the same thing with Nick Grant in North Carolina, and Hugh McKee and A. C. Epps in Georgia, and others. His phenomenal mind enabled him to grasp so much material. He never forgot a detail. He was an administrator after the pattern of Ronald Reagan with implicit trust in his associates.

Help was added about a decade later in 1963 when the Reverend Don Nichols, one of our older students from the Florida Conference, was placed in charge of recruitment.

SUPERVISED MINISTRY

I inherited the concept of field work from Professor James W. May who had followed the pattern established by Professor Emmett Johnson. Emmett Johnson, along with Dr. Arva Floyd, who had been a missionary to Japan and now professor of missions at Candler, devised the popular Cuba project to send seminary students for experiences on the mission field. All three of us were from South Georgia. They did a fine job of developing forms and establishing relationships with

Enabling Pastors

churches and others who employed seminary students. Jimmy May created wonderful opportunities for students to work with the metropolitan YMCA sports programs for unprivileged children. Students learned a lot about discipline, responsibility, and teamwork from the professionals at the YMCA. Field work, in the view of Emmett Johnson and Jimmy May, remained finding jobs for students.

Dr. May employed and trained Helen Stowers as secretary for the Field Work office in 1952. She became for me, as she was for him, my greatest asset in this responsibility. She stayed with me for fifteen years and continued to serve Candler until her retirement. She was a genius at learning the names and families and needs of the students. She learned about the entering classes before they came by studying their application folders. Each one sent a picture and biographical information. When they arrived in her office, she called them by name and asked about their families and other personal matters. They were amazed that she knew so much about them. Helen Stowers was the most helpful friend students found at Candler. She was the "Mother Confessor," the one to whom they turned with personal and financial problems or difficulties with their supervisors. She was the solver of every problem for hundreds of students.

Jimmy May, who served as a military chaplain during World War II, was a perfectionist. Well organized himself, he insisted that students develop good work habits and fulfill obligations punctually. He drilled them in Methodist polity and practice. His major interest in those days, however, was in completing his doctorate at Vanderbilt and teaching American church history full time. He was concerned with scholarly pursuits. So he requested Dean Cannon to release him from duties as director of Field Work and permit him a full load of courses. It came at the time the dean was interviewing me.

My reputation as an advocate for the rural church inclined him to consider me for the additional responsibility. After all, student pastors would be serving country churches, he reasoned, and they might learn something from me. He consented to relieve Jimmy May from administrative duties and added director of Field Work to my position as assistant to the dean. My title changed through the years as the duties expanded.

I have never been willing to leave things as I found them. Soon, therefore, I began exploring ways to make jobs we found for students a part of their educational experience. Some few seminary students had wealthy parents. They were the exceptions. God, it seems, did not call many into the ministry who were rich. Most needed financial assistance.

After World War II a new phenomenon appeared on the seminary campus, as indeed it did on every campus in America. Veterans, having delayed their education, were now ready to pick up their lives. The GI Bill provided financial grants for further study. So they enrolled in large numbers at Candler to prepare for the ministry. Emory was not prepared either in terms of faculty or space. Discarded military barracks were moved to the campus to house students and to provided classroom space. Many of them had families by now. They were not young and callow youths graduating from college. Many were battle-hardened. They had given years to their country. In the process they added decades to their life experiences and maturity. No room was left for wasting time. Class discussions took on a different dimension, more focused, more serious. They demanded more of the professors.

At the same time, the end of the war signaled a period of growth and expansion in the church. Churches needed pastors. Large churches needed assistants. Students with families needed to earn money to pay school and living expenses. The two needs met in my office. We became an employment office assisting students and their wives to find jobs and district superintendents to find pastors for their churches. Thus began the era of older students attending seminary. The trend continues.

During the years that I was in this office, I met with the bishop and cabinet every year to appoint more than a hundred student pastors in North Georgia. Most of the time, they accepted my recommendations after interviewing the students. They realized that I knew more about the students and their abilities than they did. In my role, the district superintendents expected me to assist with the supervision of these student pastors. I was glad to do this, because I wanted the

Enabling Pastors

years to be a part of their education for ministry, to be considered an apprenticeship when they learned through guided experience the art of being pastors.

My work at Emory was never confined to the campus. Much of it was done among the churches the students served. It was necessary that I keep one foot in the academy but the other had to be firmly planted in the church. This was a fortunate arrangement for me. It gave me an opportunity to work with the laypeople, district superintendents, bishops, and faculty in supporting and interpreting the students. In many ways I had the privilege of bridging the gap between the community and university.

The seminary needed to do more in this area if we were to achieve the vision of graduating well-informed pastors who were professionally prepared to lead the church. I asked for a faculty committee to work toward achieving the goal. To my great delight, Earl Brewer was made chairman. Sam West, professor of Christian education, Gordon Thompson, professor of homiletics and a distinguished pastor and superintendent in North Georgia before joining the faculty, the professor of pastoral counseling and clinical education, and a number of others who had served local churches formed the committee. Several pastors and district superintendents and directors of Christian education were added. It was a good committee. They shaped the vision.

The name was changed from Field Work to Supervised Ministry. Credit was given toward the degree for those who were successful. A few were denied graduation until they had fulfilled the expectation.

First year students, under this new program, were required to have experience in the secular world to learn how people in other professions did their work. We arranged for students to spend some time at General Motors plants in the area to learn about labor union and management interaction in the corporate work. Others were given assignments in the Federal Reserve Bank of Atlanta to find out how the financial world functions. Opportunities were provided at the Centers for Disease Control near the Emory campus so seminary students could see disciplined and determined medical scientists hounding out the causes and prevention of epidemics. Openings were provided at Sears Roebuck so students could learn about marketing, sales, and meeting the public. Other possibilities were arranged. In addition to experiencing what goes on in worlds where laypeople spend their time, the program of Supervised Ministry called for weekly group reflection and evaluation sessions. We defined the purpose of these evaluation sessions as "finding value in experience." Regular faculty led the groups.

Students were required in the second year to be involved in the church. Adjunct faculty led these second-year evaluation sessions. Each student kept a notebook recording his or her experiences and learnings for a year. As director of Supervised Ministry I read and approved all the reports.

During the third year, students were involved in Clinical Pastoral Education courses either in hospital or teaching parish settings. Our goal was to graduate students with a working knowledge and competent skills in interpersonal relations as professionals.

Adjunct faculty members, already successful in the conference, were carefully selected as models, trained, and supervised by the Supervised Ministry office at Candler. Most of them went on to provide leadership in other areas throughout the conference.

I have already noted that more than a hundred, primarily older students, served appointments under district superintendent. The office of Supervised Ministry gave these student-pastors special attention. Not only were they learning as they studied, but they were the only pastors these congregations had. Throughout their seminary careers they met regularly in small groups with adjunct faculty members related to the office of Supervised Ministry to discuss any problems they might be having and better ways of being pastors to their churches.

Every student, therefore, was on a dual track. On one hand they were seriously involved in demanding academic requirements. On the other hand they were discovering what it was like to minister to people. At the same time they were learning about the church in its theological function, they were also being the church in the world.

Enabling Pastors

WORKING WITH STUDENTS

One of my assignments was to write and edit the catalog. It was the annual prestige publication and sales piece for the school. We did not, at that time, publish a scholarly journal. The School of Theology and Emory University were both concerned about the quality of the catalog. We competed for students with other seminaries. The catalog was a major recruitment tool for new students. They compared what we said about the program, courses, requirements, and commitments of the seminary with others. In a sense, entering students considered the catalog a contract which they expected both the school and themselves to fulfill.

The dean's office, faculty committees, and the university office of publication scrutinized the material included and made contributions. Working with the faculty in designing their course descriptions was an enlightening experience for me. As brilliant as they were, they sometimes had difficulty writing succinct and appealing descriptions. I helped, especially the younger members, draft statements for their courses to encompass what they wanted to include and at the same time attract students for them. Fewer and fewer courses were required in the newer patterns of theological education during the 1960s. Students had to be convinced to register for elective courses that they needed.

As much as I enjoyed this, my greatest delight came from working with the students. I processed all the applications, evaluated their transcripts, and read the recommendations for admission. I knew the colleges from which they came, a good bit about their family backgrounds, and the level of commitment they brought to seminary. I interpreted their psychological and personality test scores. I knew their strengths and weaknesses. Sometimes it seemed wise to guide them into careers away from the ministry. At times it caused me great pain to dismiss a student for moral or psychological disorders. Occasionally I referred one for even more serious psychiatric counseling or hospitalization.

For the major part they were wholesome, well-rounded, promising students. They were great human beings. It was a privilege to help some with academic problems, some with personal problems, some with financial problems, and some who ran into trouble with one or more faculty members. A few resented me; others became life-long friends whom I have admired across the years as they developed into stronger and stronger leaders in the church.

Some times, as I traveled or preached, I met individuals of grace and means to help seminary students. These I catalogued and later wrote to them about individuals who needed a temporary financial boost. In my office, primarily through Mrs. Stowers, we knew such things.

One day we learned that one of our student pastors was embarrassed because he did not have a suit to wear in the pulpit or for funerals or weddings. I drove to Bremen and requested an appointed with Mr. Warren Sewell, a wonderful Baptist man who manufactured suits. I had met him and several of his top executives when I preached in Bremen. His philanthropy and generosity were well known. I knew, for example, that he tailored a suit each fall and another in the spring for Bishop Arthur J. Moore. His company provided scholarships for the Church and Community Workshop each summer.

I asked to see him for three minutes. He was available. I told him I wanted two minutes to tell him a story and one minute for his response. He welcomed me graciously and listened attentively. When I told him about the student pastor who couldn't afford a suit, he asked for his measurements, preferred color and said it would be in my office within a week. Then, far more than I expected, he said with tears in his eyes that any time I found a seminary student who needed a suit that I was to let him know. From then until I left Emory in 1969, I contacted him three or four times a year. Many students benefited. He never hesitated to send the suits requested.

One fall I was invited to preach for several days at the First Methodist Church in the delightful North Georgia mountain town of Calhoun. One of the members, Clarence Jones, a carpet manufacturer, attended the services and invited the evangelistic team to dinner in his colonial style home. He told

Enabling Pastors

an amazing story about his life and conversion. It was dramatic. I was deeply impressed. Though he was still determined to live a Christian life, he declared, he was a mite discouraged with the way some church people were taking advantage of his commitment.

When he became a Christian, he realized that he was supposed to tithe according to the Bible. So he began. After a while he reached the conclusion that if he was expected to tithe his personal income his business ought to be Christian and tithe the profit from his carpet business. Months later, he was reviewing his income tax returns and felt that his business was giving too little. So he came to insight about tithing beyond anything I had ever heard. From then on, he decided, his business would tithe not what he was making but what he wished he was making. He tripled the amount the company was giving that year. To his amazement, earnings for the next tax period also tripled. So he took another step.

Word spread rapidly that Clarence Jones had money to give away. So people beat a path to his door. Appeals came from every corner. One church needed a new roof. Another wanted a new pulpit Bible. When he took a look at what was happening with God's money, he saw that it leaked away in insignificant causes.

So he reached a higher level of understanding stewardship. If God expected him and his business to tithe, then God expected him to invest sacred money for the largest possible dividends to the kingdom. Wow! What an insight!

A few months later Mr. Jones invited me for a visit to discuss the decision he had reached.

He had decided that God's money could be used to produce the most good for the kingdom by investing in the preparation of seminary students who would pay dividends for a lifetime of service in the kingdom where they served.

He wanted to start by establishing a fund for me to administer at Emory to assist students who were having a hard time. Sometimes, he said, a few hundred dollars might make the difference between whether a student could remain in seminary or have to drop out. I knew that to be the case because of my intimate work with students at Candler. Some had to leave school before they graduated simply because they could no longer pay their bills.

One year Mr. and Mrs. Jones decided to have a dinner for all the students and their wives who had benefited from his generosity. That night, one of many to follow, was an emotion-filled evening. The students did not know that others were receiving help. It was all done confidentially. The checks came from Emory University with no indication of the source.

At one point Mr. Jones asked about their backgrounds and about where they planned to serve. Even I was astounded. Three would be serving the next year on mission fields in three different parts of the world. Others were being appointed in June to churches in annual conferences around the nation.

With deep feeling, Mr. Jones told that he had only one child, a daughter. He had no son. "I can not preach no matter how committed I am to Christ," he said, "But look at you. Every Sunday of the year I will be preaching by proxy in different pulpits around the nation and overseas through you and your families." This gave him great satisfaction as the numbers of those he helped multiplied year after year.

One season I persuaded the dean that the seminary needed a professional choir or singing group. For a number of years, Professor Dewey, famous as director of the Emory Glee Club, came over to assist in the School of Theology worship services. Now he had retired. No money was available, of course, within the budget to start a new program. We did find a way to provide full-tuition scholarships for students who were willing and qualified as musicians. William M. (Bill) Adams, who grew up in Statesboro, Georgia, was persuaded to be student-director. Auditions were given. Choir members selected. Rehearsals announced. The Candler Choraliers inaugurated. Services of worship greatly benefited. They were good. We sent them on a concert tour in the spring and they sang for the Southeastern Jurisdictional Conference at Lake Junaluska in July.

When Bill graduated, other arrangements had to be made. At that point, John Reed (Jack) Crawford was brought as

Enabling Pastors

assistant professor of sacred music in the fall of 1966. He was the seminary's first full-time professor of church music. Since then, Candler has developed a very professional program of liturgical music and worship.

CONTINUING EDUCATION

In the frontier days, presiding elders prepared young preachers. There was, especially in the South, a suspicion of seminaries. When a person was called to preach, "God equipped them." The older preachers instructed them, gave them books to read, and mentored their young charges. The Methodist Episcopal Church, South, did have Vanderbilt University with a major commitment to educating preachers. When the church lost Vanderbilt in 1912, General Conference voted to create two new universities, one east of the Mississippi and one west of the Mississippi, to be tied irrevocably to the church by charter. Southern Methodist University was started in Dallas. Emory College, founded at Oxford in 1836 by Georgia Methodists, served as the nucleus of Emory University and in 1914 opened the Druid Hills campus in Atlanta. Gradually the bias against theological education disappeared.

Prior to 1940, there were two main routes to meeting the qualifications for ordination in the Methodist Episcopal Church, South. One was by graduating from seminary. The other route was through correspondence. A course of study was prescribed by the Department of Ministerial Education of the General Board of Education in Nashville. Books were assigned and instructions given. Seminary faculty members graded papers. Candler was a major link in this process.

The Candler School of Theology pioneered the Course of Study School for lay pastors. It began in 1946 as the School for Accepted Supply Pastors. Dean Trimble and others decided that it would be better for laypersons serving as pastors to spend a month on the campus several summers with regular faculty members teaching them rather than to cover the same material by correspondence. Other seminaries later adopted the plan.

Dr. E. Stanley Jones, seated at the center with Dean William R. Cannon (right) and his business manager (left) when he came to Emory University to discuss establishing the E. Stanley Jones Foundation to house the five major aspects of his worldwide ministry. Standing, left to right, Dr. G. Ray Jordan, professor of homiletics, Dr. Judson C. Ward, vice president of the university, me, and Dr. J. Ross McCain, president of the Protestant Radio and Television Center and retired president of the Agnes Scott College in Decatur. Bishop James K. Mathews became president and Dr. Freeman became vice president of the Institute.

Nashville agreed. It was so superior that the correspondence program was gradually discontinued. The Course of Study School became the second continuing education or in-service training program at Candler.

Late in the administration of Dean Franklin N. Parker, Ministers' Week was inaugurated in January of 1935 with Professor Lavens Thomas as chairman. He served until ill health forced his retirement in 1939. Duties for directing the annual activities of Ministers' Week were then assumed by Professor Arva C. Floyd who gave brilliant leadership for

Enabling Pastors

twenty-five years. I succeeded Dr. Floyd and served as director until 1969.

The mid-winter week gave alumni and other church leaders an opportunity to come to the campus, hear some of the world's most distinguished religious leaders, and renew friendships with people around the Southeast.

Reference has already been made to the Rural Pastors School, which came later to be called the Church and Community Workshop. This two-week experience brought more than a hundred active pastors to the campus each summer for twenty-three years from an average of seventeen states. It was interdenominational, and eventually became interracial.

We later added the Workshop in Communications and Preaching under the leadership of Dr. G. Ray Jordan, Dr. James W. Sells, David Abernathy, and the Protestant Radio and Television Center. While it was primarily a venture in continuing education for ministers already serving in the parish, it's impact spilled over into the training of seminary students. We introduced video camera recording and feedback components for courses in homiletics. Organization and management of this workshop was also my responsibility.

The Urban Church Workshop was a natural outgrowth of the Church and Community Workshop. It provided an opportunity to apply the same sociological skills in analysis and seeking solutions to urban church problems that we used in the rural church.

CHAPTER FIVE

Inspiring Laity

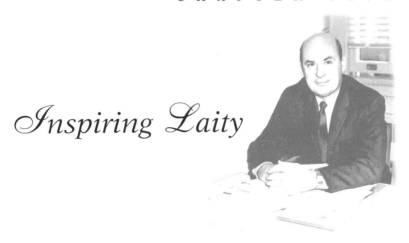

Most of my professional life involved providing and equipping clergy, but my most satisfying work has been among laity. I considered my personal assignment in every appointment to mentor and disciple several laypeople into strong leaders upon whom the church could depend. This word from Paul to Timothy was my mandate: ". . . what you have heard . . . entrust to faithful people who will be able to teach others . . ." (2 Tim. 2:2 NRSV).

My philosophy as a pastor was to build up the local church by teaching and guiding laypeople. I felt that I had failed if I did not develop several well-trained laypeople, no matter what the pastor's salary, budget, programs, and new buildings reflected. This is still my conviction. Build the people not the reputation of the pastor. After all, the church body is made up of 99.3 percent laypeople. Unfortunately, in my judgment, the United Methodist Church too often invests its resources, spends its energy and writes its rules for the benefit of professional clergy. Maybe this needs to change.

I am convinced that lay minds can grasp the teachings of the Bible, basic principles of theology, and purpose of the church. If they can master the intricacies of modern agriculture, make a living in the convoluted world of international business, and understand the mysteries of big finance, they can get their minds around the organization of the church. They only need to be trusted; they can be trained.

This excerpt from an address that I delivered to a series of district workshops in the Mississippi Conference reflects my point of view.

> The church, through its laity, is called to move with courage and intentionality into the quivering ferment of our time. Direction must be given the turbulent force unleashed in the world. Unless its energy for change is harnessed for the good of humankind, the early decades of the twenty-first century may bring social and political upheavals so violent that we will not need a seismograph to record them. In that case who can predict what terror shall stalk the earth before the dawn of a new era can chase the shadows of tyranny and oppression and fear from the human scene. In times of general unrest, the most aggressive and disciplined forces shape the outcome.
>
> Those who want tomorrow to be directed by the forces of God must risk plunging into the boiling cauldron of contemporary unrest in order to direct the future. While the world rocks convulsively in the shock waves of unbridled change and the irresistible revolution of human expectation surges toward the future, Christians are called into the storm center.
>
> All the people of God are needed to transform the kingdoms of this world into the kingdom of our God. Professional religious workers alone can not accomplish it. Most areas of struggling forces are closed to them. Only lay Christians have access to the power centers of society and are in position to transform them.

Some of the major movements of Christian history bringing vitality and enrichment to the church have been born among the laypeople. Jesus appointed seventy persons as the first lay witnesses (Luke 10:1). None of them were clergy. Sent in teams of two, they talked with convincing enthusiasm

Inspiring Laity

about the kingdom, about what Jesus was doing, and about what they were discovering in him. They came back rejoicing—in the way I have observed lay witnesses returning from a mission—amazed that God was able to use them.

In a sense, the Methodist movement is—or was—a lay movement. It's true that the Wesleys were educated and ordained. A few clergy helped. Most of his workers were laypeople who had been converted and were on fire with the love of God. John Wesley taught them, directed them, and assigned them as lay preachers.

In the 1760s, two Irish lay preachers immigrated to these shores—Robert Strawbridge to Maryland and Philip Embury to New York. Neither knew the other was in America. They collected a few people, started class meetings, and eventually organized societies. These lay Christians were the first to established permanent work in the new continent. Earlier efforts to begin societies in the colonies by John and Charles Wesley and George Whitfield all failed. Lay preachers spread the movement through the wilderness.

Sunday school was a lay movement. In its glory days, there were great Sunday school rallies. Attendance in study for most churches exceeded attendance at worship until after the 1950s when professionals took over the educational function of the local churches.

The Laymen's Missionary Movement blossomed in the first part of the twentieth century, started the Lake Junaluska Assembly, and kindled a passion for missions.

Volunteers-in-Mission, the phenomenal expression of the missionary spirit which began in the latter half of the twentieth century, is primarily a lay emphasis though pastors are involved. This well organized program continues the dream of the Laymen's Missionary Movement.

At the same time, riding the same spiritual wave in the late 1950s, Lay Witness Missions came into being.

LAY WITNESS MISSIONS

One day at Emory, a tall, good-looking preacher from Phenix City, Alabama, appeared in my office. He was a graduate of Asbury Theological Seminary and had received a master's degree from the Southern Baptist Theological Seminary of Louisville, Kentucky. He was serving a good church in the Alabama-West Florida Annual Conference. Already he was establishing himself as an innovative pastor and sought after as a revival preacher.

Ben Johnson was a force to be reckoned with even then. He told me an incredible story. Recently his work as an evangelist had grown stale. Though he preached as hard as ever, nothing was happening in the church to which he was invited.

Then he started a prayer group in Phenix City. Sometimes God intervened in the group. They learned to trust one another, to confide in one another, and to pray for one another. Ben told them in one session about his sense of futility in revivals. His sermons were not reaching the hearts of people. They prayed for him.

Soon after he was in a particularly difficult church, and there was no evidence that God was breaking through. So he sent for his prayer group to come on Thursday night at their regular meeting time. They encircled him with prayer before and during the service.

When he stood to preach, he was moved to ask several of them to share their witness. He was surprised. They were surprised. The pastor was surprised. The people were surprised. All at once, those chosen to share were anointed. The congregation was electrified. Hearing laypeople talk about what God was doing in their lives stirred the church. Ben had enough judgment—or was led by the Spirit—not to preach after that. Instead he gave an altar call. The people rushed forward to kneel. The altar service lasted more than an hour. People kept coming. It was the witness of laypeople rather than the preacher's sermon that stirred them.

That night Ben Johnson's life was redirected. The next time he was invited to preach for revival services, he arranged in advance for the prayer group to come on Thursday night. Word spread about how God was using them. More pastors urged him to come to their churches. Something new was happening.

Ben wanted to study lay movements in church history and discover, if he could, their secrets.

Inspiring Laity

So he decided to apply to Emory.

That's when he walked into my office. I was mesmerized. I guided him in the process of applying for admission for a doctoral program, suggested that he ask Dr. Claude H. Thompson to direct his studies, and urged him to get in touch with Dr. James W. Sells. His academic credentials were impeccable. He was admitted.

He asked his bishop to appoint him to attend school.

Dr. Sells, with his strange gift of believing in people, found resources to rent a house near the campus for Ben, his wife, and daughter.

So began the phenomenon of the Lay Witness Mission movement.

Even after Ben began his doctoral program, pastors continued calling him about revivals. He told them he couldn't come except for weekends. They were willing for him to come on Friday night, after his school week, and remain through Sunday night. He remembered his experiences with the prayer group, so he invited them, at first, to go with him. Later others were included in the list. At first he preached and interspersed laypeople to witness. Soon he discovered that power was released as their stories were told. Gradually the weekend schedule began to shift. His preaching was minimized. Their roles were expanded. He moderated the sessions; they provided the story. Still later, he found that these open and honest and prayer-filled laypeople could be effective in leading small groups. Sunday morning altars were filled. Prayer groups, like the ones in Phenix City, were started. The movement was launched.

While Ben was hard at work on his studies, he also took time to record what was happening and to analyze why. I met with him often during those days to evaluate what was going on and to help him think through the implications. God was doing a new thing in the church. What was being discovered had to be simplified so the experiences could be replicated if the movement was to be valid and to spread. Material had to be written. Leaders had to be identified, manuals produced, guidance given. Booklets were published inexpensively in Phenix City. I was drawn more and more into the emerging operation.

Word actually spread by word of mouth. Excited people from churches who had received such a visitation eagerly reported to others. Calls were coming from churches in Mississippi, the Carolinas, Florida, and Georgia, as well as Alabama. More and more witnesses were needed. The few who were involved in the beginning simply were not able to be gone every weekend. They had responsibilities at home and in their local churches. Others had to be found. Even more significantly, more invitations were coming than Ben could handle. So a new aspect was forced into reality. Coordinators had to be chosen and developed to conduct the missions.

Nothing much was known about the movement in official denominational circles. There was no publicity, no endorsement as the plan developed. True, Jim Sells knew. True, I was watching it carefully. After all, Emory was tangentially involved at the time.

The Southeastern Jurisdictional Association of Conference Lay Leaders program committee decided to include Ben on the agenda for the Jurisdictional Laity Conference at Lake Junaluska. So impressive was his appearance that the Association decided to become an official umbrella to champion the movement.

Institute of Church Renewal

Those nearest the movement, and closest to Ben, recognized the need for organizational and administrative accountability. It was getting too big for a full-time student to manage alone. He was operating out of the back of his car and a closet in his home. It was time to build a foundation to assure the future.

The movement was incorporated as the Institute of Church Renewal. A board was chosen. An advisory committee created. They asked me to be president. We set up an office and created a small staff. For a decade, 1960–70, I watched, sometimes nervously, over the spread of the program and its influence for renewal in the church as we became sophisticated and established a publishing arm called Forum House.

The list of witnesses and coordinators grew as more and more churches had missions. All wanted to learn. We brought

Inspiring Laity

people who were gifted with leadership ability to the campus at Emory for training. Faculty members and others designed lectures on the Bible, systematic theology, church history, and group dynamics specifically for lay witnesses and coordinators. These lectures were recorded and edited into audio teaching courses. Some materials were designed in an interactive programmed-learning format with built-in instructions for small group discussion. Churches experiencing renewal ordered these by the hundreds. Correspondence multiplied, scheduling missions was increasingly complicated, and the sale of books became a major function. I requested a faculty committee to guide the training process and provide institutional credibility.

The movement was attracting more attention. One day a representative of the Lily Foundation asked if we would like to apply for a grant. We did. The Division of Education and Religion responded positively to what was happening. Officials of the Division of Education and Religion were interested in investing some money. In addition to the answers required on the application, they wanted us to go nationwide and interdenominational. Moreover, they asked for an official connection with Emory University so that the grant could be made through Emory. All of this was done, and a three-year grant was made. For a time in the mid-1960s, the Institute of Church Renewal and direction of the Lay Witness movement spread under the aegis of Emory University.

What was the secret? Concept and program evolved out of experience. People who were converted had a story to tell. They were instructed to share honestly and to give God the credit. Teams of fifteen or twenty and sometimes more—the number depended on the size of the church—stayed as guests in homes of the congregation. Often their presence proved to be blessing in disguise as God ministered to the family.

The movement was reinforced by prayer. Prayer for the weekend started when the date was set and continued throughout the event. Every time a person got up to witness, he or she would call on someone to "pray for me."

The movement was characterized by a warm and wonderful fellowship among the team members. Before the Friday evening dinner, they would gather. After they greeted one another with hugs and joyous laughter, they talked a bit about the weekend. They prayed that they would be open to the Spirit of God. They asked that God move among them.

There was spirited and simple chorus singing. After the home folks were gone, the Team would evaluate and pray and sing "Victory in Jesus" and "How Great Thou Art." These were theme songs. Later we became sophisticated enough to sing "Kumbayah" and "Allelu, Allelu, Allelujah." Hymns and gospel songs were also used. Prayer power was real and authentic.

There was another secret. We insisted on coordinators studying so that there was understanding of their limitations, solid depth of Scripture and prayer, and spiritual integrity about what was done. Coordinators were guided through reading, listening to prescribed tapes, and serving as apprentices under experienced coordinators. A lot of time was spent in learning how to honor the host pastor and respect the spirit of the local church. Violators of this covenant were severely reprimanded. Attention was given to ways the coordinator could prepare the local church, guide the committees who were planning various elements of the weekend, and follow through after the event.

Witnesses for the team were prayerfully chosen and trained by the coordinator. One of the first rules, in true Wesleyan fashion, was "Do not harm." New witnesses would go first as observers on a mission. Experienced witnesses would help witnesses-in-training identify the best, most authentic part of their story to share.

But the thing that impressed local church members was that these people—doctors, lawyers, businessmen, farmers, college professors, homemakers, professional women, laborers, youth, long-time Christians, new converts, all kinds of people from every walk of life—would be blended into a team as if they were all the same. Each told his or her story in simple language. They didn't preach, they didn't teach, they didn't argue theology. They came at their own expense, giving up a full weekend and sometimes a workday, just for the joy of sharing "how it used to be, then Jesus came, and here's how it is now." There was power in telling their experiences.

Inspiring Laity

With new material and financial support from the Lily Endowment, the Lay Witness Missions spread to other sections of the nation, made inroads into other denominations, and were introduced into various parts of the world. Witness Teams went to the Philippines, Ireland, and Africa. People responded the same way wherever they went.

A tenth anniversary celebration was planned for the church in Phenix City, Alabama, where it all started. Representatives from many parts of the nation came. An international telephone hookup enabled those who were present to talk with people from several nations overseas about the power of lay witnesses. The occasion was a time of rejoicing for all that God was doing using laypeople in so many parts of the world.

Looking back upon those years, it is possible to record some solid accomplishments. Tens of thousands of laypeople were caught up in a new spiritual excitement during the turbulent decade of the 1960s. Lives were changed. Marriages were saved. Families were strengthened. Churches were revitalized. Literally thousands of laypeople, young and old, were given a voice to express their experiences and to find a ministry for their faith.

The teams encouraged people to collect themselves into prayer groups. Several emerged out of every mission. People wanted to study the Bible together, pray together, and support one another.

Hearing lay witnesses share their stories created spiritual and intellectual appetites. Leaders for each mission made available a selection of books and tapes on prayer and spirituality to recommend. People touched by the spirit of God went on retreats to find more truth. They bought books, and read them; bought teaching tapes, and listened to them in groups. New Christians started buying and studying different versions of the Bible, commentaries, and devotional material for going deeper with God.

A whole new market was created for Christian bookstores. Soon it was not enough just to hear others tell what Christ meant to them; people wanted to know for themselves.

There were some negatives. Some witnesses, it was reported, did more harm than good. In some churches spiritual cliques divided the congregation. A few pastors were repulsed. The "super pious" they encountered turned them off along with a lot of other people. But I also know from reading the correspondence and talking with people that literally thousands of churches were renewed and revitalized and brought to spiritual strength as a result of a few "foolish laypeople" who came to tell others about life in Christ.

Beyond the Institute

During the second decade of its existence, what started as a "movement" became "institutionalized" as a part of denominational structure. At one time, the General Board of Discipleship asked Ben Johnson to join the staff and bring the Lay Witness Movement into the official structure. He was unwilling to do it because of its growing ecumenical involvement, so he suggested one of his close friends and associates in the Alabama-West Florida Conference for the position. Walter Albritton had everything to give wings to the effort. He tried, but unable to work within the bureaucracy, he returned to the pastorate. Some new ideas were introduced, new material produced, but there was no revitalization.

Other denominations had offices to promote and guide the emphasis in their churches. The Episcopal Church called it the Faith Alive Movement for use in their churches.

In the meantime the General Board of Discipleship named Vance Archer, a layman, full-time staff member to direct the movement in the United Methodist Church.

In the 1970s things began to go wrong. When I returned to the pastorate in South Georgia, I was no longer close enough to give supervision to the work and thought it best to resign as president of the institute. Ben Johnson, who had been used of God to bless so many, made some bad choices. His marriage ended in divorce. When he remarried, some were not able to understand how such "a godly man" could justify his behavior. They became critical and lost faith in him. The association with Emory soured. The institute got into financial difficulty. The publishing arm declared bankruptcy.

Inspiring Laity

All at once, Johnson's communication with his supporters and coordinators and witnesses stopped. In a misunderstanding with the leaders of his conference, he turned in his ordination credentials and left the United Methodist Church. Thousands who looked to him for spiritual guidance as the architect of the movement felt abandoned.

At this point (1971–76) I was superintendent of the Macon District. Some of the people who had been so heavily involved in the movement—Harold Lumley, Gus Gustafson, Roy Lifsey, Lynn Utley, Walton Peabody, Bob Flanders, and a number of others—made an appointment to see me. They confessed that they felt like orphans, and wondered what to do. We decided to send an emissary to Ben to tell him the feelings and ask him what to do to straighten out any misunderstanding. They were unable to contact him after several attempts. Weeks later, they came back to see me, crestfallen. We decided to invite all the Georgia Lay Witness people we could find to a meeting at the Riverside United Methodist Church in Macon where Harold Lumley was a member. Vance Archer and several others came from the Nashville office.

We raised several questions: Has the day of the Lay Witness Mission run its course? Has its integrity been damaged? Can there be a future with a new leader? Is God still able to use it?

If so what should we do?

It was a time of heartbreaking soul-searching.

Through this dark period, God proved to be faithful. By the providence of God, the General Board of Discipleship in Nashville had established staff and procedures for scheduling missions across the church. Other denominations had likewise set up offices for doing the same thing. Coordinators kept their teams together. Some accepted invitations personally. Missions were still being conducted.

Harold Lumley and hundreds of others had been involved in coordinating missions to churches in Ireland. Harold discovered that some of the people from Ireland would be willing to come to Georgia and experience firsthand what the movement was like in the United States. Arrangements were made. A part of their itinerary called for witnesses who had

The Epworth By The Sea House Party in January 1993 was planned in our honor. Family and friends drove across the state at the invitation of Vernard Robertson who planned the entire affair with a banquet in the elegant Smith Dining Room.

gone to Ireland to gather for a reunion with them at Epworth By The Sea. That experience launched the annual Lay Witness Retreat at Epworth. It has continued for almost a quarter of a century as a rallying point for inspiration and encouragement.

The initiative begun in Macon was paying off. Other annual retreats were held in different states following this example. When the next meeting was held at Epworth, the decision was made to organize the Georgia Laity Board of Renewal and Gus Gustafson was chosen to exercise his organizational and promotional skills as executive director. The purpose was to encourage Lay Renewal Events in local churches, to publicize the results of missions, and to continue training coordinators and witnesses.

Gus was able to write a book for the Methodist Publishing House called, *I Was Called to be a Layman*. It contains his own story and those of outstanding Christian laypeople across America. With the encouragement of the General Board of Discipleship and the Foundation For Evangelism, Gus called

Inspiring Laity

together a small group of people to create a weekend retreat format for Discover God's Call—Where You Are. This movement too has spread and is now a national program. Step by step it has grown in influence and power.

Obviously, Gus had less and less time for the Georgia Laity Board of Renewal. The time came for another to be chosen as the executive director to plan the annual retreat and promote lay renewal events in cooperation with the national office in Nashville. John Woodall, Columbus District lay leader and a giant spirit, was the one identified to succeed Gus. When his health forced him to resign, Dick Williamson of Gainesville agreed to serve. Other duties made him give up the leadership as executive director. Kitty Fitzgerald of St. Simons Island has assumed responsibility since 1994 for managing the details and keeping the retreat alive.

A jurisdictional Lay Witness Retreat was held at Lake Junaluska in July of 1980, ten years after the tenth anniversary celebration in Phenix City, Alabama. It boosted the morale of the movement. Almost five hundred excited and hope-filled lay witness people registered for the event. I was, at that time, the executive director of the Southeastern Jurisdictional Council and worked diligently to make the retreat successful. Five major addresses, in addition to witnesses and workshop sessions, explored the historical, theological, and contemporary understanding of the movement. The papers were preserved. In one of them, the Reverend Danny Morris called us to examine the facts realistically.

"In the first ten years or so of the life of the Lay Witness Movement, it was like a rocket being launched through the sky," Danny Morris said in the address. Danny, Director of Emerging Ministries of the *Upper Room*, always a friend of Lay Witness, continued his address.

> At its heyday, in 1973–74, we scheduled 2,400 Lay Witness Missions from the Nashville Office. At the same time many were being scheduled for United Methodists in Atlanta, Wilmore, Florida, and other places. At that time we had an excess of 100,000 team members on our rolls in Nashville available to 1,200 coordinators for use in missions. Now we have fewer than half that many.

Numbers have declined even more since Danny made that speech, but the movement is still a valid force for renewal. When Vance Archer retired, the General Board of Discipleship put Shirley Clements in charge. She is a competent and dedicated staff member promoting and scheduling the lay renewal programs. She has been more than a caretaker, looking after details, supplying information, furnishing material for the events, certifying coordinators and keeping the movement alive at the turn of the century. She has worked diligently to infuse new life into the witnesses. Supporters of the movement are grateful for her leadership and dedication, and they are also indebted to the General Board of Discipleship and the Section on Evangelism for continuing to support the effort. Meanwhile, the movement awaits the emergence of a bold charismatic leader to thrust the vision forward.

Ben Johnson has reemerged as a spiritual leader. The Presbyterian Church recognized his gifts and ordained him for ministry. He obtained a doctor of ministry degree at the San Francisco Theological Seminary, was invited to the faculty of the Columbia Theological Seminary in Decatur, Georgia, and restored his relationship with the Candler School of Theology. Emory permitted him to pick up the Ph.D. program he abandoned and complete it. He serves as an authority and professor in evangelism for the United Presbyterian Church, continues to write books, and is again operating a publishing house.

ASSOCIATION OF CONFERENCE LAY LEADERS

The Jurisdictional Council was organized in 1945 after the Methodist Episcopal Church, the Methodist Episcopal Church, South, and the Methodist Protestant Church were reunited and divided into five regional jurisdictions and one based on race. Dr. William F. Quillian was the first executive secretary. Dr. James W. Sells was made responsible for working with small membership churches, leaders in stewardship, conference missionary secretaries, and the conference lay leaders. At one time or another he involved me in all of them to my great benefit. But my personality and

Inspiring Laity

method of operation seemed to click with the Association of Conference Lay Leaders.

Their president at the time was Howard Berg, a tall commanding figure, lay leader of the Florida Conference. His energy built the Laymen's Retreat at Leesburg from an average of two hundred a year to four different weekends with more than six hundred each session. He was a genius in organizing and motivating laity. When he became president of the Jurisdictional Association of Conference Lay Leaders, the same miraculous results followed at the Lake Junaluska Laity Conference. Less than two hundred were attending from all the conferences of the southeast at the start of his tenure. With attention to program, involvement, organization, and motivation, the crowds grew to eighteen hundred and two thousand in a few years—the largest attendance of any jurisdictional activity at the lake. Those events became the talk of the jurisdiction and of the general church. This launched an era of growing influence for the Association of Conference Lay Leaders.

I would like to claim that it was because of my reputation as a preacher that I was invited to speak several times in the mid-1950s, but it was not. In reality, however, I suspect that it was because of my relation with Jim Sells. He guided the association in planning the program. He must have dropped my name into the list of speakers. They had confidence in his counsel and took his recommendation.

The next year Howard Berg invited me to speak at the Leesburg Retreat. For several years I was a regular speaker for those events in Florida. I became part of their planning team. More importantly, Howard Berg asked Jim Sells to invite me to the Jurisdictional Association of Conference Lay Leaders when they met in Atlanta to plan conferences at Lake Junaluska.

I listened to them talk about what they wanted to see happen in the program. I made notes. Using a skill that I developed as secretary of the faculty and in committee meetings at the Candler School of Theology, I summarized the major points of their discussion and organized them into a clear outline of what they wanted to do. It was possible for me to draft a rough schedule for the program with which

Southeastern Jurisdiction Association of Conference Lay Leaders gathered in front of Lambuth Inn at Junaluska during a Laity Conference that attracted eighteen hundred people.

everybody was pleased. Later, with their permission, I helped design promotional brochures and enabled them to plan wonderful events.

I was an unpaid consultant and a fixture at the meetings of the Association of Conference Lay Leaders. They welcomed my presence and valued my contributions. Some of these lay leaders became my most trusted friends. My relationship as unofficial consultant and advisor continued several quadrennia through the administrations of Roy Black of North Mississippi, George Wright of South Georgia, Joe Pevahouse of Memphis, through my time at Emory and after I returned to South Georgia until Jim Sells retired in 1972.

The lay leaders continued to call upon me to help them design the annual Layman's Conference all during the years when Dr. Robert F. Lundy was executive secretary of the Southeastern Jurisdictional Council on Ministries. I was pleased to do it even though I had a demanding appointment in a local church and later as Macon District superintendent. Then I was elected to succeed Dr. Lundy as Executive Secretary.

Inspiring Laity

A new group of conference lay leaders arose on the horizon with a new "Pharaoh who knew not Joseph nor the things which he had done for Egypt." George Berry from North Mississippi succeeded Joe Pevahouse; Ed Montgomery from North Alabama followed George Berry. I watched as all three rose to leadership in the General Council on Ministries. I had other jurisdictional associations with whom to work and other programs to promote, so for a time my influence among the laity was diminished.

GENERAL BOARD OF THE LAITY

South Georgia sent me to General and Jurisdictional Conference for the first time in 1960. At the Jurisdictional Conference in 1964, I was elected to the General Board of the Laity as the only clergy from the Southeast. For eight years I went three or four times a year to Evanston and/or Chicago for the executive committee.

My friends, Howard Berg and Roy Black, were president and vice president of the General Board. Howard Berg was the only layperson in the church at the time that was president of a general agency. Clare Pettit of California-Nevada succeeded Howard Berg as president 1968–72. All other general boards and agencies were headed by bishops at that time. Robert G. Mayfield, a lawyer from Missouri, was the general secretary. He had assembled a splendid staff and team. To my amazement, I was named to the executive committee. They laughingly considered me a lay dropout. It was a fascinating relationship. For the next sixteen years I was actively involved as a member of two General Boards at the international church level.

I traveled across the country speaking at Jurisdictional and Annual Conference events in each of the five regions. I delivered a paper at the General Board of the Laity on "The Ministry of the Laity." The board authorized it to be printed as a booklet for distribution throughout the church.

A group of us from the General Board joined others from the United States in response to an invitation to participate in the 1965 *Kirchentag* in Cologne, Germany. After the defeat of the

A JOURNEY BEYOND

Nazis in World War II, some of the businessmen and professional men and other leading citizens began asking how such a civilized nation could have fallen so low as to let Hitler and his henchmen commit such barbaric atrocities. It was a period of soul-searching. They concluded that they had been morally asleep while it was happening, and they declared that the nation would never again allow such a travesty. They realized that the church had failed, and that they had failed the church. So they planned giant rallies periodically to be called a Rally of the Churches, *Kirchentag*. Millions turned out, many of them youth and young adults. Speeches, seminars, singing, and searching characterized the week. Major events were held in the streets. Every available space was used for meetings. The themes dealt with revitalizing Christianity in the nation that produced Martin Luther and the Reformation. It was sort of like the recent march of a million men on Washington. The media covered every facet. World leaders from other churches came.

My son George who had just graduated from high school went with us. He was fortunate enough to be housed with other young people. The son of the Lutheran leader in Cologne responsible for arranging the details was in the group.

Three million were there for the week. Between five and seven million were estimated for the open-air gathering for the weekend. All were seeking a deeper understanding of the will of God for themselves and the future. What an experience! Neither George nor I got much from the lectures or workshops. We were language-deprived. But the spirit was contagious, and enthusiasm was infectious. We found a niche among those who spoke English.

When it was over George and I joined a distinguished pastor from Indiana and the President of Illinois Wesleyan University to make a tour of the rural areas of Germany in a rented Volkswagen. We were able to stay off the beaten tourist paths and travel the country roads to the villages. Our adventure included a visit to the oldest walled city in Germany where they still locked the gates at night, trips into East Germany to see the devastation of war and communism, and through the beautiful scenery of Switzerland. Dr. Lloyd Bertholf had been a student in Munich before the war. He spoke enough German

Inspiring Laity

to ask directions and to order food and negotiate for rooms. Only he had a valid international driver's license; but only George could drive the stick shift VW smoothly.

DOCUMENTS PREPARED FOR DALLAS

My work with the General Board of the Laity led to participation in two consultations ordered by the General Conference in 1964 as a part of the conversations with Evangelical United Brethren Church about merging. One assignment was to write *A Theological Statement about the Place of the Laity in the Church*. The other was to prepare *A Foundation Statement for Christian Stewardship*.

A Theological Statement about the Laity

I delivered a lecture on "Equipping the Laity" for one of the sections of the World Methodist Conference in London in 1966. The document was distributed widely by the General Board of the Laity. Its contents became the grist for the assignment mandated for the General Board of the Laity in 1964 to prepare *A Theological Statement about the Laity*. The first full committee met at Emory where I had some influence in controlling the costs. Not enough budget or time was allowed, but we proceeded.

Our first task was to draft the scope and outline of the project. We then broke it down into manageable pieces and assigned responsibility for each section. When all the ideas were in hand, the committee met to hear the papers and determine what should be included. Decisions and suggestions were turned over to a writing team to draft the working document. It was submitted to several professors of theology and others for critiquing before the final statement was presented to the Board for approval and transmitted to General Conference.

The Legislative Committee in Dallas recommended adoption; but in the crunch of those hectic last days, the statement was included in the business approved by consensus and passed without debate.

A Journey Beyond

Foundation Statement for Christian Stewardship

The other document prepared for the General Conference in 1968 was the result of the General Board of the Laity mandate to write a *Foundation Statement for Christian Stewardship* in consultation with the EUB Department of Stewardship and the seminaries. I was part of the design team to plan a National Stewardship Seminar involving three hundred leaders in stewardship.

We met in Chicago with representatives from all Methodist and Evangelical United Brethren schools of theology, the best minds on stewardship and finance from Annual Conferences and the general agencies of both denominations. Presenters were chosen by the faculties who consulted with them in writing and delivering papers on designated topics for the consultation. Topics were assigned to cover every aspect of stewardship. Participants probed the implications of what was said in small groups. The major presenters debated the salient issues, questioned one another and responded to comments from the floor in a spirited interchange. All was recorded to preserve the collective insights and wisdom. Our task on the writing team was to digest the information and to write a document for consideration by the General Conference in 1968. The final product was adopted by the General Board of the Laity and sent through the General Conference process. Unfortunately the work was buried under other agendas at Dallas.

Though the legislative committee approved the *Foundation Statement for Christian Stewardship*, it was never presented to the total body. It was put on the consent calendar adopted by the General Conference and referred to the Creedal Study Commission. My working papers indicate that it may still be the most thorough piece of work in stewardship that Methodists have ever done.

STRONG LAY LEADERS ARE ESSENTIAL

When Robert G. Mayfield resigned as general secretary of the General Board of the Laity, I was named to head the search committee to find a replacement. It was not a duty I

Inspiring Laity

cherished. He was my friend, and I was devoted to him. Bob Mayfield had been an impassioned voice of the laity, especially for stewardship and Methodist men.

The search committee was determined to get the best person we could find for the job. We asked each bishop to nominate candidates they would recommend. Other agencies were invited to submit names. Annual Conference channels were explored to find suitable candidates. Out of the hundreds of strong people suggested, the search committee began the process of narrowing the list. It was reduced to twenty-five. Those were reexamined, their qualifications debated, and the list was reduced to a dozen. Additional information was sought, and the number reduced to five. They were invited for an interview. A schedule was developed to give them appointments.

The nationwide search led the committee to Dr. David W. Self. He was an educator with a doctorate from New York University. His wife, Helen Self, had a doctorate in special education from Columbia University. His credentials as a churchman, a leader among men and an advocate of the Lay Witness Movement commended him.

Almost before he could get started, the General Conference in Atlanta realigned the General Agencies and relocated the responsibilities and staff of the General Board of the Laity from Evanston, Illinois, to the newly expanded General Board of Discipleship in Nashville.

The effectiveness of the church in carrying out the great commission depends upon the character and commitment of the lay members in obeying. Laypeople are the carriers of the faith from the sanctuary to the world. Failure to recognize this leaves the church impotent. No matter how effectively the Good News is proclaimed from the pulpit, it has to be proven in the pew before it becomes living truth. The gap between the church's declaration and its demonstration is seen in our inability to penetrate the institutions of society with transforming power. It results in a gospel with laryngitis that does not win converts. In this case, God's redemptive word is made dumb by church people whose lives deny it.

People of faith, recognizing this, are no longer content just to be greeters at the door, receivers of the offering, payers of the bills, managers of the property, and helpers of the preacher. No longer do they feel that they are serving God merely by being handymen of the institution. They are being compelled by fresh insights from New Testament Christianity into the nature and meaning of the church. Their apostolate is to be expressed in the demanding centers of civic affairs. They want to be involved in the exciting ventures of the kingdom.

Secular society has an alarming way of ignoring the church. When lay Christians take their ministry seriously, they become the most effective ambassadors God has to send into the structures where their abilities and interests take them.

CHAPTER SIX

Relishing Ministry

During the Emory years, 1954–69, I was asked to accept the presidency of two colleges, head the Town and Country Department of the National Council of Churches, and take a staff position with the General Board of the Laity. I turned them all down. They seemed to be leading me further away from the local church. The only reason I would leave the excitement of the School of Theology was to return to my home conference in South Georgia and serve as a pastor. Bess was never unhappy wherever we lived and whatever I did. But in her heart she longed for the warmth and love we knew as the pastor of people.

During the 1960s, every campus was in turmoil. Emory was no different. All the students came through my office sooner or later. I helped with their finances, solved their academic problems, interpreted their test scores, and guided them in maintaining proper relationships to their annual conferences.

Many students came to see me in those years to tell me, "I have finally found myself and where my ministry is to be." Almost their next word was, "I have decided that the pastoral ministry is not for me." My mission, I thought, was to persuade them that real work of God takes place in the local church. I had developed a convincing argument. One day a student challenged me. "If you feel that way, what are you doing here in the safety and security of the School of Theology? Why aren't you pastor in a local church somewhere?"

I didn't sleep that night. I had been struggling with a decision about returning to South Georgia.

Dean Cannon's election to the episcopacy in July of 1968 gave me an excuse.

Associate Dean Mack B. Stokes served as acting dean during the interim to assure stability of leadership and an orderly transition. Such a Christian gentleman and churchman does not often appear who is also a theologian and scholar of the first order. He is one of my idols. Dr. Stokes was born in Korea of missionary parents, educated at Asbury College, Duke Divinity School, and Boston University. There were four sons in the family. All of them served in positions of remarkable influence as churchmen and leaders. One was a distinguished pastor, one was a missionary, and one was a college president. All of them the highest caliber.

Our friends from Baxley, Eddie Ray and Gwen Upchurch, had made a trip to Australia earlier. They were impressed by the work of Alan Walker at the downtown theater in Sydney which grew into the Central Methodist Mission—this was before he had become famous as a world Methodist and knighted by Queen Elizabeth. They urged Bess and me to investigate it. He was willing to make it possible financially.

In the year while Dr. Stokes was acting dean, he insisted that I take some vacation time after the fall term was underway. Details were falling into place. So we decided to take a month's trip in late November and early December and include more than the Australia experience. With the assistance of some other friends, we designed the trip.

We flew to Anchorage, Alaska, then to Japan, Taiwan, the Philippines, Hong Kong, Singapore, Indonesia, Australia, Hawaii, San Francisco, and back to Atlanta. Friends in the World Division of the Board of Global Missions opened doors for us to meet missionary and native leaders in all these places. The Emory alumni office personnel helped us get in touch with graduates of the School of Theology from these countries and Americans serving in these places. Many were former students whom we had helped get through Candler. Such contacts opened doors for us to information and places that we could not have arranged on our own.

We wanted to be more than tourists. We were interested in studying missions, universities, seminaries, the situation of third-world churches, the involvement of the laity, and especially the unique approach that Central Methodist Missions were making to cities in Australia. I made copious notes and wrote a series of articles for the *Wesleyan Christian Advocate* about the experience.

THE TRANSITION

I made an appointment after I returned to tell President Sanford S. Atwood of my plans to leave Emory and return to the parish. Since the academic year ended in August, I felt obligated to remain until the new dean and his administrative team was in place. Acting Dean Stokes was the next to be told. I wanted the school to move flawlessly during the transition.

With the decision made and the ties cut, I went to Bishop John Owen Smith and told him of my decision and asked for a church.

He was surprised. "What do you want?" he asked.

"I am not asking for anything, all I want is an appointment where I can be a pastor." I assured him that the place was entirely up to him.

When word got out in South Georgia, none of my friends could believe that I was serious.

Jimmy Varnell, a long-time friend, was superintendent of the Statesboro District. When I left the conference in 1951, I left from Baxley. Baxley was now in the Statesboro District. I was Jimmy's responsibility. He took my decision seriously. Ted Griner was scheduled to leave Statesboro First. Jimmy proposed me to follow Ted. Bishop Smith and the cabinet concurred. I was appointed in June of 1969 and began to make preparation to move.

A Journey Beyond

For two months that summer I had dual responsibilities at Emory and in Statesboro. Both the university and the church understood. Still it was not easy. I was committed to directing the workshops, preparing the academic schedule for the coming year, getting everything ready for my successors—my portfolio was divided among five persons—and being sure that the files were in order so that everything could be found. At the same time I had to study my new appointment, become familiar with the people and learn to preach every Sunday to the same congregation again. It had been fifteen years since I served as a pastor. The whole world had shifted. Methods and the atmosphere in the parish were different.

It was more difficult to leave Emory than I thought. Fifteen years during which our children grew up and left home gave us deep roots in the Atlanta community. Atlanta was home for them; they didn't want to leave. Only our foster daughter Nell moved with us. The faculty was gracious and gave us parties.

Ben Johnson and the Institute of Church Renewal presented me with an impressive plaque detailing some of my work with them. Letters of appreciation and warm words of friendship filled us with gratitude. Packing and moving into a new life nonetheless caused the pain of separation.

We sold our home in the Emory community for far too little. It was a mistake. We did not expect to live again in North Georgia. We planned to complete our years in South Georgia. Who can foresee the future? Within eight years, we were back in Atlanta looking for a place to live in a vastly more expensive market.

Earlier I mentioned various people who lived in our home at one time or another. One was very special. Dr. Immanuel Ben-Dor was born in Poland, moved to Vienna, Austria, where he graduated from Hebrew Teacher's College in 1921 with an abiding interest in Near-Eastern history. He continued his education at the University of Rome where he received a Ph.D. in 1927. In 1936 he accepted a position with the Palestinian Department of Antiquities. Following the death of his wife in 1954, he came to the United States to accept a post with the Oriental Institute, University of Chicago. After one year,

Relishing Ministry

however, he became a visiting professor at the divinity school of Harvard University. In 1956 he found a home with the Candler School of Theology at Emory University under the sponsorship of Boone M. Bowen.

In spite of all his acclaim and popularity at a professor, he was a lonely man during the latter years he lived at Emory. He had friends, professional associates, and admirers, but no family. As his health deteriorated, the great man was living in a sparsely furnished, almost substandard, apartment with a kindly housekeeper who came once a week. The apartment was about halfway between our home and his office. He had difficulty walking the distance. One morning Bess saw him struggling along, almost out of breath. She asked if he wanted a ride. He was very proud, and usually declined such offers. That morning he accepted. She drove him to school. After he got out of the car, she realized that he had left his lunch. So she went back to give it to him. Then she saw that his lunch for the day consisted of one cucumber.

Tenderhearted Bess wept. She concluded that he was not eating right, living alone as he did. That day, we had a family council and decided to invite him to move in with us. Anyway he would be retiring in a year. We agreed to transport him to and from his office, to have him eat breakfast and dinner with the family, and prepare him a nourishing lunch each day.

When we asked if he would be willing to accept, he wept. From that day he became a treasured member of our family until all of us moved away.

Dr. Ben-Dor's last year was spent with us. Our grandchildren loved him. This world-class citizen and famous archaeologist allowed our granddaughter to sit in his lap at mealtime and to eat from his plate. He brought a blessed benediction to our home.

The day the moving van loaded our earthly belongings for the move to Statesboro, a taxi drove Dr. Ben-Dor, two suitcases, and a briefcase to the Atlanta airport. He was leaving Emory for the last time and returning to Israel where his two remaining brothers lived. We waved a tearful goodbye to this good man.

We drove to Statesboro to begin our new life. The next day, Helen Stowers, my wonderful colleague for fifteen years and friend for the rest of our lives, called me to say that Dr. Ben-Dor had died in New York. He didn't get to see Jerusalem again.

When he arrived at the Kennedy International Airport in New York, he checked his briefcase in a locker—the suitcases had been checked through to Tel Aviv—and went to visit a rabbi friend in Manhattan during the few hours layover. He was tired and asked if he could rest for a little while before returning to the airport. He went to sleep and didn't wake up. The certificate of death issued by the city of New York medical examiner June 27, 1969, recorded that the immediate cause of death was an "acute coronary occlusive arteriolar disease. He was suffering from arteriosclerotic heart disorder and generalized heart disease."

Back on March 15, 1968, he had brought me a copy of a handwritten will which he asked me to keep. He didn't use a lawyer. He didn't have it typed though of course the school provided him with secretarial service. He wrote it out on two sheets of lined notebook paper. He was leaving that spring for an underwater expedition off the coast of Spain and wanted to be sure that everything was in order should anything happen to him. He incidentally mentioned that he was naming his friend, Alexander W. Resin, and me co-executors of his estate. Three copies of the document were made. One he gave to his friend Boone M. Bowen, professor of Old Testament, and one was placed in the office of Dean William R. Cannon. The other copy was for my files. Three handwritten codicils were later added.

In the meantime Dr. Bowen retired and moved to Charleston. Dean Cannon was elected a bishop and moved his office files and books to Raleigh. When the lawyers started searching for his will, they could find neither of the other two copies. I fished around in my unpacked boxes and the files I had brought from the office at Emory. Fortunately I located it. I still have it and the handwritten codicils he added later. Copies were made for the courts and others who had an interest. The process of settling the estate, even though the will was straightforward and simple, was complicated by the international nature of its provisions with property and bank accounts in several nations. It was completed in 1998 almost twenty years later.

Relishing Ministry

TESTING THEORIES IN STATESBORO

I didn't realize there was resistance in the Statesboro Church to "accepting that liberal from Emory."

It was a year before I knew they had tried to change the appointment the week before conference. By then they had accepted us, and we were enjoying the church and community. Statesboro! What a delight!

Dr. Ned Steele, superintendent of the Savannah District, wrote when he found out that I would be going to "the cathedral church" of South Georgia, as he called it. He had been at the Pittman Park Church across the road from Georgia Southern College and knew First Methodist well.

"You will preach to a full-house, downstairs and in the balcony, of college students and faculty as well as the community," he said. "The liturgical worship with its stately processional, great organ, and wonderful choir creates a worshipful atmosphere."

After we had been in Statesboro about six months, I received a telephone call from a group of my friends in the student body at Emory. They asked how things were going and if being a pastor was what I thought it would be. I confessed, "It is not like I remembered, is much harder than I thought, and some of the things I taught you won't work."

I was eager to test procedures I had been advocating at Emory and all that I was learning from general church involvement. Much of what I was writing about and lecturing about was based on theory. Now I had an actual laboratory to see if they would work. I relished every bit of it. Preaching to the same congregation. Being a pastor. Watching people grow. Visiting the members on their birthday, planning programs. Watching by the bedside of people who were very sick in the hospitals. Ministering to the dying and the bereaved. I even enjoyed committee meetings and planning activities.

Associations with Georgia Southern College (now University) kept me in touch with academic life. They were gracious and included me in the campus activity. Doors were opened to the students. Faculty members, some of whom were members of the church, were kind. They involved me in continuing education courses and counseling. Once they asked me to offer a continuing education course on dying for nurses and staff of the several nursing homes in the county. It was a revelation to me. Those who work all the time with the dying had great difficulty facing up to the reality of death.

Music at the church was superb, and lifted me every Sunday. When the stately robed choir began the procession in the narthex every Sunday, I could hardly walk down the aisle because of the tears in my eyes. Immense talent was available to us. Once, combining resources of the congregation, community, and university, we sponsored a Religion and Art Festival led by Johnny Hathcock, popular minister of music, and Lavinia Floyd, organist, and the committee they put together.

The broadening vision of our leaders inspired me to keep stretching. Bill Hatcher, a druggist, Martha Cain, professor, Charlie Robbins, a creative businessman, and others became conference and general church leaders. Watching them "become" was a delight.

I was elected vice-chairman of the 1968 General Conference Legislative Committee on the Local Church. At that session we hammered out the Local Church Council on Ministries Plan and guided it through the process to adoption. It became the law of the church and was put into the *Book of Discipline*. I was eager to test the concept to see if it would work. At the same time I was a member of the General Board of the Laity with a lot of research and other information available.

So I began talking about the details and teaching the philosophy to the Statesboro officials. They were willing to trust me and risk the untried innovations, so we moved immediately to implement the new organizational structure. We were months ahead of other churches.

Following the methods of the church council we approved a program of ministry for twelve months, printed it up as a guide for planning and followed it as a blueprint. It was refreshing to see what was on paper come to life in the church. The council approved a budget for advertising the church and promoting its ministry. One aspect of this effort in communication was to publish a weekly newsletter that was

Relishing Ministry

mailed to the congregation and influential leaders of the community. It became a positive force in the community beyond the congregation. We developed a campaign of ads in the newspaper and the utilization of radio spots. We flooded the airwaves with twenty-second spots on Thursdays, Fridays, and Saturdays. Each one began with "This is G. Ross Freeman with a word . . ." The "word" would then be about some aspects of the Sunday worship to encourage people to attend. I found that I could say about forty words in twenty seconds. The public relations item in the budget paid off. Our people got excited about the way the community was talking about things going on at First United Methodist.

A Lay Witness Mission and many other projects planned by the Council on Ministries and approved by the board drew people to the church and contributed to the new spirit among the people.

I discovered that there were five different groups or "congregations" within the membership of the church. They were accustomed to different patterns of worship and music in each one. An important part of my work was to blend these people from different backgrounds into a harmonious church. The very formal, liturgical form of worship on Sunday morning was one point of contention among them. Many loved it. So I decided to help increase understanding of why we expressed our worship this way. I researched and prepared a series of sermons, which took a full year, on the symbolism built in the magnificent sanctuary. It was a course in theology and worship.

My commitment to the ministry of the laity led to another experiment as a way to further this purpose. I invited a dozen strong people to meet me one day for a barbecue lunch at the church to discuss a new idea. Though they were busy people with important responsibilities, all of them came. I presented a plan for using lay liturgists to assist in worship each Sunday. I promised to instruct them so they would know what they were doing and not be embarrassed.

During the teaching periods, we studied the history of worship, the meaning of various elements in the order of worship, and how they were used in reaching God.

We studied the theological and psychological progression of worship and how to lead them.

We studied the language and form and ways of preparing prayers for the congregation.

The liturgists practiced before each other, were critiqued by the group, and watched how the others performed. They were comfortable in the role before they were assigned to take their place before the congregation.

Those who agreed to do it had duty once every twelve weeks. All of them took it seriously. They robed, processed with the choir, and shared leadership of the service with me. We would alternate in leading different parts of the ritual. Sometimes I would do the call to worship, lead the responsive Scripture, present the announcements. On those Sundays the lay liturgist would offer the morning prayer, officiate in receiving the offering, and guide the service. We would switch on other Sundays. I preached every time, unless we had a visitor in the pulpit, but we rotated responsibility for the rest of the service. They quickly felt at ease ministering before the altar.

There were several benefits. First, it demonstrated another fulfilling role for the ministry of the laity. Second, we had a dozen or more strong laypeople in the congregation every Sunday who understood what was taking place in the service and who helped create the atmosphere for worship. Third, persons in other congregations noted that these outstanding citizens were participating unashamedly as spiritual leaders in the church.

Not long before he retired as executive secretary of the Southeastern Jurisdictional Council, Jim Sells created a mobile unit for recording audio and video material. Al Weston, a graduate of Candler, was put in charge of this. He traveled around the Southeast trying to convince the church to use this new technology. His specialty was making video teaching tapes on location. Al persuaded Dean Frank B. Stanger of Asbury Theological Seminary in Wilmore, Kentucky, to deliver a series of lectures on "The Ministry of the Holy Spirit." Al converted the video into a teaching manual. The Jurisdiction offered the tape along with a workbook for use in local churches.

Relishing Ministry

It was right on target for us to introduce in Statesboro. We planned a weekend program on the Holy Spirit. Al came down from Atlanta. We set up monitors in a half dozen rooms, trained leaders for each room, and assigned the participants to the rooms. There were three congregational-type sessions with time for questions, spirited music, and worship Friday and Saturday and Sunday. But the real teaching was done in the classrooms. The plan was to have Dr. Stanger, via video, deliver a thirty-minute lecture; we followed in the workbook, and then discussed the concepts and absorbed the teachings in the class. The impact on the Statesboro congregation was phenomenal. When the weekend was over, some were so deeply affected that they did not want to stop. Al, fortunately, had an audio tape of the lectures which he was willing to leave with us. So those who wanted to continue decided to use their workbooks and meet weekly to listen to a segments of the tape. The only time they could all meet was at 9:00 P.M. Wednesday. Those sessions ran an hour and a half. My, they were revealing and growing times. They continued more than two years, added others who were captured by the same spirit. Bill Hatcher was in that group. His growing spirituality and commitment was a marvelous thing to observe.

When I accepted Dean Cannon's offer to join his administration in the School of Theology, I had to learn how to be an administrator and function among the best in the nation. I talked with persons on the campus that could help me. I subscribed to a book club for executives. I devoured these books and followed their suggestions.

When I went back into the pastorate, among an educated and sophisticated congregation, I had to learn the skills of a counselor. I was amazed at the number and complexity of problems people were having. I found myself spending a lot of time counseling people at the college, people referred to me by physicians, and many in the community who simply called for appointments. So I applied for membership in a very elite book club for psychologists and psychiatrists to help me with the heavy load of counseling which was thrust upon me in Statesboro.

A JOURNEY BEYOND

During this time I was secretary and budget chairman of the Conference Council on Finance and Administration. We changed the method of determining the salary of the district superintendents. Previously, these were set by a vote of the annual conference each year. Occasionally, when the conference was displeased about some of the appointments, motions were made to reduce salaries of the superintendent. Sometimes the wrangling was bitter and hurtful. My work at Emory included attending five or six Annual Conferences each year to represent the School of Theology, so I knew that other conferences did not have these embarrassing debates. I prepared a plan to establish those salaries automatically. The Council of Finance and Administration, under the chairmanship of E. L. Cowart, approved the proposal and recommended it to the conference. It passed. The conference has not changed the method since 1970; neither has there been a public debate over the salary of the superintendents in thirty years.

During much of his twelve-year tenure in the Atlanta Area, Bishop Smith was occupied with the issue of merging the North and South Georgia Conferences and the Georgia Conference. The statewide Georgia Conference was made up of the black Methodist churches of the Central Jurisdiction, established during the Plan of Union in 1939 which placed all those black churches established by the Methodist Episcopal Church after the Civil War into one jurisdiction. The General Conference in 1968 mandated that the Central Jurisdiction, based on race, be abolished as a part of the Plan of Merger with the Evangelical United Brethren. Bishop Smith was eager to complete the merger of the Georgia Conference. North Georgia adopted a plan and moved forward. South Georgia, with only seventeen black charges, felt that it could not accept some of the provision. The recommendations made by the first Merger Committee under the chairmanship of Dr. Zach Henderson, president of Georgia Southern College, was defeated. A motion from the floor passed calling for the Merger Committee to be re-constituted with different leadership to be named by the bishop. Bishop Smith named Frank L. Robertson. They labored mightily. When the vote was taken the following year, the second Merger Plan also failed. Again, a motion was made to reconstitute another Merger Committee to reconcile differences and bring an acceptable proposal to the conference.

I had just moved to Statesboro and was elected to head the South Georgia delegation to General Conference. The bishop asked me to chair the third Merger Committee. We determined to draw up an acceptable plan that both conferences could accept and approve. Our work was presented at a called session of the annual conference in Porter Auditorium of Wesleyan College. The debate was spirited and forceful. When the vote was taken in late afternoon, the conference approved the third plan of merger. The seventeen charges of the former Georgia Conference were merged into the nine geographic districts of the South Georgia Conference at a moving ceremony during the annual conference of 1971—in time for the mandated deadline of General Conference in 1972.

We were in Statesboro only thirty months when Bishop Smith called. He had to replace a district superintendent in the middle of the year and wanted me on the Macon District.

THE MACON DISTRICT

Morale among United Methodists was a growing concern in the district. The former district superintendent's use of authority and problems with his personal behavior created a lack of trust among the churches. I was appointed to take over November 1, 1971, to complete the routine of Charge Conferences and to begin the appointment process in January for the following June.

My first assignment was to begin the healing process and to restore confidence in the church hierarchy.

Before the end of the conference year, General Conference met in Atlanta. News reports from proposals and debates caused quite a stir among Georgians. Our folks needed answers. Some non-Methodists were openly attacking us. It became necessary for us to convince our people that the General Conference delegates would make the right decisions and keep us on course. We began an aggressive public relations campaign.

People and pastors needed reassurance. I made time for special services in local churches for revivals, workshops,

Bess and I welcome Dr. and Mrs. Nishimura from Tokyo to the Macon District Conference in 1972. The Nishimuras, who single-handedly started a ministry in one of the worst slums of Japan, hosted us for three days in Tokyo. Two of their sons, Ken and Shin, earned advanced degrees from Emory University with the assistance of the Freemans.

seminars, and renewal experiences, and in many other ways got among the people. Young pastors and those serving smaller churches received special attention.

We used the District Council on Ministries for planning and giving people an opportunity to be involved in decision making. I was able to get from the general church ten thousand copies of useful material for distribution through the churches. We began having rallies to generate enthusiasm.

Bob Brenner, a very talented graduate of Duke Divinity School, was appointed director of Macon Urban Ministry before I came. Its work was underway. Through this structure, we created a safe place for runaway and at-risk teenagers called His

Relishing Ministry

House; ministry of older adults called PaceSetters; organized the Church of the Exceptional with an award-winning ministry among the retarded, and launched *Good News TV*. In all of this, except the creation of His House, Cliff Wallace played an important role. When I first met Cliff he was one of the managers of Penny's Department Store in Macon. His heart was touched by a group of retarded youth who visited the Forest Hills United Methodist Church during a revival one year. He investigated who they were and who was responsible for bringing them. The more he learned, the deeper he wanted to be involved. Arrangements were made for him to rent an abandoned Mormon Church that had been purchased by the trustees of Cherokee Heights United Methodist Church in the same block. Cliff started searching for families with mentally impaired persons and inviting them to a special church designed just for them. They responded. I urged him to seek credentials as a United Methodist pastor. He did and later resigned his work with the Penney organization to devote himself to ministry.

The Church of the Exceptional developed a ministry to the visually impaired, a ministry to the hearing impaired, as well as to the families of the mentally impaired. Their concern for the physically impaired resulted in them bringing the people and resources together to start the first Good Will Industries in Middle Georgia. The remarkable story was written up in the *Atlanta Constitution* Sunday paper. Somebody sent the story to the staff of the NBC *Today* show, and they dispatched a crew of cameramen and reporters to Macon to see if the story had merit. They devoted an entire ten-minute segment of the *Today* show one morning to the congregation of mentally retarded people and their remarkable pastor, the Reverend Cliff Wallace. A woman in Birmingham, Alabama, saw the *Today* show, and wrote the editors of *Guidepost* magazine about it. They sent their most prestigious writer to investigate. He spent a week following Cliff Wallace and checking out the authenticity of the facts. He was so impressed that he not only wrote the story for *Guidepost*, but he recommended that the Church of the Exceptional be named the *Guidepost* Church of the Year. Think of it. Previous recipients of this award were all large city churches with enormous resources and programs. Now this

Dr. Norman Vincent Peale and myself, just before Dr. Peale spoke at the Macon Coliseum and presented the Guidepost Church of the Year Award to the Church of the Exceptional. Governor and Mrs. Jimmy Carter joined with ten thousand others to congratulate the congregation of forty mentally retarded persons in the moving ceremony.

tiny congregation of mentally handicapped persons was recognized across the world. Dr. Norman Vincent Peale himself was to preach and to present the award. The congregation decided that it would not be fair to have this distinguished preacher to come just to their little church. They decided to share the occasion with the entire city. They rented the new Macon Coliseum that seated ten thousand people. We filled it for the service of recognition so that the community could watch as they received the *Guidepost* Church of the Year award in March of 1974. In addition to Dr. and Mrs. Peale from New York, Governor and Mrs. Jimmy Carter from Atlanta were featured.

When a vacancy occurred in the staff of the Macon Urban Ministries, I used my influence as district superintendent and

Relishing Ministry

appointed Cliff to be the director. It was a fortunate choice. Not only did he develop the Church of the Exceptional, but he also led in the organization of the Ministry of Older Adults and recruited Marie Williams to direct that program. Together they proposed the concept of calling the program Ministry *of* Older Adults rather than Ministry *for* Older Adults or *with* Older Adults. Ms. Williams became the leading practitioner and champion of the Ministry of Older Adults in the South Georgia Conference. Dr. S. Walter Martin, at that time president of Valdosta State University, was the head of the conference committee. It won such recognition that he was placed on the national committee named by the General Conference to create a denominational Ministry of Older Adults.

Good News Television grew out of this same Macon Urban Ministry. It started in His House when some of the young people demonstrated a talent for music. We used them at times in district meetings. Bob Brenner, director of Macon Urban Ministries, and his wife caught a vision of asking the Cox Broadcasting Company, just opening cable television in Macon and Warner Robins, for a channel which could be used by the United Methodists. A cable channel was not worth very much at that time, so they consented. Channel 7 was set aside for Good News TV in Macon and Warner Robins. We still have that access channel. We had no equipment, no professionals, no resources. Eddie Ray Upchurch of Baxley, who has risked several times to help with some dream of mine, made us a grant of seventy-five hundred dollars as up-front money. With that and the skills of some of the people who lived at His House, a small black-and-white camera was purchased, and with a homemade studio, we began telecasting thirty minutes a day. The Cox Company gave us a switch so that we could broadcast whenever we had something to broadcast.

Again when Cliff Wallace became Director of Macon Urban Ministries, he inherited this fledgling ministry. New quarters were obtained. More equipment was bought. Longer hours and more programs were possible. But responsibility for so many new enterprises became a heavy load for him. So as I was leaving the Macon District for my assignment with the Southeastern Jurisdictional Council on Ministries, we

Governor Jimmy Carter (center) welcoming Bishop William R. Cannon to the Atlanta Area of the United Methodist Church from Raleigh in 1972. I am on the bishop's left along with Dr. William H. Ruff. On the Governor's right are Bert Lance who headed the Georgia Highway Department in Carter's administration, and Dr. Guy K. Hutcherson from Columbus.

found a way to bring Don Wood from the Central Pennsylvania Conference to be the director of Good News Television. What a fortuitous move that was. Don Wood is the genius behind the growth of the full-powered, commercial television station, the development of the video production studio that is the envy of the denomination, and the communications prowess of Georgia Methodism.

On another occasion we scheduled a huge Pentecostal celebration in the Macon Coliseum. We featured the Junaluska Singers in concert, the world editor of the *Upper Room* (Wilson Weldon) to preach, had daily readings from the *Upper Room* at

Relishing Ministry

12:00 noon on WMAZ, and gave away thousands of copies of the *Upper Room* to people who requested them.

We wanted to show that United Methodists are "a Bible believing people." We conducted a saturation campaign based on the gospel of Luke. Since we used so many, the American Bible Society printed a special cover to tell our Macon District story. We handed out ten thousand copies to people in shopping centers and malls throughout the district.

At the same time, we arranged for the public reading of Luke by members of local churches in these same shopping centers. The names of the readers were well publicized in advance. Loud speakers helped get attention and enabled them to be heard. As people gathered we asked them to participate in a public writing of Scripture. Individuals copied verses from Luke by hand on large sheets of paper . . . the completed book of Luke was then bound and preserved.

Following the weekend of public reading and writing Scripture and the service at the Macon Coliseum, we scheduled four nights at Mulberry Street United Methodist Church for people of the district to gather. There was a lecture each night on Luke by Professor David Naglee of LaGrange College, four great musical pieces based on passages from Luke and performed by various choirs. Throughout the day visitors attended a Festival of Scripture and Art displayed throughout the building. Families loaned treasures of religious art and memorabilia so the community could see them—included was one of the extremely rare and valuable Gutenberg Bibles still in existence. Other Bibles and prayer books with unbelievably early

Hooded and robed and awarded a Doctor of Divinity degree by LaGrange College in 1959.

imprints were included. Busses loaded with school children were escorted through the exhibits.

We designed a Neighborhood Bible Study as a positive evangelistic tool. The plan was to have David Naglee video a series of thirty-minute lectures which would be telecast on Thursday nights at 7:30 over our Good News television channel 7.

Fifty different homes were designated in communities of the different churches with leaders trained to lead discussions. Neighbors were invited for refreshments, to view the television program, and discuss the topic. Pastors selected the homes and trained the leaders.

The publicity surrounding all these district-wide events helped convince people that our pastors and churches believe in the Bible and the Holy Spirit.

The Lenten Living Affirmation of Faith was started to utilize more than a hundred certified lay speakers in the district. Pastors cooperated by agreeing to substitute a five-minute statement by a lay speaker trained to give a witness on one or more of six subjects for the traditional Affirmation of Faith.

To support communications within the district and among the churches, we started a Macon District Edition of the *Wesleyan Christian Advocate* and scheduled radio time on WMAZ every Sunday morning at 9:05, immediately after five minutes of CBS news. It was called "Spotlight—on Methodist News and Events of the Macon District." It reached most of Middle Georgia. Two pastors were in charge of collecting the news and broadcasting it: Jack Arnold and Willis Moore.

All this activity was supported by a strong force of laypeople inspired and led by Judge Taylor Phillips as district lay leader. His ability and prestige enabled him to get things done. Without him, little would have been accomplished. He knew whom to call, and he had access to any leader in the community. He met with me almost weekly for counsel and planning. He spoke regularly in churches of the district, and indeed across the state. He considered himself the counselor of pastors in the district; thus resolving many problems.

Taylor was elected conference lay leader with the plethora of ex-officio positions that entailed; president of the

Relishing Ministry

Southeastern Jurisdiction Association of Conference Lay Leaders; president of the National Association of Conference Lay Leaders; member of the General Board of Discipleship; member of the General Council on Ministries for eight years and vice president for a quadrennium; and member of the General Council on Finance and Administration for eight years. His affable spirit and wealth of knowledge put him in positions to influence the life of the church.

WORKING AGAIN WITH BISHOP CANNON

In 1972 Bishop William R. Cannon was assigned to the Atlanta area for the next eight years. I served in his cabinet with great satisfaction during the first quadrennium. During that period he was in high favor throughout South Georgia, and remarkable achievements were made.

Soon after his return from four years in the Raleigh area, he asked me to chair a task force for the Atlanta area on Key 73, an interdenominational and national effort to highlight evangelism in 1973. The task force prepared a program booklet called *Ten Steps to Evangelism for Georgia United Methodism* and called a statewide rally to be held in the Macon Coliseum to launch the movement. It was well organized, and ten thousand people came. This emphasis turned a membership loss for twelve years into an eight-year gain in both North and South Georgia Conferences. Growth continues in North Georgia—at least through 2000—with annual increases larger than any conference in the nation.

Since I was the leader of the General Conference delegation and helped shape the merged structure of the United Methodist Church, Bishop Cannon asked me to chair a blue ribbon task force that he appointed to restructure the conference in keeping with General Conference action. Previously we had operated as a Program Council in South Georgia. General Conference gave no directions and only hinted at suggestive guidelines for organizing an annual conference. The local church organization was only four years old. Nomenclature was new. There was reluctance to rename everything again, so we decided to project the local church

Bishop William R. Cannon and his South Georgia Cabinet in 1973 (left to right): McCoy Johnson, Gilbert Ramsey, me, Guy K. Hutcherson, Bishop Cannon, A. C. Epps, Cardy C. Edmundson, C. Eugene Cariker, Alvis A. Waite Jr., Edward H. Carruth, and J. C. "Jimmy" Varnell.

structure to the District and Annual Conference levels. It made sense. Other conferences copied our pattern, and the plan has served us well for a quarter century.

Jack Braucht, a member of the task force, was the first chairman to begin implementation of the new structure. Reverend H. W. Scoates was the council director. His energy and wisdom were invaluable in implementing and guiding the conference through the new structure. After Jack Braucht's term as chairman, the council nominated me to succeed him. It was a time of increasing membership, planting new churches and paying 100 percent of the apportionment to the general funds of the denomination. A positive feeling pervaded the district and conference.

As president of the cabinet, I wrote the report for Annual Conference in 1976. The method of preparation was for each superintendent to submit material about the accomplishments of his district. These were given to the president of the cabinet who drafted the report. It was then examined line by line by the full cabinet. When it was finally approved, the

Relishing Ministry

document reflected the combined judgment of us all. Excerpts from the report to the Annual Conference reflect some of the activity and direction in the conference during my years on the Macon District.

> Four years ago, the cabinet sought to give a sense of direction for the future. Then the bishop and superintendents were convinced that the time has arrived: (1) for us to be more concerned about what the church is and what God has called us to do than we are about criticism or opposition from individuals or groups; (2) for each congregation to reaffirm the value of the church to society so that its emphasis will be respected and its spokespersons heard; (3) for us to declare persuasively what we believe and why; (4) for an open style of operation, planning and administration with more women and youth involved at all levels; (5) for a vigorous emphasis in every church upon the essentials of the faith, the grandeur of our heritage, and our contribution to civilization.
>
> We called upon our pastors and lay members, institutions and agencies, boards and commissions, districts and local churches to launch bold and imaginative projects with power to thrill our people. Suggestions were detailed:
>
> - Set specific goals and make definite plans for winning new members.
> - Provide varieties of worship experiences that appeal to our people.
> - Develop competency and devise methods for advertising and public relations to get Christ's message beyond the walls of the church.
> - Create fresh and workable approaches to the educational task.
> - Accept as our primary, though not ultimate, task of nurturing our members.
> - Guide our people in working through the Social Principles.
> - Engage our people in a systematic study of the Bible.
> - Use the 'Theological Statement' in the *Book of Discipline* as an instrument for increasing the theological awareness of our people.

A Journey Beyond

- Help our congregations discover the resources available to them for determining their mission.

The conference responded. We restructured the conference and find that it is working.

We installed a new Bishop in Georgia with a banquet that brought together the professional, educational, business, political and religious leadership of the state in unprecedented fashion.

We mobilized a massive statewide Convocation on Evangelism in the Macon Coliseum to launch Key 73 for Georgia Methodists.

We stopped agonizing over merger and went to work building a four-year record of genuine cooperation and mutual ministry which has strengthened black and white congregations alike. We have put to rest the specter that haunted us, and realized the advantages that beckoned us.

We participated in the Bishop's Consultation on Parish Reformation and put a Task Force to work planning for the future.

We discovered the power of involving our people in planning and program development.

We moved toward a mature operation and concept of the Council on Ministries, and, in many ways, led the church.

We accepted and utilized a strategy for setting priorities so that our program resources and budgets could be focused.

We empowered District Councils on Ministries to become instruments of planning nearer the local church.

We involved key lay leaders in the nomination process to broaden representations and enhance the election procedure.

We established the Pastoral Counseling Service and are learning to take advantage of its skills.

Relishing Ministry

The Pension Funding Crusade, the largest financial campaign in our history, resulted in our people pledging and paying more than a million dollars beyond the goal.

There is a healthy, singing, enthusiastic spirit among us as we begin the third century of our national life and come to the end of this quadrennium.

CHAPTER SEVEN

Encouraging Men

Methodist men of Macon adopted me when I was attending Mercer University. They made opportunities for me to speak. They arranged for me to attend the South Georgia men's retreat, paid my expenses and included me in the carload who drove from Macon to Yellow Bluff on the Atlantic coast. There I heard grown men talk about their experiences with Jesus Christ and tell how much they loved the church. I still remember the men singing with gusto. Again I was introduced to a wider horizon than I had known. I was beginning to become a churchman. Perhaps this is the major reason why I have always felt an affinity for the men of the church.

I remembered how important it was for men to take up time with young people. So while I was at Emory, I was pleased when the jurisdictional youth leaders invited me to lead retreats and youth weeks at Lake Junaluska; colleges asked me for Religious Emphasis Weeks; local churches scheduled me for retreats. Youth have trusted me for some reason. These were good experiences, but nothing equaled what happened one year at Epworth By The Sea.

Leaders of South Georgia youth asked what they would like to have at a retreat. The council found that local church young people wanted to study what the Bible teaches about the Holy Spirit.

"Our classmates at school are always talking about the Holy Spirit, the baptism of the Holy Spirit, the gifts of the Holy Spirit, the fruits of the Holy Spirit. We don't even know what they are talking about. So we want to spend a weekend studying what the Bible teaches about these topics."

They wanted a few of us older types around, not to teach them or to tell what we think but to answer specific questions if they ran into roadblocks in the process. They did want help in selecting the scriptural passages to be studied and determining the method to be used. I was honored to be included among the adults whom they trusted to participate.

Dr. William Mallard, professor of church history at the Candler School of Theology, was chosen as the platform speaker. He is always a favorite among young people, and, as a matter of fact, in any group. So full of fun, so animated, so eager to communicate, Bill Mallard makes any presentation a delight.

Chairs in Strickland Auditorium were placed in a semi-circle around a low platform on the side facing the marsh. There must have been over three hundred—maybe more—young people attracted for the weekend. Arrangement of the room put all of them in seeing and hearing distance for the singing and speaking.

Mallard's first session caught their attention.

He told of giving one of his classes on the early church a choice of assignments. They could either write a term paper and sit for a final examination, or they could work as a group and condense the entire New Testament to one sentence. They chose the latter. After all, it sounded easy. Anything was better than researching and writing a scholarly term paper to be analyzed plus the agonizing ordeal of preparing for a final.

Then they discovered that it would not be easy. First they had to read the entire New Testament to understand what it said. The class had to reach agreement on the essential

Encouraging Men

message. Then they had to choose words, and fashion one sentence to capture the essence and the spirit of the early church. The young people were captivated by Dr. Mallard's humorous and dramatic account of what the students went through in fulfilling the requirement.

When the term was over and the report presented, he approved their work.

Then he told the young people the sentence they prepared: "Listen! A whole new world is breaking in, and taking us along with it." That's it! The New Testament is all about the kingdom of God.

Running through the weekend was a serious search of what selected passages teach about the Holy Spirit. It was more than an intellectual adventure. It became a profoundly moving spiritual experience.

Saturday night I was asked to direct an altar call. It was 9:00 P.M. before I started. They had been sitting a long time. I knew they needed to move around. So I invited them to walk across the campus in silence, kneel quietly at the altar of Lovely Lane Chapel, transact business with God, and leave so that others could come. Deeply moved by the presence of the Holy Spirit, these young people walked slowly from the dimly lighted auditorium to the dimly lighted little church. I didn't know whether they would do it or not. They had had a long, full day. They could have slipped out in the night and gone to their rooms. When I was able to get free about thirty minutes later, I was astounded at what I saw. All of them had gone immediately. The chapel was full. The altar was full. The path leading up to the door of the chapel was also full of young people, kneeling four abreast, inching forward as space became available, waiting for an opportunity to kneel at the altar. The line of praying young people continued until after 2:00 in the morning.

I have been a part of only one other such experience in my lifetime. It was in the Philippines at a Catholic Church while people crawled on their knees for blocks to kiss the toe of a black Jesus on a cross which had been brought there from South America.

A Journey Beyond

WOMEN

I have always worked well with lay men and women—well, not always, with some women. A few leaders of the United Methodist Women chastised me for some of the positions I took.

It was not always so.

In the early years of my ministry, I was partial to the Women's Society of Christian Service (WSCS before the name was changed to United Methodist Women). Work in the local church prospered when they were active. They were the most dependable, best-trained, totally committed members of the church. We organized units in the small churches we served where they did not exist. Bess and I participated in their studies and projects.

At that time and in those places the women were not always organized. In Appling County they named one of the circles of the charge-wide organization for Bess Freeman. It still bears her name. As my understanding of the sociological importance of the rural church expanded, I studied it more in depth and taught the course on the rural church and community for the Schools of Mission and in many local churches in Georgia. The women of the conference, in cooperation with the National Division, assigned Armine Davis to the Appling County churches as the first deaconess to serve as a church and community worker in the South Georgia Conference. This was the beginning of the Altamaha Larger Parish which involved ten United Methodist Churches in the county. (Bert Winters was the first church and community worker assigned to North Georgia. Others were working in conferences across the church).

Armine Davis taught me a lot and flavored my rural church ministry. She was a brilliant, vivacious, caring young woman who made a place for herself in the hearts of the people of Appling County. She was a teacher of uncommon skill who related well to all age groups and broadened our vision of what the church should be.

While we were at Emory, Bess was very active with the Glenn Memorial women. She was an officer and served on the executive committee of the North Georgia Conference as

Encouraging Men

director of student work. For many years I regularly addressed their conferences and taught in the Schools of Missions.

Looking back I can not remember when I fell out of favor with the remarkable women in the leadership of the United Methodist Women. It may have been when I spoke to an Annual Conference of United Methodist Men, and sought to goad them to more effective leadership. The meeting was pathetic. Few people were there. Less than twenty were present for this conference-wide event. Planning was poor. Promotion was poorer. I had driven from Atlanta to address them. Frankly, I was disappointed.

In an effort to stir men to assume more responsibility and assert themselves in the church, I spoke with uncommon force. "Unless men take their place in the leadership of the church, the women and children will have to assume responsibility for the future of the United Methodist Church."

Well, as a matter of fact, I still believe it. The voice and strength and point of view of men are essential to a well-rounded church. I certainly did not intend to disparage the vision and commitment of either the women or the youth. I have only admiration for the leadership they provide in the denomination and local churches.

The editor of the conference newspaper, wife of a pastor, was not present. One of the younger men gave her his interpretation of what I said. Based on his account, she wrote a front-page story attacking what I had said. She didn't check her facts with me or with any of the other men present.

Those good men were dismayed. They believed in me.

She reported in the story that some people in the Southeastern Jurisdiction were mentioning me for the episcopacy. Elections were a year away. Delegates had not even been named. She vigorously opposed my election "for fear that I might be sent to her conference and work against interests of women and young people."

She used the influence of her paper to blast me. Members of the Commission on the Status and Role of Women spread reprints of the story. Copies were distributed to a national meeting of United Methodist Women, and used widely against me.

She never talked to me about the incident, never apologized for maligning me without investigating. Later, when I became an editor, it was always hard for her to face me. She never mentioned the episode; neither did I. I just smiled when I saw her, and said nothing.

Still, women who knew my work continued to believe in me and appreciated what I did for the church.

There were valid reasons why I ought not to have been a bishop; but my determination to motivate the men of the church was certainly not one of them.

MEN HAVE A LOT TO GIVE

Throughout my ministry I have tried to build up the weak places, to encourage the floundering movements. Those who were going great did not need my help. I spent my energy on the Macon District with the weaker charges preaching, visiting, teaching, planning, and working with the pastors. Vital churches with effective pastors and competent staffs did not need reinforcement from the district superintendent. Like a parent who always pays more attention to the struggling child, my disposition was to assist congregations who were having a hard time. My heart went out to small membership churches.

That may be the reason I spent so much time trying to build up United Methodist Men. When I was discovering which segment of the church needed my attention in the Macon District, I found that the work with men was the weakest.

We called a meeting of men to discuss how a stronger district organization could be effected. Judge Taylor Phillips was chosen president and started us in the right direction. He served for a year before he became district lay leader. Roy Lifsey replaced him. Reginald Broxton replaced Roy when he was elected conference president.

What God-directed choices these men were.

While Lifsey was district president, he gave the time, became the dreamer and engineered a program of United Methodist Men in a few years that was recognized nationwide. We encouraged each local church to have a fellowship, to have

Encouraging Men

Three stalwarts of United Methodist Men. Left to right: Roy Lifsey, Al Suttles, Judge J. Taylor Phillips.

two monthly meetings at home with the third meeting each quarter attending a subdistrict motivational and inspirational event. One of the quarterly subdistrict cluster meetings was to be used as a district rally to generate enthusiasm. Guidelines and program suggestions were provided the local fellowships. While the pastors participated in all the meetings, they were especially urged to attend the district rally to show enthusiastic support of the men.

In addition, Roy Lifsey devised a scheme to charter each local church fellowship with the national office and thereby support the work of men in the general church. He proposed a plan for every man to purchase a share in the work of United Methodist Men. I don't remember how much a share cost, probably five dollars. The income from the sale of these shares provided enough money to pay the charter fees for the local fellowships and money to fund projects of United Methodist Men in the district. Within two years, the Macon District had more chartered fellowships of United Methodist Men than any district in the nation. We led them all.

Later, at a national meeting, the plan for EMS—"Every Man Shares"—was adopted for the whole church as a way to fund United Methodist Men. The improved version cost fifteen dollars and included five dollars for support of the national office, five dollars for a subscription to the *MensNews* publication, and five dollars to be divided between the jurisdiction and Annual Conferences. Membership in EMS costs more now.

With such imagination and leadership skill, it was inevitable that Roy Lifsey would attract the attention of the South Georgia Conference United Methodist Men. Dr. S. Walter Martin—former academic dean of the College of Arts and Sciences at the University of Georgia, former president of Emory University, and former vice-chancellor of the University System of Georgia—had returned home to South Georgia. Now president of Valdosta State University, Dr. Martin was persuaded to assume the leadership of United Methodist Men of South Georgia. The conference Board of the Laity named him director of UMM. A man of sterling credentials as a churchman and man of statue, he was a genius at organization and administration.

In the restructuring following General Conference in 1972, even though at the national level men were downgraded to a department in the combined General Board of Discipleship, the men were given a more significant role in the governance and life of South Georgia.

Bishop Cannon appointed me chairman of the South Georgia Conference Task Force on Restructure in 1972. Walter Martin was a member, as were all the elected leaders of the conference plus some others. Under his guidance the men emerged as a structured and important force.

All the while Roy Lifsey, as one of the district presidents, was increasingly respected as a thoughtful planner. He became the obvious choice to succeed Walter Martin as conference president when the men elected officers in 1976.

Encouraging Men

Reginald Broxton succeeded Roy Lifsey as district president. He likewise had a long, fruitful tenure.

Lifsey gave admirable leadership to the conference and served until 1980. During this time, he was a member of the Southeastern Jurisdiction Association of Conference Presidents of UMM and was elected president 1980–84. His presidency also made him a member of the National Association of Conference Presidents of UMM. When he was elected vice president of the national association, he became an ex-officio member of the General Board of Discipleship assigned to the Section of United Methodist Men. For the next eight years, Lifsey was elected by the Jurisdictional Conference as a regular member of the General Board of Discipleship. His influence in the opinion-making bodies of the world church continued to increase.

He was honored March 6, 1999, as chief architect and engineer guiding legislation through the General Conference for the creation of the General Commission of United Methodist Men as a free standing part of the church structure.

Roy Lifsey went from being president of the Macon District men to being president of the South Georgia Conference men, to being president of the Southeastern Jurisdiction men, to being chairman of the Section of United Methodist Men of the General Board of Discipleship, and to influencing the program of men worldwide.

In the meantime another South Georgian, Jim Snead, was chosen for the staff of the General Board of Discipleship as director of the United Methodist Men in the Section of the Laity.

Dr. David Self from Alabama was giving visionary leadership as general secretary of the General Board of the Laity until the General Conference restructured the board and agencies in 1972. In so doing the General Board of the Laity was merged with the Board of Evangelism and with sections of the Board of Education to form the new General Board of Discipleship. Jim Snead had been a lay staff member of the South Georgia Conference Council on Ministries building a reputation in stewardship training and the work of men. David Self knew of his work and invited him to Nashville for an interview in 1974. He was offered the choice of two positions: director of Stewardship or director of United Methodist Men. He chose the latter. Thus began an international career with the General Board of Discipleship on July 1, 1974, that lasted over twenty years as a lay man in the bureaucracy of the church.

Lifsey was an elected member of the decision-making executive committee of the General Board of Discipleship and chair of the Section until he was no longer eligible to serve. His influence is still available, however, as a member of the United Methodist Men Foundation. Snead continued giving superb leadership to the men of the church as the employed staff serving as national director.

For twelve years, Roy Lifsey and Jim Snead stood side by side in the general councils of the denomination. What a tandem! What strength! What leadership!

EMPOWERED TO STRENGTHEN

During the fifteen years at Emory I had the opportunity of working with the Jurisdictional Conference lay leaders and being involved in retreats for men in several annual conferences. What a joy to see this network unfold as men with enormous capacity united across conference lines to accomplish things for the church.

What I found in the Macon District and South Georgia Conference reinforced my discoveries. Men have the capacity to grasp the truths of the Bible, to master the intricacies of theology, and to understand the inner structure and mission of the church. They find, however, that concentration in the business world leaves little time to cultivate the inner life. The answer for them is in retreats, accountability in small spiritual search groups, and a spiritual friend who will mentor and guide them. Men need men who will journey with them.

When I moved to the jurisdictional office, I found the need and possibilities still present. As with the Annual Conference, the Jurisdictional Association of Conference Lay Leaders named a director of United Methodist Men. Alex Woodall of Birmingham was put in that position.

Roy Lifsey was elected president (1980–84) to succeed Alex Woodall. Tom Mallonee from Western North Carolina was the third SEJ president (1984–88). Ernie Wendell from the North Carolina Conference followed (1988–92); Robert Powell from Alabama-West Florida was next (1992–96); Denver King from Holston was sixth (1996–2000). Ron Hardman from Virginia is now the seventh at the turn of the century. Each administration built on the foundation laid by the others and increased the influence of the men.

United Methodist Men are stirring across the church. Working through General Conference, the men now have an independent General Commission of United Methodist Men. As one Bishop put it, "The sleeping giant is waking up."

In response to these developments, and other needs, the SEJ Council on Ministries and the College of Bishops called three convocations in 1979. One of these was for the men. The SEJ Association of Conference Lay Leaders, ever generous and eager to encourage this new effort, provided up-front money to organize a convocation of United Methodist Men to be held at Lake Junaluska, July 6–8, 1979. The design team called it Convo 79 and planned an inspiring, event-packed session including some of the elements of the international event. Jim Snead and the national office gave guidance.

Response was encouraging. The decision was reached to call one every four years between the International Congress of United Methodist Men meetings at Purdue University. We have now held six: 1979, 1983, 1987, 1991, 1995, and 1999.

The second convocation of United Methodist Men for the Southeast was better organized. We now had some experience. It was one of eight convocations, called by the College of Bishops and sponsored by the SEJ Council on Ministries in 1983, leading up to the bicentennial observances of the Methodist Church in America in 1984. A special task force, guided by the SEJ Association of Conference Presidents of United Methodist Men and the Section of United Methodist Men from the Board of Discipleship, designed it. Bishop Joel McDavid and Roy Lifsey co-chaired the task force.

Studies by Lyle Schaller, reported in the *Presbyterian Survey* in 1982, reveal that "men are disappearing from many churches." One reason is that older adults constitute the most rapidly growing segment of the population. Church membership

The logo and centerpiece for the 1983 Jurisdictional Convocation of United Methodist Men at Epworth By The Sea.

is older than the general population; women tend to live longer than men; so there are naturally more women in church than men. A second explanation for fewer men in the church is that people usually identify with small groups before they become active members of the congregation. Most churches have more small groups—ports of entry—for women than they do for men (almost ten to one); it is easier, therefore, for women to "break into the church" than it is for men. Still another reason that

Encouraging Men

Schaller discovered why men are disappearing from the church is that churches tend to honor persons with verbal skills—that is, persons who can speak, or teach, or preside, or make reports, or make motions. Women tend to excel in these skills while less than 20 percent of the men have them. Men, therefore, tend not to feel comfortable at church where the emphasis is on talking.

The theme for the convocation held at beautiful Epworth By The Sea, April 23-24, 1983, where John and Charles Wesley both ministered, was *Heritage Weekend for Men*. The place was a reminder of our history, but it was more than a nostalgic look at our past. The penetrating insights of Lyle Schaller haunted everything that was planned. The design team took these concerns seriously. They became convinced that men want to be in the mainstream of the church where decisions are made, involved in significant ministries at the exciting edge of mission, investing themselves in efforts to influence the quality of life in the future. They need tools and handles.

If men want to be more than greeters at the door, receivers of the offering, payers of the bills, keepers of the property, helpers of the preacher, and hearers of the Word, what can the church do to inspire and guide them in becoming "doers of the Word and not hearers only."

Five major objectives were announced in the invitation of the men to come: (1) Deepen the spiritual life of men who attend and send them home better husbands, fathers, citizens, and churchmen; (2) Magnify the strategic role of men in the church; (3) Help men find ways of influencing and being involved in the mission of the United Methodist Church; (4) Provide men with a new awareness of the program and organization of the United Methodist Church; (5) Call men to strengthened commitment of what they can accomplish through district and conference organizations.

The call went out. The men came in response to the call of the bishops. The opening session was a parade of flags led by the bishops and conference presidents from the nine states. The nine governors provided the state flags for the event. They were impressively placed around the stage for each session. Registration was three times as large as four years ago. Sessions pointed the way for men to be involved in ministries that might shape tomorrow as we move toward Methodism's third century. The bishops or a designee met with the men in episcopal areas to hear the concerns of men. Attractive workshops were led by prominent pastors and laypeople to stimulate lively discussion.

Men need not only to hear, but they need to speak to the church if the findings of Schaller reflect what is actually happening.

SPEAKING TO THE CHURCH

During the convocation, men were provided avenues for speaking to the hierarchy of the denomination. That doesn't happen often. Permission was provided in small groups. Careful notes were kept. These were assembled and categorized. Appropriate concerns were sent as petitions to the bicentennial General and Jurisdictional Conferences. Summaries of the convocation were printed and distributed to the College of Bishops, to the Annual Conference Councils on Ministries, and to leaders of United Methodist Men at all levels. My condensation of the notes indicate that they still have important words for church leaders:

You have said . . .

That we need a strong emphasis on men in the United Methodist Church that is totally backed by the bishops, the district superintendents and the pastors.

That we need specific programs to guide the monthly local church Fellowships; men want to know more about the Bible and need some help in its study.

That we are hungry for spiritual direction and experience so that our lives can be pleasing to God.

That we want to know more about the *Book of Discipline* and what it means to be a United Methodist, especially what place men are expected to have in the system.

That we believe the General Conference should mandate an

Encouraging Men

organization of United Methodist Men in each local church and lay the responsibility upon pastors and district superintendents for getting them started.

That we need more and better communications reaching each local Fellowship so that our men will know what issues are facing the church and the possibilities for action.

That we have men larger than their faith—hear it?—men larger than their faith; help them develop a faith big enough for them and their experiences.

That we need more "ports of entry" for men to get into local churches.

That we need more gatherings of men at every level.

That we need the church to show men the way to break old ways and old habits in order to adopt Christian ways and Christian habits.

That we need first-class, lively, spirit-filled music to stir our hearts and move our spirits—not draggy, dead, death-producing sounds.

That we need a full-service church providing total ministry for total man.

That we need help in being good spiritual leaders in our homes.

That we need to find ways to promote harmony between the races, to share our deepest spiritual experiences with one another, and to prayerfully consider the views of minorities as we plan for the total body of United Methodist Men.

That we need to cultivate a positive attitude among men of the church to combat the negative voices and influences.

That we need to clarify the position of the church on issues that are troubling and disturbing to us in our society—issues like how the church spends its money, what causes to support, attitudes toward abortions, the increasing demands for the rights of homosexuals, marital abuse, neglect and mistreatment of children, drug and alcohol addiction, and others.

That we need to involve men in forming new churches, in rebuilding some of the older ones, and in sending United Methodist Men as missioners to help revitalize churches that are declining.

That we need to increase our understanding of stewardship with the goal of having individuals give a minimum of 10 percent of their income through the church, and with a congregational goal of using 50 percent of what we give for the local church budget and 50 percent for missions beyond the local church.

That we need to require more from our men so that they do not feel it is so easy to be a part of the United Methodist movement. One of you commented on the song used during the offering, "My House is Full, but My Field is Empty." The line which says, "all of my children want to sit around the table, but they don't want to get out into the vineyard and work" is a disturbing characteristic of our men.

The experience was so unique that the decision was made to publish the addresses by Bishop William R. Cannon, Dr. Ezra Earl Jones, Red Bond, and George Berry along with findings from the workshops and listening sessions. Copies were studied, filed, and referred to often.

Though I was part of the planning team for 1987, I actually was not involved in the operation. By then I had moved out of Jurisdictional Council office. Tom Mallonee of Western North Carolina was the new jurisdictional president. He was unfailingly thoughtful, sought my counsel, and included me as much as possible. My mind, however, was drawn to my new career. Though I attended, others were in charge.

GROWING OUT OF PURDUE

For eight years while I was a member of the General Board of the Laity (1964–72) I was a member of the executive

Encouraging Men

committee and served on the program committee for the International Congress of United Methodist Men at Purdue. It was my honor to work with the program committee every four years from 1965 to 1993, helping them select the themes, design the programs, and process ideas for the events. The vision and competence of these men thrilled me.

Even after I was no longer officially involved, they continued to include me. Especially did Jim Snead and Roy Lifsey open doors for me to serve through the National Association of Conference Presidents of UMM including *A Spiritual Journey for Men* and *A Transforming Journey for Men*. Now, *A Ministry Journey for Men* has been produced by the men of North Georgia and the General Commission of United Methodist Men as the third program in the trilogy. Don Wood and GNTV recorded and edited a video to enrich the experience.

These programmed spiritual growth experiences got started in a rather unusual manner. The executive committee of the National Association of United Methodist Men had felt for some time that some effort should be made to enrich the spiritual life of men. The idea lay there as a part of the incomplete agenda.

I had been invited to spend a week in Nashville with a national task force on ways to improve the Sunday school. I was about ready to leave Friday afternoon when I received an urgent plea from Danny Morris. His leadership for the Conference Prayer Advocate retreat was in the hospital. Could I possibly delay my return to Atlanta and fill in for him?

The Conference Prayer Advocates were a part of the United Methodist Men program to support the toll-free Upper Room Prayer Center. They come to Nashville once a year for training. In a quick consultation with Jim Snead, I adjusted my schedule. We decided to involve the Prayer Advocates in a consultation for developing spiritual life among the men. Though it was not what they expected, they were willing. Thus began the two-year research and testing program in each section of the church that resulted in the program *A Spiritual Journey for Men*. The rest is history.

What an inspiration it has been working with strong men from across the nation to make these outstanding programs and events a reality. Many good things were launched because the men gathered every four years at Purdue. In preparation for the 1993 Congress, on the verge of my retirement, the design team came up with the theme of *A Man Sent From God*. They asked me to tie the theme together and build bridges between the major addresses by preparing and delivering six twelve- to fifteen-minute scriptural segments at the beginning of each plenary session using the story of Peter. The men gave standing ovations after each statement. In the evaluations, participants requested that these be made available to the men of the church for use as a study guide for monthly meetings. Since they were videotaped by Don Wood and GNTV, it was not difficult to grant the request. John Bulew, a member of the design team from the North Central New York Conference, skillfully prepared study questions to follow each address. Don Wood packaged the video and booklet for distribution through the system as a program resource by local fellowships of United Methodist Men.

The men have honored me in so many ways. Whoever the leaders, they continue to invite me to the Jurisdictional Association and the National Association of Conference Presidents meetings every year. I am especially indebted the Robert Powell of Alabama-West Florida and Denver King of Holston, outgoing presidents of the two associations, for their many courtesies along with their executive committees. The UMM made me a life member, a member of the "Society of John Wesley," and at the 1999 Jurisdictional Convocation, they named me only the second "United Methodist Man of Distinction" ever awarded in the history of the Southeastern Jurisdiction.

CHAPTER EIGHT

Enjoying the Larger Church

Bess and I grew up in South Georgia; we began our ministry there; our three children were born there. We lived thirty-four years, however, in North Georgia, primarily in Atlanta, before our retirement in 1993. Half of these, seventeen years, I had an office in Atlanta's downtown United Methodist Center as executive director of the SEJ Council on Ministries and as editor of the *Wesleyan Christian Advocate*.

We maintained active ties with South Georgia. We were likewise very involved in North Georgia. We attended both Annual Conference sessions unless the dates conflicted, as they have since we divided into the North Georgia Area and the South Georgia Area. As a result both conferences claimed me.

North Georgia claims that I'm from South Georgia; South Georgia claims that I'm from North Georgia.

Both have been good to me. Our son, Dr. George R. Freeman Jr., is a member of the North Georgia Conference; one daughter and her husband, Rev. and Mrs. J. Stephen Posey, are members of the South Georgia Conference.

My membership has remained in South Georgia. They received me when I had little to commend me and their gracious welcome opened doors to ministry for me.

A Journey Beyond

During the fifteen years I was at Emory and the ten years that I served the jurisdiction, it was my responsibility to attend four or five Annual Conferences each year to present the causes I represented. It was never a hardship. The truth is I love going to Annual Conferences, observing how they operate, and watching the interaction. Warm and wonderful friendships emerged in each one across the years. I felt quite at home anywhere in the nine states.

During these years I was given the opportunity to address many of the conferences, lead retreats, consult with committees, and preach in revivals.

GROWING CONCEPT OF EVANGELISM

All my energy at the beginning of my ministry was aimed at winning people to faith in Christ. That's what I thought ministry was about at that stage of my life. I was revival oriented. I didn't know anything else. While I was in Macon as a youth, we had a citywide crusade with Gypsy Smith and another with Bishop Arthur J. Moore. These services fanned my imagination. On the coast serving some of the churches Arthur Moore served in his first appointment and learning about some of the people who helped his ministry get started filled me with visions of what I might become. I flourished on the legends of his early days. I studied the biography of Lorenzo Dow, Peter Cartwright, Sam Jones, and early circuit riders who were important in the Methodist tradition. Their stories enflamed my zeal to win converts.

Constant preaching developed latent skills in verbal communication. Word spread that I enjoyed it. Invitations came for me to lead revivals in local churches. Pastors for whom I preached told others how their churches had responded. One year while I was serving the Darien Circuit, in addition to the heavy load I carried at home, I preached in twenty revivals for other pastors.

This early experience resulted in a reputation for evangelism in local churches, in camp meetings, and in retreats. I would go anywhere to preach in small churches, large churches, close at hand, or at great distances. There was joy

Enjoying the Larger Church

Here I am pictured preaching in a revival series at the First United Methodist Church of Conyers during the first pastorate of Dr. Nat H. Long.

and freedom in the pulpit. This enthusiasm for revivals continued in every assignment, and I studied everything I could find about evangelism.

Almost every week for fifty-two years, God has given me the awesome privilege of being in the pulpit on Sunday, and often between, for revivals, camp meetings, retreats, and conferences. For more than half a century I have averaged preaching five times a week for at least forty weeks a year. My methods became more sophisticated, more solidly founded in the tradition of the gospel, and more intellectual in my approach to evangelism.

As my reputation grew, opportunities came to preach in many places and opened doors into larger ministries. My administrative duties during my fifteen years at Emory limited the amount of time that I could spend away from the campus in evangelism. Dean Cannon recognized the public relations value of my speaking around the southeast, and he encouraged it. He and Associate Dean Mack Stokes also kept heavy schedules of preaching. It cost the university nothing and benefited the school, attracting students and sometimes gifts. Our exposure to churches around the Southeast paid off during the "God is dead" controversy. People who had heard us in their local churches were not disturbed over what was happening at Emory. They believed in us.

My duties compelled me, however, to restrict engagements away from the campus to one week per quarter. Sometimes I could squeeze another between quarters if there was a long break. Since my evenings were my own, I could preach at night within a radius of one hundred miles and still be in the office every day.

During these years when there were far more invitations than I could accept, I stumbled, quite by accident, on a plan for weekend revivals that enabled me to get into many more local churches. I adapted it for the rest of my years at Emory.

I was invited to Cocoa Beach, Florida. The pastor and chairman of evangelism said that because of their proximity to Cape Kennedy and the demands made upon the schedules of their people, they could not set aside four or five days in the week. Rather they wanted to try a full weekend, urging their families to set all of it aside for the church in the way they would plan for a camping trip, or football weekend, or a retreat. The idea caught on. They scheduled thirteen different events between Friday night and Sunday night. Not all the people were expected to attend all thirteen, but there was an obvious build up of spiritual momentum that had quite an impact.

The chairman of evangelism in the church who engineered the weekend was a young businessman, Robert Fannin, whom I had met at the Leesburg men's retreat. In a few months after I returned to Emory, he wrote to ask if he could enter the School of Theology and study for the ministry. He was accepted, completed his Master of Divinity degree, remained for a Doctor of Sacred Theology (S.T.D.) degree and returned to have a brilliant career in the Florida Conference. He is now

Enjoying the Larger Church

the resident bishop of the United Methodist Church in North Alabama until he retires in 2004.

I learned some things along the way. Some discoveries are from books I have read and observed from contemporary masters. I have examined the published sermons of selected evangelists like Jonathan Edwards, Charles H. Spurgeon, Dwight L. Moody, Sam Jones, R. A. Torrey, Billy Sunday, Billy Graham, and countless effective evangelists who are lesser known. Primarily, however, these are insights growing out of my own experience.

Effective revival sermons are scriptural, doctrinal, logical, educational, and positive.

People still want to know what the Bible says about the fundamentals like God, Christ, the Holy Spirit, man, sin, salvation, life, the ultimate outcome of the human struggle, and immortality.

They want logical sermons that appeal to the mind, struggle with real questions and are as direct as a lawyer's brief, as reasonable as a debate insisting upon a decision.

While the major purpose of an evangelistic sermon is to persuade and not to educate, a congregation has a right to expect that the investment of a week of preaching will unveil truth and impart insightful information.

Above all they expect the sermon to be positive. Ralph Sockman, in one of his more revealing sentences, helped me with, "Jesus came primarily with an invitation and not a warning."

Even with a carefully crafted sermon, the preacher must give attention to the principles of communication, the needs of the congregation, and the psychological laws governing revivals. The delivery is important. The best lines, garbled, leave us cold.

GENERAL CONFERENCE

I thoroughly enjoyed the rigors of General Conference and the larger church. It was grueling, demanding, exhausting—often frustrating. I relished the give and take of honest debates, shrewd parliamentary battles, and skillful maneuvers to sway votes.

Each time I won some friends and made some enemies, but I came away uplifted and inspired by the way this church functions. Always I had an agenda and was working toward something that seemed important. Seldom did I work against anything, though I did vote negatively occasionally.

I listened to members of our delegation on issues where they were better informed than I, courted allies from other jurisdictions, and sought counsel from the most knowledgeable persons I could find. Then I voted my convictions regardless of how others voted.

Through watching the process and the results I came to believe in the wisdom of the body. General Conference seldom makes serious mistakes in directing and governing the church. Delegates are often moved by the pain which others feel. I remember listening to a plea for understanding from Joseph Lowery back when he was serving a church in Alabama. He spoke with pain in his voice about the way African-American people were embarrassed and hurt. I cried that day at General Conference.

Delegates are good people who love the church and serve their communities. As I got to know them, regardless of where they were from, I liked them. I learned to trust their hearts. We could laugh together even though we disagreed and voted on opposite sides of an issue.

Approximately one thousand delegates gather from around the world. The first week is given over to impressive ceremonies during the plenary sessions. Most of the time, however, is spent in legislative committees. There is always a heavy load of work for these committees. When the entire *Book of Discipline* is open for revision, every agency of the denomination given free reign to reshape its paragraphs, and every caucus or local church or individual invited to submit legislative proposals or resolutions, the accumulation is massive.

The committees are required to examine and handle every petition referred to them from whatever source, recommend to the full body modifications or approval or referral or disapproval. Many dealing with the same subject matter can often be linked together and acted upon at the same time.

Enjoying the Larger Church

Each of the legislative committees has between seventy and one hundred persons who have to understand and vote upon the suggested changes. This often requires extensive debate on some of the petitions within the committee. Usually lobbyists for or against the proposals are in the room watching and sometimes silently influencing the outcome. Sessions of the committees, when the workloads are heavy, start early and last until after midnight. Sometimes the better part of the week and weekend are required to complete the agenda. No wonder delegates walk around bleary eyed from lack of sleep.

No one person can keep up with everything that is happening. Fortunately the rules require each delegation to have at least one delegate on each legislative committee if they have enough to go around. Persons choose these committees in order of their election and in keeping with their special interests. Sometimes large conferences can have several on committees dealing with matters crucial to them. Within the delegation, therefore, there is usually one or more persons able to inform the others about the issues to be decided.

The second week is given to plenaries. Each item dealt with by the legislative committees has to be reported to the total body. These recommendations require explanations and sometimes entail debate. Skillful presiding officers who insist on following well-defined procedures and carefully drawn "Rules of Order" are essential to getting the massive business done. Time is reserved in the agenda for worship and other high moments as special Orders of the Day.

South Georgia clergy first sent me to General Conference as a delegate in 1960. After that they elected me every four years—sometimes barely—until I asked them not to include me on the ballot for 1988. (I decided that I ought to be an unbiased reporter rather than an actively involved delegate after I became editor of the *Advocate*.)

What an honor. Seven times they gave me the privilege of going, plus the two called sessions while delegates hammered out details of the merger with the Evangelical United Brethren and restructured the new denomination. I was a delegate in Denver, 1960; in Pittsburgh, 1964; in Chicago, 1966; in Dallas,

A Journey Beyond

1968; in St. Louis, 1970; in Atlanta, 1972; in Portland, 1976; in Indianapolis, 1980; and in Baltimore for the bicentennial, 1984.

In 1960 I was goggle-eyed with wonder before we ever reached Denver. A first time delegate, number five and last in the clergy elected by South Georgia, I wanted to do a creditable job. I read and marked material in the *Advance Editions of the Daily Christian Advocate* and other documents mailed to the delegates. I wanted to be informed when I arrived. I had even decided how I would vote on the legislative proposals. How naïve to think that I could decide without hearing the explanations, considering the debates or understanding the mood of the conference.

That first time I was in the legislative committee on pensions. I knew the decisions were important. But when I heard the knowledgeable experts from the staff and delegates, I realized that I had little understanding and nothing to contribute. Two or three times I tried to speak in the group, but my ignorance embarrassed me. By the end of the week I had decoded the major questions to be voted up or down.

During the plenary session, I stood to challenge a point made by the distinguished and brilliant Harold Bosley. He was speaking in favor of General Conference going on record favoring civil disobedience to laws that violated Christian conscience. The South Georgia delegation was seated near the front. I stood to ask for the floor. The chair recognized me. When I had identified myself, I asked Dr. Bosley and the conference if we should take such a position as a world church when it might place some of our delegates from communist countries at risk when they returned home. He had no answer. The question stalled action on his proposal a day and a half until reasonable language could be found to resolve the dilemma. That was my initial venture on the floor of General Conference.

STUDIES OF THE MINISTRY

A quadrennial study of the Methodist ministry had been made for each General Conference by the Department of Ministerial Education since unification in 1939. Three of

Enjoying the Larger Church

My first General Conference in 1960 when I challenged Dr. Harold Bosley on a point he was making about civil disobedience. The debate delayed action for a day and a half to reconcile the language.

these (1944, 1948, and 1952) had been done by Professor Murray H. Leiffer of the Garrett Evangelical Seminary in Evanston, Illinois.

The department engaged Professor Frederick A. Shippey of Drew and Professor Earl D. C. Brewer of Emory to make the fourth study for 1956. Neither of these was available to do the statistical study and analysis for 1960. Dr. J. Richard Spann and Dr. Gerald O. McCulloh of the Department of Ministerial Education, asked them to suggest someone.

One by-product of working in the Religious Research Center at Emory with Dr. Brewer was his reference to me of projects that he couldn't accept. The quadrennial statistical study and analysis of the ministries was one of them. It was important. Legislation presented to General Conference for action was based upon the findings of the report every four years.

Always opening doors for his young friend, Dr. Brewer recommended that I be invited to do it. He promised to assist if the Department of Ministerial Education assigned the project to me. His offer assured that they would ask me to do it. Brash and eager, I thought that if Dr. Brewer considered me competent, I would attempt it. To be sure that I did not mishandle the formidable task, I carefully examined the four previous studies to discover trends and procedures as points of reference. There had to be continuity in the results.

The design for the report to the 1960 General Conference was broader in scope than the others had been. It included chapters on recent developments in theological education, in-service training, and ministerial recruitment as well as a statistical picture of the pastoral leadership available to the church.

The publication included a brilliant essay on "The Struggle for a Trained Ministry in the Methodist Church" by Bishop Paul N. Garber. Before he was elected to the episcopacy in 1944, Bishop Garber had been professor of church history and dean of the Duke divinity school. He was eminently qualified for the assignment. A chapter was included on "Recent Developments in Theological Education." Another chapter described the "Inservice Training Opportunities for Continuing Education." Still another chapter made an appeal for "Ministerial Recruitment."

But the major portion of the report was given to the statistical study and my recommendations growing out of it. Basic data were obtained about the number of pastoral charges, fully ordained and qualified pastors in full connection, pastors on trial and just beginning, pastors who were approved to supply churches and other pertinent information through a questionnaire. All the information was broken down by jurisdictions, by level of ordination, by educational attainments, and by age, by the number of members served, by salaries, and by the number of new pastors needed in the next four years. Comparisons were included in each of the categories with studies made in 1952 and 1956. Twenty-one tables and twenty-three bar charts and other graphic representations were analyzed and conclusions drawn from each one to inform the General Conference legislative process. The study was painstaking and required the better part of a year. Dr. McCulloh wrote of his appreciation of my work in the foreword of *The Methodist Ministry 1959*, this analysis "shows the thorough and extensive quality of his research."

Working with the Candler School of Theology for eight years as chairman of the Conference Board of Ministerial Qualifications, combined with this project for Dr. McCulloh and Dr. Spann and others gave me a perspective into the needs of the church for ministers that few had. By the time I finished the study I had a wealth of statistical and factual information. The report was distributed at General Conference and disseminated widely across to the church to bishops, cabinets, Boards of Ordained Ministry, and others concerned about the supply and qualifications of our pastors.

As a result of the problems highlighted by the research, the 1960 General Conference ordered the creation of a top-level committee to study every aspect of the ministry during the next four years. The Department of Ministerial Education chose representatives to the Study of the Ministry Committee from among the bishops, the ministers, the theological schools, the Board of Missions' Division of World Mission, and the Board of Education's Division of Higher Education. Bishop Donald H. Tippett was elected chair, Bishop Paul N. Garber was elected vice-chair, and Dr. Gerald O. McCulloh was elected secretary. I was asked to direct the collection and tabulation of data and to write an interpretation of what they mean.

Others named to the committee reflected the seriousness with which the mandate was taken: Bishop Fred G. Holloway; Dean William R. Cannon of Candler School of Theology, later a bishop; President Dwight E. Loder of Garrett Biblical Institute, later a bishop; Professor Harvey H. Potthoff of Illiff Seminary; President Charles T. Thrift of Florida Southern who was a member of the committee to evaluate the seminaries during the last quadrennium; and active pastors Norman W. Clemens and Thomas M. Pryor, later a bishop; Tracey K. Jones Jr., general secretary of the Board of Missions; and John O. Gross, general secretary of the Board of Higher Education.

A JOURNEY BEYOND

The committee had a fourfold purpose: (1) seek a clearer understanding of the meaning of the church; (2) clarification of the roles and responsibilities of those persons, ordained and unordained, to whom has been entrusted the preaching of the Word and the pastoral and priestly service to the people; (3) evaluate the institutions and ecclesiastical structures of the denomination to see their function in accomplishing the work of the church; and (4) continue the survey of ministerial resources to discover future personnel needs and outline guiding principles for preparing effective ministerial leadership.

When the scope of the investigation had been determined, members of the committee were assigned to write papers on various topics. When the full committee met, these papers were read, questions raised, conclusions examined. They were then rewritten and mailed to the seminaries, bishops, and other knowledgeable clergy and laypersons for evaluations and comments. Finally a writing team was designated to bring the report together for the General Conference in 1964.

My assignment was to determine the general characteristics and trends in the ministry. Three questionnaires were developed and employed. One was mailed to every person under appointment in the Methodist Church: those on-trial, full ministerial members of the annual conferences, and all approved supply (or lay) pastors. A second instrument gathered data from a scientific sample of clergy and laypersons on the functions and work of the minister. Still a third phase of the study sought information from persons licensed to preach in 1962. We considered it important to understand why they answered the call to preach. Useable responses from the mailing to all pastors numbered 18,887—a whopping 64.2 percent return—providing the most complete statistical study of the Methodist ministry since unification. Copies of the instruments, data graphically presented in fourteen tables and nine charts, my analysis of the information along with the seven other documents which were finally approved for transmission by the committee. Dr. McCulloh wrote, "A special thanks is extended to G. Ross Freeman for his work in connection with the planning of the questionnaires and the processing of the data in the statistical section of the report."

Enjoying the Larger Church

Bill Parks, leading the Lay Delegation to the General Conference in Pittsburgh, and I giving careful attention to the debate in 1964.

The book includes thirty-nine summary recommendations that went forward to General Conference from the study committee. Some of them made for lively debate at Pittsburgh.

The entire report with its recommendations was assigned to the Legislative Committee on the Ministry. Theological giants from over the church were in that committee. It was a major battlefield. Dean Cannon was chosen chair in a hotly contested election. Because of my work, the South Georgia delegation assigned me to that committee to interpret and defend the report.

One far reaching proposal growing out of the study, in light of discussions about union with the Evangelical United Brethren Church was the elimination of dual ordination of clergy. The EUBs had only one ordination. The Methodist tradition was to first ordain candidates as deacons and to ordain them elders two years later. Both the study committee and the legislative committee were divided over the issue. Those favoring only one ordination finally won out in 1996.

Dean Cannon began his work in the chair. In presiding over the faculty in the Candler School of Theology, he frequently entered debates and issued decisions during meetings. Faculty members sometimes didn't like it; but they were his faculty and he was in charge. These tactics were not acceptable to a General Conference Legislative Committee. The first day he forgot his responsibility for presiding impartially and joined the debate. That angered some in the committee. I learned after the session that a few were so incensed that they planned to take him out of the chair the next morning. Another legislative committee had actually replaced their chairman for doing the same thing. I got to Dean Cannon, along with Mack Stokes who was also in the committee and some other friends, with a strong word that he not debate the issues but preside following precisely the Standing Rules of the Conference and *Robert's Rules of Order*.

The next morning he disarmed his antagonists by apologizing for his behavior and assuring them that he would strictly abide by the rules for presiding over such a body. He had memorized Robert's rules in their entirety during the night so that he would know what it said. He was saved from the embarrassment of being removed from the chair. For the rest of the conference he was a model presiding officer. The lesson served him well after he was elected a bishop.

THE PLAN OF UNION

We were in constant discussions over the Plan of Union with the Evangelical United Brethren Church. Understandings and agreements had reached the point that in 1966, the two General Conferences would meet to vote the plan up or down. If the constitutional majority required by both denominations approved, the two General Conferences arranged to meet in Dallas. There they would take whatever action was necessary by each body separately, and then proceed jointly with approval of a new *Discipline* and consummate the merger in a glorious celebration of union. Some details had to await a second called session of the General Conference in 1970 in St. Louis.

Delegates assigned to the combined legislative committees in Dallas met to organize. A church renewal caucus schemed and organized to name a slate to head all the legislative committees. The strategy succeeded. Their nominees were elected chairs of all the committees except three. Two

Enjoying the Larger Church

were designated by the General Conference the first day for persons from the EUB side. Neither could they control the strong-willed Committee on the Ministry. Dr. Dow Kirkpatrick was the chief instigator of the effort and was elected chairman of the Committee of Chairmen—the group that determined the flow of business to the floor and dominated the conference.

Three of us were nominated to chair the Committee on the Local Church. Dr. Merlyn Northfelt, president of the Garrett Evangelical Institute, was on their list. He was elected. I was elected vice-chair.

A special session was called for St. Louis in 1970 to complete the unfinished business about the merger. The same persons were on the legislative committees, but new officers were elected.

This time I was elected to chair the Legislative Committee on the Local Church. Dr. Northfelt was elected vice-chair. We were preparing for the historic General Conference of 1972 in Atlanta. Among other things we had a preview of the plan for restructuring the General Boards and agencies.

The 1972 General Conference met in Atlanta.

I was back in South Georgia on the Macon District when elections were held in 1971 at Epworth By The Sea. I was the first clergy elected to the General and Jurisdictional Conference delegation. Frank Robertson was second. Our usual procedure was to support the first clergy delegate as the nominee for the episcopacy. Instead Frank Robertson was chosen. He was elected a bishop in July at the Jurisdictional Conference.

George Wright was the first lay delegate elected. According to our custom of rotating the chairmanship of the delegation, he was the leader.

Change was in the air. Union with the EUBs had been accomplished. The Central Jurisdiction—the nationwide jurisdiction created in 1939 based on race—had been merged with the geographic jurisdictions by action of General Conference. General Boards were being reformed. No attention had been given in the plan, however, to provide a structure for the jurisdictions nor the Annual Conferences. No effort was made to harmonize the whole.

Presiding over the South Georgia Committee to restructure the Annual Conference.

I was again elected to chair the Legislative Committee on the Local Church. We dealt with fifty-one bona fide calendar items and a host of others, which were lumped together because they were all about the same subject.

I was still on the Macon District when elections were held in 1975 for delegates to the General Conference in Portland, Oregon. Bishop Cannon had named me chairman of a task force to restructure the South Georgia Annual Conference. Since General Conference had left us without a uniform structure in 1972, each annual conference was free to design its own. I persuaded the task force that we should pattern the South Georgia plan after the local church organization designed by General Conference in Dallas and Atlanta. It had gone well. The plan was approved by a called session. It worked so well that several conferences based their plan of organization on it and it served us well for a quarter century with only minor alterations.

Again I was the first clergy elected. George Mayo was the first lay delegate. In many ways the conference in Portland was disturbing. In others it was personally gratifying. Bishop

Enjoying the Larger Church

Cannon preached the third day on "The Place of the United Methodist Church in the Total Christian Heritage." It was classic Cannon and brought a standing ovation. He was my bishop and asked me to be the liturgist and offer the prayer.

Since I had my choice of legislative committees, I selected number eight, the Council on Ministries. This was a new concept in our tradition, brought into the union from the EUB side of the house, but it was already working well in South Georgia.

When the legislative committees convened to organize, I was chosen to chair the Council on Ministries Legislative Committee. We had a heavy agenda and some tough issues to decide. We examined and reached decisions and presented seventy calendar items to be considered by the total body. We organized the committee into sub-committees in order to give proper attention to each petition and utilize the talents of each person. Each sub-committee had to defend its recommendations before the entire committee and win a majority vote for action. As chair I had responsibility for presenting the recommendations from the committee to the plenary. I called upon the sub-committee chairs to assist in the interpretation and to argue the case if there was debate.

The caliber and commitment of the committee members, assisted by the excellent staff of the GCOM, guided me, though we did not always do what the staff wanted. Along with all the other petitions that had been submitted by the church, our Legislative Committee was to recommend a missional priority for the church. The GCOM had proposed the ethnic minority local church. Pleas for the continuation of the ethnic minority local church priority were reinforced by petitions and a general mood in the church. The committee had no problems with approving it.

We did run into strong support in petitions handled by one of the sub-committees demanding World Hunger as a priority worthy of a world church. Massive starvation in sections of the globe made a strong case for the church to mobilize resources in response.

Another sub-committee received a petition from a small church near Chattanooga, Tennessee, asking that the United

Methodist Church establish evangelism as the priority. A number of similar petitions requested the same thing. Our serious decline in membership—losing almost a million members since union in 1968—was disturbing much of the church.

The proposals, well thought out and documented, had much to commend them. After lengthy and sometimes heated argument, the committee voted to send all three to the floor of the plenary session for debate. We expected the body to vote down two of the proposals and leave only one priority.

The arguments for each, however, were so compelling that General Conference approved all three. We came away from Portland with the church committed to (1) strengthening the ethnic minority local church, (2) a campaign to relieve world hunger, and (3) calling every board and agency and unit of the church to evangelism.

GENERAL COUNCIL ON MINISTRIES (1976–84)

After the General Conference in Portland in 1976, I was elected by the Jurisdictional Conference to be a member of the General Council on Ministries. Many of those who had been on the Legislative Committee in Portland had also been elected to GCOM. About half of us were new. The others had served four years. We accepted our committee responsibilities without knowing much about the duties at the time, but the course was set for the next four years.

Few specifics had been given for the priority on evangelism. Details had to be worked out. I was assigned by the General Council on Ministries to serve on an interagency task force to develop a program. Bishop Ed Tullis was chairman. I was vice chairman. When I was elected executive secretary of the Southeastern Jursdictional Council on Ministries that fall, Bishop Tullis and I worked with a task force named by the council and the SEJ Association of Conference Leaders in Evangelism. We were able to translate many of the concepts from the interagency task force in the jurisdiction.

Another of my special assignments with the General Council on Ministries was with the task force on designing a

Enjoying the Larger Church

twenty-five-million-dollar television presence for the United Methodist Church. A lot of energy went into this effort. We worked diligently and had some big names in the communication world to dream with us. Our plan was to follow the pattern of the Mormons. The Latter Day Saints are able to influence the networks because they own TV stations in major markets on all three networks. In this way, when the network owners sit down around the table to make programming decisions, the Mormons have enormous influence. So we thought that the way forward for United Methodists would be to buy a TV station, make it profitable and buy another until we might own several around the nation. Some of the ideas were good, but we were never able to get the denomination excited about the dream. As a matter of fact, United Methodists have never caught the vision of mass communications. Here and there it happened. But the vision splendid was aborted because of our inability to raise the twenty-five million dollars. When the Good News television station in Macon grew from a CATV channel under the leadership of Don Wood and his Board to a full-powered, commercial TV station, it was the only television station owned by any unit of the Methodist Church. Two or three local churches have since started low-powered stations.

Another assignment I was given was the task force for New Church Development. We arranged a national consultation on strategies for planting new churches and revitalizing churches in changing communities. The results were shared with district superintendents and conference Committees on Church Extension around the denomination in an effort to spark new interest in this method of church growth. So much of the church's energy during this time was spent on other concerns that little was left for initiatives in beginning new congregations. Some of the major learnings from this experience are included as a part of the jurisdictional story in chapter 11. We were not as successful in mobilizing the rest of the church as we were in the Southeast under the guidance of Bishop Robert M. Blackburn. There are some great stories of conferences budgeting huge amounts and approving specific plans to reach out to new and unchurched communities.

But my assignment in the area of planning and futuring with Ezra Earl Jones was probably my most enlightening and beneficial experience during my eight years with the General Council on Ministries. Our report on "The Future That Can Be" was presented to the General Council on Ministries, November of 1983, and transmitted to the bicentennial General Conference in Baltimore.

I remember the exhilarating sessions as we stretched our minds and our imaginations around such topics as the consequences of trends in family patterns, changing patterns of leadership, economic interdependence with the rest of the world, the impact of technology, the shift in America from an industrial to an information society, the revolution in communication, and the momentum toward decentralization. We brought some of the leading minds of the nation to help us grapple with these trends and guide us in thinking about responses that the church should make to each one. All of this was probed against the biblical and theological understanding of the mission of the church.

My mentor Professor Earl Brewer was also deeply involved in futuring. As a social scientist he was an early leader in the theory and practice of the Futuring Society and served as president of the Southeastern Futuring Society. He inspired me to study trends and project alternative futures from them for organizations and movements. Continuing the trend lines ten or more years, it was possible to read the future if things did not change. Alternate futures could be predicted as different events or changes intervened. It became a fascinating hobby for me and very useful in my work.

It was against this background that we planned our work in studying and reflecting on trends in the Southeast that determined initiatives by our Annual Conferences. It is inspiring to contemplate the scope of the vision in these papers even today.

My fortunes in South Georgia changed again. In the twenty years that the conference had sent me to General Conference, I had carried heavy responsibility in my own conference:

Enjoying the Larger Church

- Chaired the Conference Board of Ministerial Qualifications (1960–68);
- Chaired the Conference Budget Committee as vice-chair of the Council on Finance and Administration until I was invited by Bishop John O. Smith to be a part of his Cabinet (1969–71);
- Chaired the South Georgia Merger Committee and was able to get merger approved after the conference had voted down two previous plans (1971–72);
- Chaired the South Georgia Structure Committee that completely reorganized the conference after the pattern of the local church (1972–73);
- Chaired the Bishop's Consultation on Parish Reformation for the Atlanta Area (1972–73);
- President of the South Georgia Cabinet (1976);
- Chaired the Bishop's Task Force on the Missional Priority of Evangelism for the Atlanta Area (1976–80);
- Chaired the South Georgia Council on Ministries (1976–80);
- Member: Board of Managers of Georgia Pastors School (1960–68); South Georgia Coordinating Committee (1966–68) until it was replaced by the Council on Ministries; South Georgia Board of the Laity (1964–76); South Georgia Council on Finance and Administration (1969–76); South Georgia Board of Missions (1968–72); South Georgia Board of Evangelism (1972–76); Georgia Commission on Higher Education (1972–76).

While I was at Emory, when I returned to South Georgia as pastor of the Statesboro First United Methodist Church and as superintendent of the Macon District, it was of course possible to spend time on committees and attend events that kept me in contact with the conference. Some involvement continued after I first was elected executive director of the SEJ Council on Ministries. Quickly my time and energy and involvement were required over the sixteen annual conference area with four or five months—all the summer—each year spent at Lake Junaluska. Not much was left for my own conference. As a matter of fact I could only spend a couple of days at the South Georgia Conference each year because of obligations at the other conferences. I was no longer around to exercise leadership or influence. Other leaders came to the front.

So when conference met in Tifton in 1979, I was almost a visitor. Though my voice was still respected on the floor, I was no longer in contention to lead the delegation. Besides there was an uprising against the bishop and cabinet and all who were close to them. In spite of this, my friends hung in there until I was finally elected in position number seven. But I was glad to go.

The General Conference of 1980 met in Indianapolis.

Though I was last in the rotation for choosing legislative committees, the delegation did save the place on legislative committee number 9, Council on Ministries, for me. Though I was not an officer this time I was able to get some things done. It seemed important for me to be there because of my work with the SEJ Council on Ministries. The Jurisdictional Conference elected me for another four-year term as a member of the General Council on Ministries.

Earlier the General and Jurisdictional delegation had voted that I would be the favorite son of South Georgia for the episcopacy. When Annual Conference met in Valdosta, June 2–5, 1980, the delegation asked the conference to endorse the nomination. It was an honor, and I appreciated it. There was no unity in the conference, and there was no chance of an election from South Georgia.

These were the wonder-years in American Methodism leading up to the historic bicentennial conference in 1984. Work in the jurisdiction was flourishing, with my greatest satisfactions ahead.

THE BICENTENNIAL GENERAL CONFERENCE

Sixty Methodist circuit riders rode away from the Baltimore Christmas Conference in 1784 claimed by the vision of a lofty purpose. Authorized by John Wesley, they had established the Methodist Episcopal Church on American

Enjoying the Larger Church

shores, elected Francis Asbury to be their leader and consecrated him a bishop, voted to begin Cokesbury College in honor of Thomas Coke and Francis Asbury, and launched the Methodist Publishing House.

When they asked the question about why God had raised up a people called Methodist, they concluded that it was to "spread scriptural holiness over the land and to reform the continent." They spread from Baltimore to begin the task with a will. A lot has transpired since those beginnings, and Methodism is now a mighty world force.

A thousand delegates from around the world met again in Baltimore in 1984 to celebrate the two-hundred-year history of what has happened as a result of that resolve. It was a time of celebration and rejoicing at what God has done. Bishop William R. Cannon gave the episcopal address with historical perspective, a penetrating analysis of what we have accomplished, and a ringing challenge for the future. Powerful, erudite, moving. J. Taylor Phillips, representing the National Association of Conference Lay Leaders, explained that a representative committee from the association had drafted the Quadrennial Address of the Laity. The address was presented by Sue A. Guzman, Ramon C. Lopez, and Mai H. Gray, with Phillips himself presiding and delivering the final section. Since Phillips was also president of the Southeastern Jurisdiction Association of Conference Lay Leaders, he was selected to write and deliver the Bicentennial Address of the Laity for the Jurisdictional Conference in July.

Taylor Phillips was chair of the delegation. William R. Key was the first clergy elected, followed by Charles Wilbourne (Handy) Hancock. I was number three in this delegation to Baltimore. Again I had the privilege of serving on legislative committee number 9, Council on Ministries. Since I was completing eight years as a member of the General Council on Ministries, I had a number of assignments to steer through the Legislative Committee and the General Conference.

Phillips was elected by the Jurisdictional Conference to succeed me for eight years on the General Council on Ministries. William S. Hatcher, who also succeeded Phillips as

Members of the South Georgia Delegation to the 1984 General Conference in Baltimore who were available for a picture.

Conference lay leader, followed him as a member of GCOM for eight years and made a brilliant record for himself.

When the South Georgia Annual Conference met in June at the First United Methodist Church in Albany, I was endorsed by the conference as a favorite son for the episcopacy.

Three different times I received votes for the episcopacy. It was an honor. I have the utmost admiration for those who were elected and serve the church in this larger sphere. The

Enjoying the Larger Church

only time when I might have had a chance was in 1976; but no bishops were to be elected in the Southeast that year.

It may seem strange to those who do not know my heart, but I never ran very hard, nor was I willing to use positions entrusted to me to promote myself. I was never convinced that God could best use me in that way. To be honest I did not consider myself equipped to be a bishop of the church. Neither did I have the temerity to ask people to vote for me. I disappointed my friends who did believe and worked hard.

One day a friend who had heard talk about the possibility of my being supported asked, "Why were you never a bishop?"

I answered honestly, "I didn't get enough votes."

CHAPTER NINE

Understanding the Jurisdiction

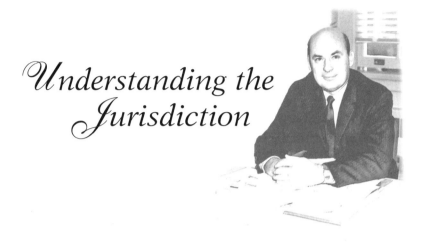

Persons called to the ordained ministry in the United Methodist Church often invest themselves in either the structure of the church, the institutions of the church or the movements of the church. Some have the opportunity of expressing their ministries in society beyond the church.

My official assignments and dominant commitments at various times involved me in three of these areas.

Along with appointments as pastor and district superintendent, in the course of my journey, it was my privilege to be chosen for responsibilities within the two major United Methodist institutions belonging to the Southeastern Jurisdiction: Emory University and Lake Junaluska. From this base, doors opened into significant movements that affected my life.

When the Methodist Episcopal Church, the Methodist Episcopal Church, South, and the Methodist Protestant Church finally reached reunion in 1939, the Methodist Church was divided into six jurisdictions. Five were geographic. The sixth, the Central Jurisdiction, was based on race.

The Methodist Episcopal Church, South, started two universities after the loss of Vanderbilt. One was established

A Journey Beyond

west of the Mississippi River, Southern Methodist University in Dallas; the other was east of the Mississippi, Emory University in Atlanta.

Decisions made in negotiations leading up to 1939 lodged ownership of these universities, along with the two assembly grounds, within the jurisdictions in which they were located. Thus two major institutions which belonged to the Methodist Episcopal Church, South, at unification—Emory University and Lake Junaluska—became the property of the Southeastern Jurisdiction.

These two institutions played significant roles in the evolution of my life from country preacher to retirement. Their welfare and development commanded most of my energy for twenty-five years of my life. I have already discussed the ways in which Emory enriched and extended my ministry. Junaluska did the same.

LAKE JUNALUSKA ASSEMBLY

Several streams, arising from various sources, converged to produce a conference and retreat center of incomparable beauty in the mountains of western North Carolina. They all contributed to the distinctive character of the assembly.

One of the streams goes back to an ecumenical Layman's Missionary Conference in New York City in 1900. A sizable contingent attended from the Methodist Episcopal Church, South. They were deeply impressed by the latent spiritual force in such a movement. One morning, as they met for prayer in the hotel lobby where they were staying, someone suggested that it would be great to have such a gathering among members of the Methodist Episcopal Church, South. Those present agreed. They decided to organize one.

The first Methodist Layman's Missionary Conference in the South met in New Orleans in 1903. Great energy for missions was released. Their enthusiasm translated into an offering of fifty thousand dollars. That fund was used to start Soochow University in China. When the communists took China, the nationalists fled to Taiwan with many valuable art and cultural treasures. These were housed in an elaborate

Understanding the Jurisdiction

museum in Taipei. Among the treasures that they carried was Soochow University. It is still there. Bess and I were guided through both the museum and the university. We were permitted to purchase three beautiful paintings. They hang in our living room.

Plans were announced for the second Layman's Missionary Conference to meet in Chattanooga in 1908. Out of it came the historic resolution calling for the establishment of a center for the "rallying of the church and the evangelization of the world." A committee was appointed to identify a place and to begin the work.

During the same period another stream was emerging. James Atkins was elected a bishop in 1906. The great thrust of his ministry had always been Christian education. He made his home in Waynesville, North Carolina, and served as the head of the Sunday School Board of the Methodist Episcopal Church, South. The board had only five members to guide the educational program of the denomination. In an effort to learn as much as possible Dr. Atkins decided to visit those responsible for the educational work in the Methodist Episcopal Church in the north. He learned in his travel that one of the leaders had been instrumental in launching the influential assembly ground at Lake Chatauqua, and he set out to discover as much as possible about the way it operated. He was stirred by a vision for a southern assembly ground modeled after Lake Chatauqua. At an appropriate time Bishop Atkins called the five-member Sunday School Board to meet in his home at Waynesville. They took care of business expeditiously. Most of the meeting, however, consisted of Bishop Atkins driving the board members to attractive mountain and valley sites near Waynesville in an effort to convince them that Haywood County would provide an ideal location for a southern assembly ground. All the while he extolled the virtues of the Lake Chatauqua program.

The third stream was flowing out of Birmingham, Alabama. Dr. George R. Stuart, the legendary pastor of First Methodist Church in Birmingham, had a vision of beginning a great Methodist campsite and assembly ground in the mountains of

East Tennessee, primarily as a preaching and evangelism center. He was gaining support and looking for a site.

Leaders of the Layman's Missionary Movement were looking for a place in response to the resolution passed in 1908. Bishop Atkins had convinced the Sunday School Board that a great educational and cultural center for the Methodist Episcopal Church, South, would make training for Sunday school workers so much easier. Dr. Stuart and his friends were convinced that an assembly ground would make possible large gatherings of the church for preaching and evangelism. The church could move forward with such a place.

So the stage was set. A small committee was formed. John Pepper of Memphis represented the laity. He was joined by Bishop James Atkins whose original dream grew out of his responsibility for the Sunday School Board, and George Stuart because of the work he had already done. The decision was made to build a southern assembly ground in the beautiful valley surrounded by mountains near Waynesville.

Money was raised. Farms were purchased. A dam was envisioned to turn the small creek that ran through the valley into a lake. An open-air auditorium was built. Hotels were planned. John Pepper, Bishop James Atkins, and George Stuart built homes on the grounds to show their faith in the enterprise. Others joined them. Today there are more than five hundred homes on the property.

When it was time for the third Layman's Missionary Conference in 1913, the new southern assembly ground was ready, albeit very rough. Pictures of the time reveal how barren and unpromising it was. There was no lake, yet. People camped or stayed in Waynesville. Those who stayed in Waynesville rode over daily on the train. They were deposited, walked across the dry fields, stepped across the stream, and made their way to the open-air auditorium. In spite of the inconvenience, the reported attendance was four thousand. Speakers of missionary vision and experience delivered stirring addresses. The plea was sounded for missions in various parts of the world. These were published in a book and still have the power to move people. Those attending brought an offering for missions from local churches and conferences.

Understanding the Jurisdiction

More than $150,000 was given. Missionaries were consecrated and sent out from the gathering, financed by the offering. It was an auspicious beginning for the southern assembly.

A frame hotel was erected across the street from Stuart Auditorium where the administration building now stands. The first burned mysteriously. The Terrace Hotel was shifted a little and rebuilt. A hotel was built on the hill where the cross now stands. It was called Mission Inn. It too burned. Twice. Mission Inn was also rebuilt.

World War I diverted attention. Financial problems consumed the energies of those who cared. The Layman's Missionary Movement faded. The assembly passed into the hands of the receivers. The bank appointed an administrator who sought to salvage it.

During the 1920s, before the Great Depression paralyzed the nation, new life was breathed into the vision. A spirit of optimism dominated decisions in every enterprise, including the southern assembly. Negotiations enabled the Methodist Episcopal Church, South, to take over the facility. Along with the new surge of enthusiasm, the center was named Lake Junaluska Assembly in honor of highly respected Chief Junaluska of the Cherokee Nation who lived nearby. The Sunday School Board, headed by the son-in-law of Bishop James Atkins, fulfilled its original intent by building Shackford Hall as a model for Christian education. Mission Inn, now owned by the Board of Missions, was renamed Lambuth Inn in honor of Bishop Walter R. Lambuth, elected in 1910, the vastly-traveled energetic and visionary missionary bishop of the Methodist Episcopal Church, South.

So Lake Junaluska symbolized the concerns of missions and evangelism and Christian education—the interests of three major boards of the Methodist Episcopal Church, South. Whatever the changing situation or structure, the emphasis at Lake Junaluska continued to be missions and education and evangelism and Chataqua-like features. But a new dimension has been added. Junaluska has become the heart out of which the most progressive and liberating influences for the church have been pumped throughout the jurisdiction. Here we have been at the growing edge, creating a new mood for the witness of the church.

Conversations toward the reunion of the Methodist Episcopal Church, the Methodist Episcopal Church, South, and the Methodist Protestant Church had been going on for decades. One or more of the three denominations voted down every plan put forward. One question facing the Methodist Episcopal Church, South, as the historic Uniting Conference in 1939 approached had to do with the future of Lake Junaluska. Lambuth Inn belonged to the Board of Missions. Shackford Hall belonged to the Sunday School Board. A heavy indebtedness continued to burden the assembly. An agreement was reached that these two boards would give the title of the properties to the trustees. A financial campaign was approved to pay off the indebtedness so that the denomination could go into the union with all the property under the control of the trustees and with a debt-free assembly.

As proud as the Southeastern Jurisdiction has been of Lake Junaluska, not much was done to support the assembly financially after union. It is true that the jurisdiction has given far more than the Methodist Episcopal Church, South, ever gave with an item included in the jurisdictional fund for program and capital improvement. This amount has steadily increased.

The trustees struggled, doing the best they could, until 1972. The Jurisdictional Conference that year approved the voluntary Junaluska Advancement Fund based on twenty-five cents a member. Only 48 percent was paid. But it was a start. When the 1976 Jurisdictional Conference met, the fund was continued and doubled. Fifty cents per member was approved as a goal. Response increased to 53 percent. Results were so apparent and positive that delegates to the 1980 Jurisdictional Conference voted to continue the fund, and during the 1980–84 quadrennium, payment reached 82 percent of the goal.

The Jurisdictional Conference of 1976 made another decision which impacted Lake Junaluska. A study was made by the Jurisdictional Council of all the programs and agencies of the jurisdiction. As a result of this study, the council presented a structure document to the Jurisdictional Conference. Some

Understanding the Jurisdiction

Dr. James W. Sells, right, welcomes us to the Southeastern Jurisdictional Conference at Lake Junaluska in 1976.

slight modifications were made from the floor. Then it was adopted. That document fixed responsibility for all the programming at Junaluska, as well as for the jurisdiction, in the hands of the SEJ Council on Ministries. It fixed responsibility for the physical operation of the assembly in the hands of the trustees.

Lake Junaluska is a jewel. It is easy to wax poetic in describing the beauty and importance to the church of these acres in the mountains of Western North Carolina. Both sides of Bess's family roots are deep in these mountains. She has loved them from the first time she saw them. She claimed everything she could see looking from "my picture window, at my mountains, with my moon shining across my lake." In a poignant moment one day as we drove through them, she said with tears in her eyes—she always cries when she sees beauty

A JOURNEY BEYOND

Bishop William R. Cannon stopping for a visit to our Junaluska cottage.

so majestic that it cannot be absorbed—"Thank you for giving me the mountains."

The first time I saw their grandeur, I was a country preacher from the flatlands of South Georgia. I also had ancestors from these mountains. A branch of my Freeman forebears settled in Surry County, North Carolina, just north of Haywood County where Junaluska is located, on the family trek from the southern part of England to Massachusetts to Virginia to North Carolina on their way to Georgia. More than a little mountain blood flows through my veins. Not until recently, however, did I learn this part of my heritage. The knowledge is a result of research into our family tree by my brother, Ramus, after he retired from the South Georgia Conference.

For more than a half century, I have been familiar with the Lake Junakuska Assembly and its summer programs, especially in the town and country church movement and with the laity. My close association to Lake Junaluska began in 1964 when I was elected to the board of trustees at the Jurisdictional Conference. I continued to serve the Assembly

Understanding the Jurisdiction

from that time through my years as executive director of the Southeastern Jurisdictional Council on Ministries through 1986. For twenty-two years I was active on the board of trustees and its committees. During my ten years as executive director of the Southeastern Jurisdictional Council on Ministries, I shared responsibility for the welfare of the assembly and the success of its programs with two Directors, Dr. Mel Harbin and Barry Rogers.

THE JURISDICTIONAL COUNCIL

When three denominations of the Methodist movement in America reunited in an historic step in 1939 to form the Methodist Church, some opposed it. One of the solutions to allay fears and overcome objections was the creation of the jurisdictional structure. Leaders of the Methodist Episcopal Church, South, moved quickly to organize the Southeastern Jurisdictional Council. In some ways the Council replicated the organization of the Methodist Episcopal Church, South. In the beginning the jurisdictional boards of evangelism, education, missions and church extension, and lay activities, were freestanding and independent of the Council. That quickly proved to be unworkable and expensive.

The SEJ Council met to organize June 27, 1944, during the Jurisdictional Conference in Atlanta, after the meetings and reports of the jurisdictional boards. Bishop Arthur J. Moore, Atlanta, was elected President; Bishop Costen J. Harrell, Birmingham, was elected vice president; Dr. A. R. Perkins of Harlan, Kentucky, was elected recording secretary. Bishop Moore announced that the Jurisdictional Council would meet at Lake Junaluska, August 23.

This first meeting of the council made several strategic decisions. Fifty-four of the sixty members were present. They found funds to operate and approved a budget. The executive committee was instructed to incorporate the council. The council approved a motion for a mid-quadrennium convocation in Birmingham early in 1946 to be used as inspiration for the Crusade for Christ phase of evangelism. The council approved the use of radio and news releases as communication efforts.

The council endorsed the plan to build a memorial chapel at Lake Junaluska to honor men and women who served in World War II from churches in the southeast. Heady and ambitious plans were made in these years following the end of World War II.

They then proceeded to elect an executive secretary by written ballot. Seven names appeared on the first ballot: R. Z. Tyler, William F. Quillian, J. Emerson Ford, F. S. Love, Bachman C. Hodge, A. R. Perkins, and Lester Rumble. On the second ballot, R. Z. Tyler received nineteen and William F. Quillian received twenty-eight. Since the number necessary to elect was twenty-six, Dr. Quillian was elected.

Dr. William F. Quillian was a distinguished South Georgian with broad experience and a premier administrator. He had been president of Wesleyan College in Macon and general secretary of the Board of Education, Methodist Episcopal Church, South. This first executive secretary proved to be a superb choice. He and Bishop Arthur J. Moore, the first president of the council, gave strength and direction to the council. The office was located in the Wesley Memorial Church on Auburn Street in Atlanta. Bishop Moore and Dr. Quillian were next door to each other. They consulted frequently and supervised the new structure and program.

Dr. James W. Sells from Mississippi was elected in August 1945 to join the team to begin January 1, 1946, and given the title of extension secretary with special responsibility for radio and communication.

Jim Sells, for more than a quarter century, was the idea man and executive for the laity, small membership churches, stewardship, missions, radio, and later television, and in all things he included me. Jim was my friend, my mentor, my guide, my confidant, and my sounding board for thirty-three years. He died in our Junaluska home October 3, 1979. We traveled with him back to Mississippi where he was laid to rest in the site he had chosen years before in Jackson. Others were my teachers and counselors along the way, but Jim was more.

The first broadcast of the *Methodist Hour* was Sunday morning, February 17, 1947, at 8:30 A.M. (EST) live over a

Understanding the Jurisdiction

network of telephone lines from Atlanta to cooperating radio stations. Thus began the broadcast ministry that has continued fifty-four years into the third millennium with an international reach.

Dr. Quillian led the council until 1952. Dr. Sells continued to serve the jurisdiction a quarter of a century, until 1970 as one of the executive secretaries with Edgar Neese, George Clary, and Trigg James.

Dr. Edgar H. Neese Sr. was chosen to succeed Dr. Quillian August 1, 1952. An unfortunate automobile accident, in one of Dr. Neese's trips from Junaluska to Atlanta in the process of beginning his work, curtailed his tenure. At the same time, Dr. Sells was also elected executive secretary so that there were two executives of equal rank and responsibility. When it became apparent that Dr. Neese could not recover enough to undertake the arduous work and extensive travel, the council, with sensitivity and tenderness, received his resignation with sadness. A new executive would be necessary to replace him.

Bishop Moore wrote the Council members about the situation, explained how limited the funds were, and asked that permission be given the Executive Committee to search for a successor.

Dr. George E. Clary Sr. of South Georgia, was elected April 1, 1954. He served with Dr. Sells until June of 1958 when he returned to Georgia to become the executive director of the newly formed Methodist Commission on Higher Education to consolidate the promotion and fundraising efforts for the Methodist colleges and Wesley Foundations in the state. He was imminently successful in this, as he was in all his appointments in South Georgia.

Dr. D. Trigg James was elected July 1, 1958, and served during a period of giant strides until his retirement. One accomplishment on which he spent major hours during his administration—along with D. W. Brooks, Dean William R. Cannon of Candler School of Theology, Dean Robert E. Cushman of Duke Divinity School, and university administrators—was birthing the Jurisdictional Ministerial Education Fund. The purpose was to provide operating funds for the two seminaries in the jurisdiction and to support seminary students. (Gammon Theological Seminary was added when the Central Jurisdiction was abolished.)

Dr. James was the "man in the middle" during the negotiations between Duke and Emory and the legislative process guiding the plan through the Jurisdictional Conference. Later adopted by the 1968 General Conference for the whole church, the Ministerial Education Fund provides unprecedented financial resources for the theological school and ministerial scholarships.

The executive committee, on January 29, 1968, approved the constitution and bylaws of SEMAR—the Southeastern Methodist Agency for the Retarded—and recommended the agency to the Jurisdictional Conference. Robert M. Pitzer, a staff member of the General Board of Hospitals and Homes, working with Charles D. White and Carlisle Miller, had drawn the plan in response to action taken at the beginning of the quadrennium. SEMAR was incorporated as an agency of the Southeastern Jurisdiction with Dr. Pitzer as director.

The organizational meeting of the Jurisdictional Council for the 1968–72 quadrennium met July 27, 1968, and elected Bishop Roy H. Short, president, to succeed Bishop Garber. Other officers included Joel D. McDavid and R. H. Bond as vice presidents, and Carl Sanders as recording secretary. Jim Sells and Trigg James continued sharing responsibility as executive secretaries.

The retirement date set for Jim Sells was July 31, 1970, with a dinner honoring him during the council meeting October 19–20, 1970, with generous plaudits expressing grateful appreciation of the jurisdiction. He was several years past the age of retirement, but need necessitated that he stay at his post. Trigg James was asked to continue as the one executive secretary until the Holston Annual Conference met in June 1971.

Dr. Robert Lundy was elected to succeed them at that same meeting October 20, 1970, to assume office January 1, 1971. Dr. Lundy was a member of the Holston Conference serving under the Board of Missions as a missionary in Singapore. Four years earlier, he had been elected a bishop by the Methodists in Malaysia. In the interest of the global church, Lundy had a strong conviction that the indigenous church should elect one of their own to lead them. After serving as a bishop for four years, he refused to allow them to re-elect him. The Board of Missions brought him home and assigned him responsibility as liaison for furloughed missionaries. From this position he was elected executive secretary of the Jurisdictional Council. For the first time since Dr. Quillian, the council had only one executive secretary. Dr. H. T. Maclin and Dr. Israel Rucker were added as program counselors responsible for communications and missions and ethnic minority concerns.

The mood of the church, and of the jurisdiction, was redefining and restructuring. Merger with the Evangelical United Brethren Church in 1968, the elimination of the Central Jurisdiction, and the redesign of the general church agencies compelled a fresh look at the Jurisdictional Council. A resolution passed by the Jurisdictional Council January 30, 1968, created a "Committee to Study the Structure, including the naming of Members." Almost as soon as Bob Lundy took office he was faced with working on a new structure. A draft of the proposal was made to the executive committee March 18–19, 1971. The document, as modified and approved by the full council April 20, 1972, was prepared for submission to the jurisdictional conference.

Significant changes were made in the way membership of the council was determined, the formation of COPALD—the Committee on Program and Leadership Development—as a major part of the council, and the decision to have one executive secretary with two program counselors.

Membership of the council was defined as:

- One ministerial and one lay representative from each constituent annual conference (these members shall be elected by the Jurisdictional Conference upon nomination by their respective Annual Conference delegations to the Jurisdictional Conference, but nominations shall not be limited to such delegations);
- The effective bishops of the Jurisdiction;
- The executive secretary of the Southeastern Jurisdictional Council;

- The president of the Board of Trustees of Lake Junaluska Assembly;
- The president of the Jurisdictional United Methodist Women;
- Ten members at large elected by the Council.

The following members were ex-officio without vote: the program counselors of the council; the executive director of SEMAR; the executive director of Hinton Rural Life Center; the executive directors of the Lake Junaluska and Gulfside Assemblies.

The COPALD membership was comprised of seven lay members (at least two of whom were to be women), four clerical members, one youth member, and one from the College of Bishops. Beyond these members of the council, the chairpersons or designated representative of each of the associations or fellowships of annual conference boards and agencies as defined by the council, the president of the council and the jurisdictional president of the United Methodist Women. Members of COPALD without vote included the executive secretary of the Jurisdictional Council, the program counselor(s) of the council, the executive director of the Hinton Rural Life Center, the executive director of SEMAR, the executive director of Junaluska, the executive director of Gulfside Assembly, the chairperson of the Jurisdictonal Committee on Communications, and one representative each from Duke Divinity School, Candler School of Theology, and Gammon Theological Seminary.

The nine associations and fellowships of conference leaders were: the conference lay leaders, the conference directors of education, conference leaders in evangelism, conference Boards of Missions and Church Extension, conference Boards of Church and Society, Conference Boards of Health and Welfare Ministries, Conference Committees on Communications (TRAFCO), and Conference Directors of Program Councils (renamed Councils on Ministries by General Conference in 1972). Several important areas were not included, for instance, the Association of Town and Country Leaders, the Association of Stewardship Leaders, and others. Provision was made for additional associations as the council deemed wise.

Understanding the Jurisdiction

It was a turbulent time for the church. The Jurisdictional Council on Ministries and the executive secretary had rough sledding. Serious structural, financial, and administrative problems continued. Too many independent, uncoordinated agencies within the jurisdiction competed for the same resources of time and money. A strong desire emerged to bring all of them under one umbrella. By mid-quadrennium, frustration led to yet another structure committee chaired by Duncan Hunter of North Alabama. Bishop Kenneth W. Goodson had succeeded Bishop Short and was president of the council 1972–76.

Significant changes again were made in the membership. The executive directors of Annual Conference Councils on Ministries automatically became the clerical members from the Annual Conferences. Lay members were elected as before. This placed in the SEJ Council the program leadership of each conference.

From time to time over the years, changes were made in the working relationships and authority of the council. From the beginning, until the Jurisdictional Conference in 1972, the membership was comprised of the first lay and clerical delegates elected to the General Conference from each Annual Conference plus the bishops and other ex-officio members. The number from each Annual Conference depended on the size of the conference. Those designated were considered the most influential leaders in the various conferences able to generate support for the programs and work of the council.

The structure was studied in 1968 with modifications in 1972 and more changes approved by the Jurisdictional Conference in 1976. Merger and restructuring was in the air. Restlessness and dissatisfaction were everywhere. Not all was well at Junaluska or in Atlanta. Dr. H. T. Maclin had become a staff member for Division of Interpretation of the Board of Global Ministries with responsibility for the southeastern region and left the council.

The jurisdictional Committee on Communications, already incorporated and semi-independent, opted out of the council and employed Dr. David M. Abernathy to direct its

A Journey Beyond

Jeanne Page being honored by the Southeastern Jurisdiction Association of Conference Lay Leaders for her long years of service to them and the Jurisdictional Council on Ministries. (Left to right): Joe Pevahouse, president of the Association, me, Executive Director of the Council, Mrs. Page with her husband Harold and her daughter Neada.

work on a part time basis. Aware of mounting tension, Bishop Allen offered Dr. Lundy a splendid church back home in the Holston Annual Conference in June. He took it.

ANOTHER STRUCTURE

The Jurisdictional Conference, hoping to resolve the issues, in July voted for the new structure. A three-fold purpose was approved by the Jurisdictional Conference: (1) To coordinate and to help make effective the ministries and agencies of the General Church as they work within the Jurisdiction; (2) To study the changing missional needs of the Jurisdiction; and (3) To give oversight to all program agencies of the Jurisdiction. In order to achieve these purposes, the conference outlined the following eleven functions:

Understanding the Jurisdiction

- To implement and coordinate all programs authorized by the Jurisdictional Conference.
- To give oversight to all program agencies created by the Jurisdictional Conference, or who are receiving funds for programming from the Jurisdictional Conference.
- To provide staff personnel when ordered by the Jurisdictional Conference.
- To study and coordinate the budget askings of the Jurisdictional Conference program agencies and to make recommendations regarding the same to the Commission on Finance and Administration.
- To give leadership in research and planning, to aid general boards and agencies in understanding the needs of the region, and to assist Jurisdictional Conference boards, commissions, and committees in discovering and responding to programmatic needs.
- To assist in training Annual Conference and District leaders within the region.
- To coordinate the ministries of the General Board staff persons assigned to the region.
- To be the liaison agency for all staff members assigned to the jurisdiction.
- To cooperate in ecumenical projects and events which are compatible with the basic policy of the United Methodist Church.
- To evaluate programs and agencies which are under the direction of the council.
- To provide inspirational opportunities at the jurisdictional level.

The search for a new executive to succeed Dr. Lundy could not be completed until the council met in the fall. For six months, therefore, the council was without an executive secretary. Bishop Ellis H. Finger was the new president, succeeding Bishop Goodson. He set about putting things in order. He spent a lot of time in the Atlanta office, and was in constant contact with Dr. Rucker and Jeanne Page until the new executive came.

A Journey Beyond

I was elected Executive Secretary, October 14, 1976, to become the chief executive of the newly designed Jurisdictional Council on Ministries.

Bishop Finger suggested that I make a formal response to my election. Some of my enthusiasm is seen in the statement that I made to the Council:

> I recognize the honor which your trust imposes, and I am aware of the enormity of the task before us. I accept it with humility and with determination to justify your selection.
>
> The Southeastern Jurisdictional Council was authorized by the Jurisdictional Conference in Atlanta in 1944 and organized the following summer. I have stood in awe of those who had the courage to create the council and to make it work for thirty of the most turbulent years of our national history.
>
> The intrepid Bishop Arthur J. Moore, whose mastery is reflected in so much of world Methodism and whose genius is still apparent in this council, was chosen to be the first president. The second president to guide us with that bundle of intelligent and disciplined enthusiasm [was] Bishop Paul N. Garber who added to the world vision of the council. That marvel of organizational skill and engineer of achievement, Bishop Roy H. Short, who led us through difficult times with a strong and steadying hand, followed Bishop Garber. Then came Bishop Kenneth Goodson, whose ability to inspire others to significant achievement and whose grandeur of vision guided the creation of the new structure into purposeful organization. Now you have elected Bishop Ellis Finger whose attention to detail and passion for fiscal responsibility promises an administration of incomparable skill and devotion to the ideals of the council.
>
> Along with these who served as president, to counsel and assist, has stood the College of Bishops and the remarkable array of talent elected to the council from the Annual Conferences. How fortunate we have been in the leadership made available to the jurisdiction. And think of the imagination and courage of staff members who have served us.

Understanding the Jurisdiction

I confess that this illustrious train intimidates me. The task fills me with awe. I have been in every conference and love every corner of the jurisdiction. From the Atlantic Ocean to the Mississippi River; from the Gulf of Mexico to the Ohio River; from the vigorous explosion of Florida to the unbelievable developments on the outskirts of Washington, D.C.; from the coasts to the mountains to the lakes of western Kentucky; from the Golden Crescent to the space centers to the atomic energy plants to the strip cities to the golden triangle to the rich agricultural stretches to the matchless strength of our growing metropolises, we are at work!

At every place we have a church, trained leadership, community respect, and an army of volunteers ready to be mobilized for the work ahead. Not a foot of ground exists in the entire region where we have not fixed responsibility for someone in the church to be planning ways to represent God. The pluralism of the United Methodist Church represents the racial, cultural, [and] economic diversity that makes up the region.

The expanse frightens me; but the diversity intrigues me. The quality of our leadership, the strength of our churches, the richness of our heritage, and the cohesiveness of our purpose places heavy obligations upon this council. Dedicated leaders in the College of Bishops, a strong corps of District Superintendents, competent pastors and a host of informed laity promise hope for the future. We are blessed with more than our share of colleges, universities, seminaries, Wesley Foundation directors, campus ministers, and ministries beyond the local church.

Action of the General Conference, mandates of the Jurisdictional Conference, and the charge given this Council on Ministries dictates our mission for the quadrennium; therefore,

- We will operate as a unit of the United Methodist Church—not independent of it.
- We will serve the Annual Conferences and the institutions that have created us.

A Journey Beyond

- We will strengthen Ethnic Minority Local Churches.
- We will mobilize our resources in the Crusade Against Hunger.
- We will call our people to the primacy of the evangelistic task—and try to add 350,000 to our membership by 1984. (This is our share of the increase of one million members to which the Council of Bishops has called us.)
- We will continue our compassionate commitment to the mentally and physically disadvantaged.
- We will give increased attention to communications, interpretation, and public relations. Our aim shall be to make the church visible, make our people proud, and make the public aware of what we are doing.
- We will utilize the best techniques for goal-setting program planning, and leadership development.
- We will work to put the Junaluska Advance over the top.
- We will cooperate with Annual Conference Councils on Ministries.

Of course I will move cautiously. That's my nature. This is how I see my beginning months.

First, I want to meet with the staff and General Agency people assigned to the region for briefing, overview, and establishing our pattern for working together.

Second, I want to seek counsel from the Bishops, Executive Committee members, Committee Chairpersons, Association, Fellowship and Organizational leaders, and members of the Council to find out what they see as the opportunities ahead.

Third, I want to visit United Methodist Institutions, the General Boards and agencies within the region to begin a working relationship.

Fourth, I want to study the region in order to understand its diversity and discover the strength of its conferences.

Fifth, I want to work closely with each Conference Council on Ministries to see if we can devise a vehicle for sharing the best of what they have learned with each other.

Understanding the Jurisdiction

Sixth, I want to visit each Annual Conference Session, on a rotation schedule arranged with other members of the staff.

Seventh, I want to form a pattern of research and planning as soon as we can. I realize that we are in an austerity budget, but for now, at least, we need ideas more than we need money.

That is the vision with which I began. My tenure as executive began in January of 1977 with a mandate to consolidate all the activities in the jurisdictional budget including Lake Junaluska.

"These have been busy weeks as I have sought to find my way," I wrote in a special report to leaders of the Annual Conferences in the SEJ. "Incessant travel, long roads, crowded airports, lonely motels, irregular hours, innumerable meetings, impossible schedules, unavoidable conflicts, prove to be just petty annoyances compared with the enticing opportunities beckoning from every direction and the exciting discoveries as I visit with conference leaders whose dreams outrun the possibility of achievement."

Our first task was to get our finances in order. We were in debt. We could not pay bills. Even travel expenses for council members had to be delayed. Our salaries were deplorable.

Our second task was to hammer out relationships between the council and Lake Junaluska and establish a style of operation with previously independent agencies that were forced into the council when Jurisdictional Conference approved the Structure Document. None of the implementing details had been worked out.

Our third task was to create a sense of direction and unity in the various programming units of the jurisdiction.

Soon after I came on board in early 1977, we had a meeting of COPALD to project a program for the remaining years of the quadrennium. Five major thrusts were agreed upon:

- Coordinate the planning process so that activities and events could all be moving in the same direction;
- Devise a way to let the jurisdiction know about things being done;

A Journey Beyond

- Rekindle hope in the Ethnic Minority Local Church;
- Involve our people in the Crusade Against World Hunger;
- Influence tomorrow through evangelism today.

The last objectives were related to the three missional priorities adopted by the 1976 General Conference in Portland and we were determined to cooperate fully in the Southeastern Jurisdiction.

Our report to the 1980 Jurisdictional Conference reflected progress, but more challenging opportunities were opening.

CHAPTER TEN

Cooperating with Leaders

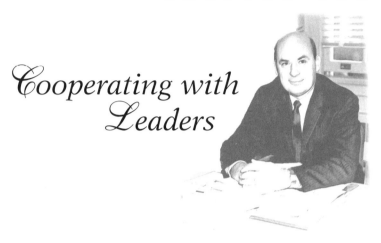

My method of creating programs was to bring together the most knowledgeable people I could find to stimulate ideas and concepts. This was easy to do while I was at Emory. Big people responded just as quickly when invitations were extended in the name of the jurisdiction. Keen and informed minds were usually eager to participate. Because they were, imaginative plans came into being and objectives were realized. Dreams became realities. Their thoughtfulness and reputations brought credibility to our work.

Members of each group knew more about the subject than I did. I was content to explore their minds, to serve as an expediter, to function as a facilitator, and to summarize the sessions. The mix of interests, the combination of information, the interaction of active minds produced splendid results for the kingdom. My role in most instances was to make notes, keep track of the ideas, and organize them into logical and sequential outlines. These were fed back to the group to see if they agreed. As programs were perfected, the group felt good about the process.

Conference and jurisdictional leaders who were involved felt responsible for implementing the projects. They claimed ownership for the programs because they helped to birth them. Credit was given the association, the commissions, the task force or the "think-tanks" consultations.

TALENT AVAILABLE TO THE COUNCIL

The Jurisdictional Council primary staff was small. In the beginning there were two executives with secretaries to do all the work. Along with the elected staff there were competent and committed secretaries to whom the jurisdiction is forever indebted: Ethel Barber, Louise Pierson, Ray Moore, Jeanne Page, and others who didn't stay as long.

Because we existed, however, resources were available that far exceeded our ability to provide. The SEJ Council on Ministries reported to the 1980 Jurisdictional Conference the wealth of skill and leadership ability coordinated in the southeast.

- The primary staff was made up of the executives and support persons paid by the council.
- The extended staff was made up of persons who worked full time in the jurisdiction through the council and its units but whose salaries were paid by other agencies.
- The related staff was made up of general board staff persons whose major responsibilities were elsewhere but who worked with one or more of the associations or fellowships in the Southeast as experts or consultants or resources persons.
- The Annual Conference Council on Ministries staff, more than a hundred professionals, provided a phenomenal pool of skilled and effective leaders. Each of them was involved in planning and promoting programs of one or more jurisdictional associations or fellowships.
- The associations and fellowships, made up of designated Annual Conference leaders, worked creatively and unstintingly for jurisdictional programs and activities. They generated ideas, promoted their special interests, and planned training and inspirational and promotional events. They were the vehicles to get ideas from and

Cooperating with Leaders

programs to Annual Conferences. By the end of the first quadrennium, there were twenty-five associations and fellowships in the networks making very significant contributions on a volunteer basis. Individuals were funded by their conferences. They were the keys to attendance and success of jurisdictional events.

In addition to the standing committees, there were four Commissions of the Council on Ministries. Each commission had a core group from the membership of the council in addition to at-large persons who were added because of their special expertise or to represent a segment of the constituency. A member of the primary staff served as director of the Commission. They met regularly to think and plan for the sixteen Annual Conferences of the nine-state area. The list of activities and achievements each year is still impressive.

- The Commission on Archives and History, Brooks B. Little, director.
- The Commission on Communications, David M. Abernathy, director.
- The Commission on Missions and Ethnic Minority Concerns, Israel L. Rucker, director.
- The Commission on SEMAR, Robert M. Pitzer, director.

Our vision continued to outstrip financial resources. We depended upon the energy and commitment of the remarkable men and women who were willing to bring their gifts to regional cooperative planning. Consider these groups who were a part of the SEJ Council:

- Members of the College of Bishops with broad experience, total church view, record of leadership, prestige and respect in the Southeast and across the church.
- Conference Council directors with proven planning and programming ability, competent staff and heavy responsibilities in the conference they serve.
- Lay members of such prominence and varied talents that they were nominated by their annual conferences

and elected by the Jurisdictional Conference to provide leadership at this level of the church.
- At-large members, nominated by a selection committee at the Jurisdictional Conference and elected by the Jurisdictional Council, brought balance and special knowledge to our work.
- Presidents of the Jurisdictional lay organizations led thousands and caused things to happen across the Southeast.
- Designated representatives of United Methodist institutions that belong to or are related to the Southeastern Jurisdiction added a depth dimension to the Council.
- Additional members of the four commissions were chosen to bring expertise and specialized information to the work of the council.
- Presidents of the SEJ associations and fellowships that plan the missional and programmatic thrusts of the jurisdiction were members of COPALD and therefore available to the Council.
- Representatives of the General Agencies assigned to advise and resource our work kept the denominational focus before us.

Plans for a mid-quadrennial convocation were written into the structure of the Southeastern Jurisdictional Council initially. These convocations brought hundred of church dignitaries to various cities of the Southeast. They were finally judged to be too expensive, so they were discontinued.

Had we planned one in 1982 to include the council members, commission members, association members and the categories of staff leaders outlined above, almost a thousand would have attended. That many people were involved in jurisdictional leadership through the grassroots. All of them, except for the council executive and support staff, were volunteers.

ASSESSING RELEVANT TRENDS

One of the assignments given the Jurisdictional Conference in 1976 was to "Study the changing missional needs of the

Cooperating with Leaders

jurisdiction." Among the eleven functions assigned the SEJ Council on Ministries that year was, "To give leadership in research and planning, to aid General Boards and Agencies in understanding the needs of the region, and to assist jurisdictional boards, commissions and committees in discovering and responding to programmatic needs." This task we took seriously.

While I was a member of the General Council on Ministries (1976–84), I served on the National Task Force on New Church Development (1980–84), the National Task Force for Developing a United Methodist Television Presence, and numerous Futuring research projects. I was on the writing team for a document on "The Future That Can Be" under the leadership of Ezra Earl Jones, at that time a staff member of GCOM and later general secretary of the Board of Discipleship. Our task was to analyze world trends and project appropriate responses United Methodists should make as we moved into our third century.

To begin our assignment, the executive committee of the council spent an evening and morning with Professor Earl Brewer of Emory. We asked him to lead us in understanding what was taking place in the Southeast and especially in the United Methodist Church. A broad outline for a research program was sketched. Under the tutelage of Ezra Earl Jones and the General Council on Ministries, we identified fifty societal trends and twenty trends within the church—a total of seventy—that would impact the future of conferences in the Southeastern Jurisdiction.

The seventy trends were selected from four major research documents and organized to be provocative and stimulating: (1) A working paper prepared by the General Council on Ministries of trends and characteristics with possible implications for the United Methodist Church in the Southeast as part of a research design for United Methodism as it enters its third century; (2) Statements prepared for the Delpi Project of the General Council on Ministries that most members of the special panel agreed were likely to occur by 1984 or 2000; (3) Research documents prepared by the Southern Growth Policies Board, Research Triangle, North

Carolina; (4) Research documents prepared by ACTS (Association for Christian Training and Service), Nashville, Tennessee.

We were convinced that programs for the future needed to be in response to these trends. The College of Bishops and the SEJ Council on Ministries led the massive effort. Each bishop was asked to create a blue ribbon committee to analyze the trends and propose responses. A document was prepared for the bishops and their study-reflection-planning committees to help them assess relevant trends with possible implications for their conferences. An instrument was designed to help them determine which of the trends would be positive for the conferences in the SEJ and therefore should be encouraged, and which would be negative influences and should be counteracted. Each committee was asked to address three questions to each of the trends: Is this trend strong in our area? If so, what will be its impact upon our churches? What initiatives should we take in response?

The bishops were invited to bring three persons from their areas to a three-day Jurisdictional Consultation at Junaluska to share the results of their discoveries and recommend programs for the consideration of COPALD. Dr. Earl Brewer from Candler and Dr. Ted McEachern from the ACTS organization in Nashville served as consultants and reflectors.

Participants worked diligently, seeking understanding and insight. Responses were written and digested. After all the data were processed, Dr. Roy C. Clark, chairman of COPALD, gathered the information together and wrote the findings.

Dr. Clark's report to the Jurisdictional Conference in 1980 on the process and results was a moving address entitled, "Facing the Future in the Southeast." The subtitle was "Assessment of relevant trends in the church and society in the Southeast to which United Methodists should address themselves during the remainder of the twentieth century." He described the background of the study, examined the situation in the church, detailed conditions in society confronting the church, and summarized suggestions for United Methodist responses. Programs to be considered by appropriate committees of the Jurisdictional Conference were referred.

Cooperating with Leaders

Fifty-six assignments were made by the Jurisdictional Conference to the SEJ Council on Ministries out of this process. These, along with proposals from the Task Force on Evangelism, commissions and staff, became the blueprint for action. The council shaped these data into seven objectives:

- Strengthen the ethnic minority local church
- Strengthen the local church
- Strengthen Methodist connectionalism
- Involve our people in Missions
- Project a positive public image
- Develop lay and pastoral leadership
- Outreach to the unchurched.

PROCLAIM THE WORD

The General Conference in 1976, disturbed by the declining membership nationwide, called the church to make evangelism a priority along with the ethnic minority local church and world hunger for the next four years.

The Council of Bishops in 1976 urged the church to reverse the downward trend and again emphasize growth. The bishops established a goal of adding one million members by 1989. The SEJ share of the million based on our size and projected growth in the region was 288,000 new members. That was our target.

Statistical studies revealed that conferences of the SEJ, with occasional exceptions, continued to lose members, declined in average church attendance, and showed an alarming loss in the church school. There was obvious need.

The Southeastern Jurisdictional Conference authorized a response to this challenge by establishing the objective to "help every local church become a functioning center of evangelistic ministry." The SEJ College of Bishops asked that evangelism be a major emphasis of the Jurisdictional Council on Ministries. COPALD (the Committee on Program and Leadership Development) recommended that one of the five major objectives of the 1976–80 quadrennium be "Influencing Tomorrow through Evangelism Today." The SEJ Council approved and created a task force to design a "simultaneous, coordinated, high visibility proclamation evangelism event for the Southeastern Jurisdiction" and urged each local church to participate. We called it "Proclaim the Word."

Bishop Edward L. Tullis chaired the task force. It included representatives from the College of Bishops; the Division of Worship, Stewardship and Evangelism of the General Board of Discipleship; the SEJ Association of Conference Leaders in Evangelism; the General Interagency Coordinating Committee on Evangelism; pastors and young adults.

Personnel of the task force to design the program included Bishop Tullis, chairman of the General Board of Discipleship Division of Evangelism, Worship and Stewardship; John B. Carroll, treasurer of the SEJ Association of Conference Leaders in Evangelism; Gladys Fitts, member of the General Board of Discipleship and the Core Group of the SEJ United Methodist Women; Jack L. Hunter, president of the SEJ Association of Conference Leaders in Evangelism; Clay F. Lee, pastor of Galloway Memorial, a grand old downtown church experiencing a new birth of evangelistic ministry, in Jackson, Mississippi; John Ed Mathison, pastor of Fraser Memorial in Montgomery, one of the fastest growing churches in America; Tom Murphy, pastor in Virginia and member of the executive committee of the SEJ Association of Conference Leaders in Evangelism; James C. Peters, vice president of the SEJ Council on Ministries and vice president of the United Methodist Publishing House; Syd S. Cleland, young adult member of the SEJ Council on Ministries and secretary of the Commission on Communications and Public Relations; Robert M. Temple Jr., Florida pastor and secretary of the SEJ Association of Conference Leaders in Evangelism; Eddie Fox, staff member of the General Board of Discipleship Section on Evangelism; and G. Ross Freeman, executive secretary of the SEJ Council on Ministries.

Bishop Tullis had been elected chairman of the General Interagency Coordinating Committee on Evangelism. Since I had been chairman of the Legislative Committee that steered the evangelism priority through the 1976 General Conference, I was made vice-chairman of the Interagency Coordinating

Cooperating with Leaders

I am in front of one of the Proclaim the Word banners in Greenville, South Carolina. Rev. W. W. "Bill" McNeil (placing the banner) was pastor.

Committee. I was expected to have a role in decisions of the SEJ Task Force and to serve as staff director of the work.

The task force designed the program and developed a calendar. The proposal was presented to the College of Bishops, Association of Council Directors, Association of Conference Leaders in Evangelism, COPALD, and the SEJ Council on Ministries.

The task force was then instructed to perfect the plan for the simultaneous emphasis and create the Proclaim the Word material for the Annual Conferences. Carefully developed handbooks were printed and distributed without charge for (1) the Annual Conference Steering Committees—five thousand copies; (2) Local Church Committees—eighty thousand copies, and (3) the Pastors—twenty thousand copies.

Each pastor was requested to participate by setting aside two weeks during Lent of 1980—February 24–28, the Week of Evangelism on the United Methodist Calendar and the Sunday for launching the World Methodist Council Evangelistic

One of the 878 highway billboards in the SEJ advertising local churches who participated in the Lenten Prayer and Visitation program in nine states as a part of the Proclaim the Word effort to have 200 million intercessory prayers in forty days for five million persons.

Mission to North America, and March 23–27, Passion Week in the Christian calendar. One of these weeks the pastor would host and direct the event in his or her own church. The other week, the pastor would serve as the visiting preacher in a church to which he or she was sent. The cabinets were asked to assign the visiting preachers to the pulpits in whatever manner seemed wise to them. Pastors covenanted, as a part of the massive connectional effort, to accept only their expenses for the week. They agreed not to expect or receive an honorarium.

The entire plan was presented to Annual Conference Councils on Ministries in the fall of 1978. Their leaders in evangelism requested that they build the schedule for full participation into their 1980 planning process.

One important feature suggested that the visiting preacher, following guidelines which were provided, meet for four to six

Cooperating with Leaders

hours with the local church Council on Ministries to study their evangelistic performance for five years, to help them set goals for 1981–84, and to build programs to achieve these goals.

The high publicity media campaign made the general public aware that the United Methodists were serious about evangelism. The task force employed a professional advertising agency in Charlotte owned by Parker Duncan, son of a pastor in Western North Carolina, to design and supervise the production and distribution of the media campaign material.

Elements of the media campaign consisted of (1) a reproducible logo to provide identification and to tie it all together, (2) five themes that were used in ads for radio, television and newspapers, (3) a common design for highway billboards, posters and bumper stickers, (4) five thirty-second TV spots, five thirty-second radio spots, and five attractive newspaper ads.

Each Annual Conference Steering Committee was sent free of charge five sets of the TV spots, three sets of the radio spots for each district, ten sets of the newspaper ads and five outdoor billboard ads for each district. Additional material was available for the asking at no charge. The professional services of Parker Duncan Associates were offered without charge in placing the ads in each conference where they would do the most good.

Local churches were asked to order, for a nominal fee to cover production costs, the number of posters, bumper stickers, radio spots, and newspaper slicks they could use. District and Annual Conference Steering Committees paid only for placing the material in the media where there was a charge.

What an impact!

Imagine: 157 sets of the five TV spots for a total of 785 spots played over and over in each market; 758 sets of the five radio spots for a total of 3,790 spots used again and again; 216 sets of the five newspaper ads for a total of 1,080 ads; 878 highway billboards with each one seen by thousands of drivers each day for months; 122,831 bumper stickers displayed on United Methodist cars for six months or more; and 40,474 posters in communities over the Southeast. The cost of producing and distributing the media campaign material was $47,734. Other expenses, including the publication of the three handbooks and the final report to the Jurisdictional Conference, was $24,336 for a total of $72,070.

This was just the beginning. The imagination and creativity of the task force paid dividends in other evangelistic efforts during the next five years.

How was it financed?

Pastors declined honoraria. Receiving churches paid the travel and other expenses. Each local church, in addition, was expected to receive an offering each night of the proclamation event. They were requested to send the collection received on the second night to the Annual Conference treasurer. The total amount sent in by the local churches for this one offering was almost $250,000. Sixty percent of the amount was given to the Conference Steering Committee to pay for broadcasting the TV and radio spots and publication of the newspaper ads. Almost $150,000 was distributed. This means that those conferences participating had an average of $10,000 from this source—depending on the size of the conference and the level of involvement—to spend for mass media plus the amounts spent by district committees and local churches for publicity. The other forty percent of the one-night offering was forwarded to the Jurisdictional Council on Ministries office to defray the cost of the campaign. The amount sent to the SEJ office through the Conference Treasurers amounted to $96,408. After paying all the bills a balance of $24,338 was left which was used to provide up-front money to begin the next step in Proclaim the Word.

MOBILIZE A MILLION

Actions of the Jurisdictional Conference became the marching orders for units of the SEJ Council on Ministries. Seven major objectives came out of the Jurisdictional Conference in 1980. The seventh had to do with outreach. Specific programs were mandated: establish two hundred new congregations, involve a million laypeople in the next step of Proclaim the Word, reach out through mass media, start new Sunday school classes and outpost Sunday schools, develop intentional ministries to persons with handicapping

Cooperating with Leaders

conditions, make an effort to establish contact with half the adult population who are not members of any religious body, and champion the causes of the oppressed and unrepresented as we reach out to them in the name of Jesus.

Calendar Item 11 of the 1980 Jurisdictional Conference became the mandate. The subject: "Strengthening the Local Church for its Evangelistic Mission in the World" was adopted with directions for the SEJ Council on Ministries to devise an emphasis which would involve one million lay members in the evangelistic task of the church during the quadrennium.

One million! That's quite an army of volunteers! An army of redemption! Recruits had to be inspired, organized, trained, disciplined to become the channel through which God can work.

For months I had been praying each Sunday morning for the one million persons who worship in churches of the Southeastern Jurisdiction! What will it take to mobilize a million in some spiritual or evangelistic activity?

The assignment was taken seriously by the SEJ Council on Ministries and the Association of Conference Leaders in Evangelism. Other staff members and units of the SEJ Council were assigned responsibility for the first six objectives. The seventh was the continuation of the task force on evangelism with which I had been working. So it continued to be my major commitment.

We decided to move forward in five areas: (1) The next step of Proclaim the Word, (2) Discovering and emphasizing Church Growth principles, (3) Set membership goals for conferences, districts, and local churches, (4) Involve a million laypeople in some spiritual or evangelistic activity, and (5) Discover the secrets of church planting and establish new churches.

Each of the objectives called for two kinds of Goals: result goals and effort goals. We acknowledged that evangelistic *results* are in the hands of God. The evangelistic *effort* we put forth, however, is up to us.

Each local church was asked to make the effort to organize itself into "a functioning center of evangelistic ministry." This was to be accomplished by having the Administrative Council authorize the creation of CORE

A Journey Beyond

(Committee on Renewal through Evangelism) with responsibility for working toward the numerical result goal. Detailed guidelines were furnished in a booklet, *PROCLAIM THE WORD—Next Step to Involve a Million*, prepared by the SEJ Association of Leaders in Evangelism and distributed by the SEJ Council on Ministries.

Second, each local church was urged to do its part in involving one million lay members at some level of evangelistic ministry. At that point in history there were approximately three million United Methodists in the Southeastern Jurisdiction. On any Sunday morning there were almost a million and a quarter attending services of worship in the annual conferences of the Jurisdiction. These are the ones we count on to achieve the effort goals.

Not every person is comfortable talking about spiritual experiences or witnessing in any traditional sense. Neither is every member "gifted" in leading others to make a decision for Christ. Every Christian, nonetheless, is expected to obey the commission to "go . . . make disciples . . ." No one is excused. But how can these worshipping members be mobilized to do it?

After much soul searching and agonizing struggle, the SEJ Association of Conference Leaders in Evangelism decided on a plan. John B. Carroll of South Georgia succeeded Jack L. Hunter of the North Carolina Conference as president of the association. They both had been on the task force chaired by Bishop Tullis. The association did not miss a beat. Plans moved forward.

The decision was reached to design a Lenten program of intercession and visitation in 1983. The plan would seek to enlist members of the worshipping community to do three things: (1) Pray every day during Lent for five nonchurch persons. (2) Visit those five persons during Holy Week, preferably on Good Friday. (3) Report to the pastor any response they make. The SEJ Council on Ministries agreed. With the program approved, work proceeded to perfect the details.

Research was done primarily in the minds and spirits of persons attending a consultation I was leading during the Prayer and Bible Conference at Lake Junaluska, July 18–22, 1982. About eighty persons registered. Among them were prayer leaders from around the nation. The Reverend Kay Barger of the

Cooperating with Leaders

Baltimore Conference, chairperson of the Upper Room Committee of the General Board of Discipleship, was among them. She offered the assistance of the professionals on the staff of the Upper Room Division.

The Reverend Danny E. Morris, staff member from *The Upper Room* who directed the Prayer and Bible Conference, was an essential catalyst and imaginative expediter in the whole process.

In no way is it possible to convey the sense of spiritual energy and excitement that was felt in these sessions.

Basic decisions were reached early.

Average church members would need a manual to guide them. If they were to participate, five simple "How To" helps would have to be written and provided: How To Pray—for persons who are not practiced in the art of prayer; How to Pray for Others—for persons who need guidance in intercession; How to Pray Forty Days for Five Persons—for persons who need suggestions of what to pray about; How to Visit—for those who have not had an occasion to visit in the name of the church; How to Start the Conversation—for those who have never thought about beginning a conversation about the faith with another person.

Initially the purpose was to develop a guide that could be placed in the hands of church members who chose to participate in the Lenten Prayer and Visitation program. But the concept quickly moved deeper.

It was quickly revealed that we would have to write a daily guide for intercession lest the prayers tire of simply asking God to bless the five, day after day, for forty days. It was decided that the daily guide should reflect progressive intercession.

The themes were chosen. Each intercessor would ask God to grant the five rich fulfillment of life, to set them free from anything which hindered them, to release a dawning desire for spirituality, to lead them to a community of believers, to nudge them to enter life abundant, to help them claim the promises that God has for them, to enable them to grow in grace, and to develop Christlike qualities. Each theme built on the others. The progression was beautiful.

A Journey Beyond

But we had missed a step. We saw that whatever was asked for the five must be based upon scriptural promises. We had to be sure that God had already promised to do it. So we began a search of the Bible to find Scripture on which to base our intercession. More than that, we added an interpretation of the significance for intercession in the selected Scripture. Then we wrote models for intercession each day.

By the time we reached consensus on all of this, the Prayer and Bible Conference was over. Our participants had to go home. Still a lot of work remained to be done. Two weeks later, however, the Week of Evangelism was in session, sponsored by the SEJ Conference Leaders in Evangelism. I had committed to lead a couple of seminars. Fifty persons registered. Since all of this started with the association, they were willing for my seminars to continue the consultation.

I reviewed for them the work that had been done during the Prayer and Bible Conference. They made some modifications, but when they saw the vision, they moved with zeal to complete the manual. Forty volunteered to write the daily guides following the pattern that have emerged. Their names are written with the pages they wrote. When the Week of Evangelism was over, all that remained was to bring the writing of the various authors into a harmonious style and to design the booklet. *The Upper Room* was especially helpful in editing the material and guiding it through publication.

All stops were pulled out in publicizing and promoting the effort through the connectional structure of the church. Direct mail was sent to every pastor and local church offering basic packets giving details of the program and describing material available to make it work. Prayer assignment cards, a motivational audio tape to be played in each church, newspaper slicks, bumper stickers, banners and posters—and the *Forty Days of Prayer for Five Persons* daily guide were provided at minimal expense because they were produced in such quantity.

The first printing of the daily guide was 250,000. Nearly 2,500 local churches in conferences of the southeast participated. Initial reports received in the SEJ office from annual conferences indicated that at least 225,000 United Methodists were involved in this movement of intercessory prayer. Think of

Cooperating with Leaders

it. That many faithful church people offering 45 million prayers of intercession for 1,125,000 nonchurch persons over a forty-day period! All of this was done in one year in the jurisdiction. Some churches were so renewed by the experience that they repeated it.

Add persons in local churches who are regularly involved in visitation, in Covenant Prayer Groups, in lay witness missions and other evangelistic activities and the totals are mind boggling.

As impressive as the totals are, even more significant is what happened in individual churches. We could not record all the information which was sent in to the SEJ office—this was in the days before the magic of computers—but we lifted up some sentences at random from a few of the reports which came to us.

> The response of our people was far beyond my expectations on the First Sunday of Lent . . . We did not have enough assignment cards for all who came forward . . .

> Our faith was too small. We ordered the amount of material suggested for our size church. We didn't have enough. The response overwhelmed us . . .

> Without any arm-twisting or pressure, people came to the altar the first Sunday in Lent and picked up one hundred packets with five hundred names in them. It did something for our people . . .

> I was pleased with the way in which our families participated. One hundred thirty-eight came to the altar to receive the names of over five hundred . . .

> We prepared fifty-seven packets and thought we would do good to have thirty-five taken. But fifty-five persons responded! All the packets were taken . . .

> Our people were excited to find that friends and relatives in Atlanta, Belle Glade, Florida, and Alabama were also in this program at the same time. It gave them a new feeling of the United Methodist Church working together . . .

The greatest joy came to our young people. Imagine the delight of adults on Good Friday when they received a visit from an eleven year old . . .

One of our college professors captured the spirit of our church, "It is good to be praying for someone else instead of being concerned about what is happening to me . . ."

Several people have told me about specific answers to their prayers. Some for whom they were praying started coming to church. Attendance at Sunday school was up 20 percent. Morning worship attendance increased 17 percent during Lent . . .

One man showed up in church Easter. He had been on somebody's list of Five and had received a visit on Good Friday. At the close of the service, he thanked me for the prayers of the church. He was back the following Sunday . . .

Our church was crowded Easter. Chairs in the aisle. Chairs in the overflow room. One-third of the people who gathered were unchurched. I am convinced it was due to the Prayer and Visitation program . . .

Easter Sunday we had a moving moment when the cards were returned to the altar as an offering of our faithfulness. Over 20,000 prayers had been offered in our community for 500 persons. There has been genuine excitement and joy about our involvement in prayer. Wonderful seeds of faith and love have been sown, and God will bring in a harvest for years . . .

Reports came that persons "felt" someone was praying for them. Others commented about an "unexplained sense of support when I was feeling down." Many acknowledged "an awesome sense of responsibility that I was actually interceding for someone else," and many more testimonies of the effectiveness of intercessory prayer.

The impact of the Lenten Prayer and Visitation movement on our congregation was beautifully distilled in the comment of one of our lay members: "I hope that my forty

Cooperating with Leaders

days of prayer are as meaningful to the Five and they are to me. The suggestions and format for the prayers furnish so much spiritual nourishment . . ."

Churches outside the Southeast heard about the program and asked if they could participate as well. We had direct contact with churches in Arkansas, Maryland, West Virginia, Oregon, Arizona, West Virginia, New Mexico—to mention a few of those who communicated back to us. The East Ohio Conference had sixty thousand United Methodists in five hundred churches participating in the *Forty Days of Prayer for Five Persons* the following year.

Pastors still write to see if material is available. They remember the impact and want to use the program again. Permission has been given for hundreds of churches to reproduce the material on their copy machines. The supply has long been exhausted.

CHAPTER ELEVEN

Dreaming for the Future

I looked through twenty-five issues of the *SEJ United Methodist* newspapers in which the staff and I recorded many of the events and activities of the Jurisdictional Council on Ministries. I re-read reports that I wrote for the Council on Ministries in which achievements and visions were detailed for each of the ten years. I reviewed eight years of the SEJ Council on Ministries stewardship prepared for the Jurisdictional Conferences in 1980 and 1984. I examined the rather astounding and ambitious programs adopted by the 1976, 1980, and 1984 Jurisdictional Conferences for the Council on Ministries to implement. I took a journey through nine Junaluska program books which I designed and wrote to reflect the rich variety of our offerings each year to Annual Conference leaders. I marveled at the roster of distinguished preachers and teachers and world leaders we were able to make available to the jurisdiction. I contemplated my personal and jurisdictional calendars and remembered each year with gratitude even as I wondered how it was possible to do it all. I reflected on the budgets, remembered the struggles to pay bills, agonized over the meager salaries we paid our staff, and thanked God for their commitment to the task whatever remuneration we could afford.

A Journey Beyond

The Southeastern Jurisdictional Council had only four presidents in the first thirty-one years of its history (1945-76): Bishop Arthur J. Moore (1945-60), Bishop Paul N. Garber (1960-64), Bishop Roy H. Short (1964-72), Bishop Kenneth W. Goodson (1972-76). But in all the restructuring, the pattern changed. Somewhere the decision was made to elect one of the bishops as president for two-year terms in the order of their seniority. During my decade as executive director, we had five presidents. Bishop H. Ellis Finger led us as president (1976-78); Bishop Earl G. Hunt (1978-80); Bishop L. Scott Allen (1980-82); Bishop William R. Cannon (1982-84); and Bishop Robert M. Blackburn (1984-86). They gave wise and diligent attention to the work of the council while they were in office, but all the bishops were involved in the council and committees and commissions. Without their support, not much could have been done. With it, the council had credibility.

Our staff was hard working and visionary, cooperative and committed, and totally loyal to what we were doing. In addition to the elected staff, the secretarial staff made it all possible. There were some temporary and part-time persons used at peak seasons, but the following persons wrote their names large in the fifty-year history of the council: Ethel Barber, Ray Moore, Louise Pierson, and Jeanne Page. The jurisdiction could never pay them what they were worth. They continued in the job because of their commitment to what we were attempting. All had different gifts, but together we made a team.

In the Advance Edition of the *Daily Christian Advocate* which the staff prepared with our reports and recommendations for the 1984 Jurisdictional Conference—as we did for the one in 1980—we listed the names and categories of the membership, the conferences which they represented, the members of the Committee on Program and Leadership Development (COPALD), and the members of the four commissions. We had reports from each commission as well as my quadrennial report.

One of our goals for the quadrennium was to "project a positive image of the United Methodist Church." This was in

Dreaming for the Future

the hands of Dr. David Abernathy and the Commission on Communications. Their four years of work staggers the mind. For example, Dr. Abernathy reported that we produced forty-eight radio programs heard by 528 million people around the world, including the Armed Forces Network, through the Protestant Radio and Television Center just off the campus of Emory; edited and published and distributed four books of sermons through Abingdon Press; participated in the production of seventy-two award-winning television programs called *Perspectives* seen by 870 million; produced the complete Heritage media campaign for use during the Methodist Bicentennial; printed four inspirational and informational pamphlets, ten major reports on convocations and consultations distributed around the jurisdiction; and published a brief history of the colleges and universities started by Methodists in the SEJ, *Higher Education in the Southeastern Jurisdiction*. All of this involves twenty-four books and booklets produced during the four-year period by the Jurisdictional Council.

TOWARD AN URBAN STRATEGY

Still we were never satisfied, especially when reminded of the potential in these nine states.

"The golden age of church growth and social impact of Methodism in this country came prior to the Civil War," Dr. Earl D. C. Brewer, professor of religion and sociology at the Candler School of Theology, said in an address to the 1980 Southeastern Jurisdictional Conference. "There are doubtless many reasons for this faltering of faith and evangelistic practice," this modern day prophet continued.

"The heyday of the growth of the church came during a period of rapid increase in the population based upon high birth and immigration rates. Yet the denomination outgrew the rapidly growing population. It was a time for the primacy of the frontier. Our spiritual ancestors forged both a structure and a spirit that provided dynamic encounters with the personal and social needs of people moving into the wilderness and developing small towns. It was also the period of the highest English-speaking immigration into this country.

"Following the Civil War, the urban centers of the Northeast became the new frontier in a rapidly growing industrializing nation. Our church never devised an urban strategy comparable to its earlier frontier strategy. Immigration shifted. People came to the new world from central and southern Europe, which was basically Roman Catholic. Again, as a denomination, we did not develop a usable strategy for ministering to or evangelizing nonEnglish-speaking people and cultures. In some instances we simply watched as nonEnglish-speaking followers of John Wesley formed themselves into separate language denominations.

"Much of our structure was institutionalized during the frontier days and has been slow to change in the light of new developments."

These and other observations in Dr. Brewer's address jolted the complacency of the Jurisdictional Conference delegates. They wrote, and passed, Calendar Item 13 which admitted, "We do not have a comprehensive strategy for the city, and we are not flourishing in urban areas." Delegates voted to "request the SEJ Council on Ministries through the appropriate structures to call a Consultation on the Urban Church." The purpose was to explore: (1) ways for stronger churches to assist those with dwindling resources to remain in ministry where the needs are great; (2) the possibilities for a total United Methodist witness and approach to the entire city; (3) ways for providing a ministry to subculture groups of the city in the name of the United Methodist Church; (4) special qualifications required for ministers and staff serving inner city and urban churches; and (5) development of an orientation plan to prepare pastors who are sent for the first time to an urban appointment from rural or small town situations.

Following our usual approach to such assignments, the SEJ Council on Ministries asked the College of Bishops to call a Consultation, to designate the participants after conversation with representatives of the SEJ Urban Workers Network and to assign Bishop Paul A. Duffey to chair a task force to plan it. In addition to Bishop Duffey, the task force was comprised of Denison Franklin, Louis Jones, Ted McEachern, Walter McKelvey, Cecil Myrick, Bobbie Roberts, Tom Robinson,

Dreaming for the Future

Ray Sells, Lester Spencer, Frank Windom, Israel L. Rucker, and G. Ross Freeman.

The Consultation was arranged for September 14–16, 1982. A total of 187 participants came from every conference of the Southeastern Jurisdiction to plan an urban strategy. All of them were leaders. Five were elected later to the episcopacy. An open, probing, searching spirit characterized the session. Far-reaching insights emerged from the group wisdom. A growing conviction crystallized that United Methodists need to move from strength and unity to engage the urbanization culture, to confront the structures of the city with the claims of God, and to collaborate with others in meeting human needs and working for justice. They concluded that we might have to speak a new language and learn to praise God in different settings.

In addition to normal population growth and migration, large numbers of refugees fleeing oppressive conditions in third world countries were entering the South with critical needs and markedly different languages, religions and social customs. One out of five persons in the region was below the poverty level. These sub-culture and nationality groups constituted 35 percent of the nation's poor.

The 1980 census defined twenty-three cities as urban areas in the nine southeastern states. Participants in the Consultation were divided into Urban Regional clusters for the "Think Sessions" so they could focus ideas on one specific geographic entity. Their first assignment was to identify issues which needed to be addressed in creating a comprehensive and total strategy for the city. Our task, it was agreed, was to focus on interpretation of what was happening in the city, planning to meet critical emerging needs, resource development, and deployment.

Our strategy must be whole to include each unit in the city. Success needs to be defined in such as way that the whole body can celebrate what God is doing, not just the more affluent parts. Such success has to be measured by quality of ministry, faithfulness to God's claims on us, and the achievement of goals realistic for the situation—not in terms of statistical reports. If the policy of career advancement based on statistical success continues, then the church in transitional and inner city communities in particular will continue to have a hard time attracting clergy competent to the task. Whether it is fact or fancy, there is a feeling among some clergy and congregations that these appointments are punitive. Appointing the right person to the right place is crucial. Nothing is more demoralizing to a congregation as rejection by a pastor who doesn't want to be there. Nothing can be more wasteful and destructive in the utilization of our clergy resources than to assign them to places for which their gifts and graces are unsuited.

An appropriate urban strategy will take into account that others may already be at work in a given community. Specialized ministries, community centers, churches of other denominations and agencies may exist. We have to know who they are and how we can collaborate with allies in meeting needs.

"This consultation and its findings, if we have the will to implement them, may be one of the most significant events in the Southeastern Jurisdiction in a decade," Bishop Duffey observed. "It represents a high level of cooperation between the Board of Global Ministry, the Board of Discipleship, the College of Bishops and the structures of the SEJ Council on Ministries."

ESTABLISH NEW CHURCHES

Denominations grow by planting new congregations. In the SEJ we, along with other jurisdictions, almost observed a moratorium on beginning new churches since 1960. United Methodists have not been starting new congregations as rapidly as we have been closing them. As a result we have been losing members since 1968.

The study of trends in which the Jurisdictional Council engaged prior to the 1980 Jurisdictional Conference predicted an influx of 3.5 million people. If United Methodists were to maintain the percentage of that new population which they currently hold in the southeast, provision would have to have been made to accommodate 250,000 additional members. New churches would have been required to do this.

Dreaming for the Future

Loaded with this information, delegates to the Jurisdictional Conference in 1980 approved Calendar Item Twelve, which mandated that new churches be established.

The College of Bishops took this responsibility seriously. They spent a day discussing the need and possibilities for church extension. Before deciding on a strategy, the Bishops wanted more precise information about successful models. They asked the SEJ Council on Ministries to collect information about some models that might be utilized in conference and district efforts.

A task force was created to guide the investigation and propose a plan. Bishop Robert M. Blackburn was designated by the College of Bishops to lead it. Other members of the task force were: W. S. Bozeman, Florida; A. C. Epps, North Georgia, member of the National Task Force on New Church Development; R. Beverly Watkins, Virginia; W. Robert Borom, South Carolina, organizing pastor of a new church; Fred Heleine, New York, General Board of Global Ministries; Ken Callahan, professor Candler School of Theology, with research and courses in new church development; William W. Morris, Tennessee Conference Council Director and member of the General Council on Ministries; Israel L. Rucker, director of the SEJ Commission on Mission and Ethnic Minority Concerns; and G. Ross Freeman, executive director of the SEJ Council on Ministries and a member of the National Task Force on New Church Development.

Tucked away in one of the legislative items at the Bicentennial General Conference in Baltimore was an unbelievable and serious call for the United Methodist Church to double its membership in the next eight years. The National Fellowship of Asian Americans initiated the petition. It passed. Our missionary children were challenging us to move into our third century with a worthy growth goal.

Another action that year, that did not receive much attention from the media, was in line with the emphasis on new members. General Conference adopted the report of the National New Church Development Task Force. I had served four years on that task force. It called for the United Methodists to plant one thousand new pulpits and teaching places in the next four years, to target twenty-five hundred marginal congregations for revitalization, and to mobilize resources for accomplishing these goals. These were ringing calls to the future.

The 1980 SEJ Conference—concerned over continuing decline and inspired by response to the trends study—called upon Annual Conferences to launch an imaginative effort to turn things around. Evidence of this determination was the adoption of a proposal to establish two hundred new congregations in the Southeast in the next four years.

The Task Force made six decisions early: (1) We would take full advantage of the research and other work done by the National Task Force on New Church Development; (2) We would utilize the resources provided by the General Board of Global Ministries and the General Board of Discipleship; (3) We would recognize that the locus and disciplinary responsibility for new church development is in the Annual Conference and District Committees so that the chief function of the Jurisdictional Task Force would be to resource and encourage their planning and decision making; (4) We would publish and circulate a series of articles designed to create a climate for starting new churches; (5) We would hold a Consultation on New Church Development in 1983; and (6) We would publish a report for the Jurisdictional Conference in 1984.

A detailed study was made of the sixty-nine new churches that were identified by the district superintendents. There is no common pattern, but all of them together yielded some important findings for the guidance of bishops and our conferences. They are contained in the report published for 1984 Jurisdictional Conference. Let me summarize ten at this point.

- The district superintendent and the district committee on church location are key factors in any new church planting. They can benefit, however, from overall conference and regional strategies. In many instances, moreover, their imaginations need to be prodded a bit so that they can find ways of getting the job done.

Dreaming for the Future

- The advantage of studying population movements and anticipating where new churches will be needed ten or twenty years down the road is that suitable land can be purchased when it is still affordable. Land, if it happens to be in the wrong place, can be swapped or sold more easily than exorbitant prices can be paid when it is needed. So a second important finding is for the conference and/or district to purchase land before it is needed.
- The organizing pastor must be well trained, mature, and experienced enough to provide proper guidance to a new congregation.
- While the congregation may be collected in a temporary facility, an architect's drawing of the ultimate building should be displayed quickly to serve as a reminder of where the congregation expects to go.
- A well designed plan of promotion and publicity is essential in collecting a congregation. Prospective members need to feel that the venture has denominational support, that the church will be organized with integrity, and that it will be planned with an eye to the future.
- There must be well thought out plans for funding and a carefully designed budget if the effort is to succeed. Purchasing the land, buying a parsonage, paying a pastor, providing a program, renting temporary facilities, obtaining suitable equipment, and starting the first unit; all have to be financed.
- Church planting is far too expensive for districts to undertake alone. This is why a conference-wide or regional strategy is so important. Denominational resources plowed back into new congregations will prove far more valuable for kingdom purposes than money invested in other enterprises. Why should we feel that our own future is any less promising than that of General Motors or Dupont or General Electric or any other aspect of corporate America?
- The great vision which must be transmitted existed fifty years ago. It is not new. It only needs to be reemphasized. It is the vision of an existing church

sponsoring a new church. Older congregations can measure their success by the number of new churches they have sponsored.
- Denominational leaders must find ways to organize and launch churches in racial and ethnic communities.
- Leaders must get away from the concept of new churches meaning new million dollar plants. Congregations can be gathered without a building. They can begin wherever there are people willing to meet.

Two approaches to starting new congregations emerged. One, favored by the General Board of Discipleship, was to decide where new churches ought to be located, send in leadership to start a Sunday school and collect a congregation in whatever space could be obtained. Often space could be rented from a school, a bank with a community room, an empty store building, a community center or a home. The idea was to start small, recruit people and let the church building emerge as the need for one grew.

The other, favored by the General Board of Global Ministries, was the one most often followed. Elaborate studies were made. Competent leadership was provided by the denomination. A pastor was appointed. Experienced volunteers were recruited from nearby congregations to give leadership to the new church. Resources were made available to purchase land, to pay salaries, to fund ministries, to provide an architect and allocate money to build the first unit. In those days it usually cost the conference from $250,000 to $500,000 to start one church over a five-year period. Obviously not many could be built.

I worked hard on a proposal that the National Task Force on New Church Development carried to General Conference as a way to finance land and new buildings. It called for the General Agencies to allocate some of their investment money for new churches.

The United Methodist Church has a lot of money invested in corporate America. Investing in new churches would be equally as sound financially. Very few new churches have ever defaulted—less than half of one percent—on mortgage

Dreaming for the Future

payments. Districts and Annual Conferences could have stood behind the loans. Church repayments would earn the going interest rate and protect the income from the funds. Studies show that new churches grow faster than older congregations, pay a hundred percent of their apportionments, and rapidly become strong dependable churches. We would be investing in our own future and multiplying the number of new churches we could plant. The National Task Force argued that the denomination ought to have as much confidence in its own future as it does, for example, in the future of Ford Motor Company or Dupont or any other company in America. Representatives of the General Boards were on the task force. Most of them were persuaded that the plan was feasible. But before General Conference delegates had a chance to consider the proposal, it was derailed by elements in the church with another agenda. So new churches were not built. Membership continued to decline. The plan never surfaced again.

Several conferences in the SEJ, however, received the ten recommendations from the SEJ Task Force with favor and devised plans of raising funds for new church development. Some of the findings influenced decisions by United Methodist leaders in the sixty-five urban centers of the jurisdiction.

BLUEPRINT FOR EVANGELISM

The SEJ Council on Ministries prepared plan forward recommendations in 1984 for the Jurisdictional Conference Committees. These grew out of the futuring processes of COPALD and the Council. Delegates were challenged to "launch our third century with boldness."

General Conference decisions, Jurisdictional Conference action, the thousands of people around churches who are without Christ and the mandate of the gospel all call United Methodists of the Southeast to the evangelistic task.

Calendar Item 34 of the 1984 SEJ Jurisdictional Conference called upon the College of Bishops to "give bold leadership and provide motivation for a comprehensive plan of evangelism designed to reach a goal of 3.75 million members in the next four years. We further call upon the

A JOURNEY BEYOND

agencies of the Southeastern Jurisdiction and Annual Conferences to respond to the leadership of the bishops by providing initial plans, resources and training events to achieve these goals."

That was a sweeping order. The SEJ Association of Conference Leaders in Evangelism took this action seriously. In response John B. Carroll, president of the association, appointed a task force to prepare a "Blueprint for Evangelism." The task force was comprised of, in addition to the president, Harold Bales, David Brazelton, Eddie Fox, G. Ross Freeman, H. T. Landrum, and Israel L. Rucker. Plans were drafted. Carroll requested the College of Bishops to appoint a time when they could meet with the task force. A date was set to consider the preliminary proposal.

Seven sections were included in the fifteen-page document.

1. Creating the expectation of growth.
2. Setting the goals for growth.
3. Finding the people for growth.
4. Developing the strategies for growth.
5. Informing the conferences about growth.
6. Affirmation and Recognition of growth.
7. Resources and bibliography for growth.

Nineteen proposals were spelled out for the bishops to evaluate. They allowed time to examine and respond to each proposal. Options were discussed. Several of the concepts found their way into annual conference programs. They are as valid and workable today as when they were suggested.

SETTING GOALS

By way of illustration, the section on setting goals for growth outlined three different methods for setting the goals—after the case was made for having goals. "We are convinced that if no individual church goals are set, the overall goal will not be reached. We believe that the General Conference goal correctly calls the church to its fundamental responsibility. We believe that the Jurisdictional Conference

Dreaming for the Future

acted responsibly in accepting the challenge to reach out to the undiscipled and requesting the bishops to exercise bold leadership in evangelism. We believe that each local church must analyze its outreach opportunities, set specific goals, and work faithfully to reach them."

One proposal presented to the bishops was based on Fair Share Goals. One of the fairest methods of determining the relative strength of an annual conference, or a local church, is the decimal figure by which apportionments are assigned. Computations are based on the relative strength of each church. The same method can determine the "fair share membership goal" as well as the financial goal for each church. The task force computed the four-year growth goal for each conference in the southeast with instructions for assigning the annual growth goal for each church.

An alternate method was for each church to set its own goals by using a list to determine its responsibilities. In a study requested by the General Council on Ministries in the early 1980s, research by the Lou Harris organization found that there were twenty-two million people in the United States who claimed they were Methodists. For whatever reason they claimed us, we needed to find who they were. Using the FRAN sociometric procedure was a viable way to involve the membership in establishing its list of potential prospects. Each active member would be asked to identify friends, relatives, associates, and neighbors who were not involved in another church and who lived within reach. Suppose the Sunday morning attendance was fifty. Following the FRAN method, the fifty could identify an average of four names each. This would be a total of two hundred prospects within their circle of influence. These persons already had contacts within the congregation and were therefore prime candidates for membership—especially if their names appeared on three or more lists. Then they divided the two hundred by half to establish a realistic four-year membership growth goal of one hundred persons to be cultivated and involved in participation. This would be a growth goal of twenty-five per year, or slightly more than six per quarter.

The third method suggested to the bishops was the Faith Leap Goals. We designed a way to set goals in relation to the unchurched people in the community. We were in position to provide demographic information on a county basis for each annual conference. Our data gave the number of United Methodist churches, the percentage of the population of each county that was United Methodist, and the percentage of the population that was unchurched in 1980. By multiplying the number of unchurched persons by the percentage of the population which was United Methodist we could ascertain the United Methodist responsibility. Goals could then be distributed to the churches based on their relative strength and individual circumstances. Approximately half the counties in the nine southeastern states were growing in population. The other half was stagnant or declining. Counties that were growing naturally had the larger goals.

When the Glenmary Research Center made these studies for us there were 44,213,015 people in the nine states. At that time, there were 22,779,305 persons who were not associated with any religious organization or movement. While nationally, the percentage of the population which was United Methodist was only 5.1 percent, in the states of the SEJ 8.0 percent of the population was United Methodist. Multiply the total number of unchurched persons in the southeast by 8 percent, and you have 1,786,139 who are United Methodist responsibility in the SEJ. The percentage in each state varies. So each state and each county was computed individually to determine the numbers.

With the movement of the population to the Sunbelt in the last twenty years, the possibility for United Methodist growth is staggering. That is why this method of establishing goals was called a "Faith Leap Goal."

Such details were offered for all seven of the sections. Let me call attention to Proposal 15 in section four, "Developing Strategies for Growth" as another illustration of the planning and work done in the name of the Southeastern Jurisdictional Council on Ministries.

NEIGHBORHOOD STUDY OF MARK

Studies by the SEJ Association of Leaders in Evangelism urged the development of a program of neighborhood Bible study as a way to engage nonchurch families. We expended a lot of energy in the simultaneous, high-visibility, media supported proclamation evangelism event and in the Lenten Prayer and Visitation movement. These efforts centered primarily in the church. SEJ Leaders in Evangelism were convinced that gospel preaching, intercessory prayer, and Bible study are three essential steps along the road to renewal.

Delegates to the 1984 Jurisdictional Conference called upon "the Bishops to provide bold leadership in evangelism" to guide Annual Conferences in achieving the membership growth goals set by the Bicentennial General Conference. One specific program adopted by the SEJ Jurisdictional Conference in Calendar Item 41 called for "a program of neighborhood Bible study in homes as a method of reaching out."

A successful method of outreach in the 1980s was nonthreatening neighborhood Bible study groups. In the progression of renewal movements, the time had arrived to move outside the church to nonchurched persons in the neighborhoods. If those who need the church will not come, the church must go to them.

Our research revealed a growing interest in "what the Bible says." Many who want to know are unwilling to risk themselves in "church." We discovered a readiness in many places, however, for persons to meet with their neighbors in a nonthreatening atmosphere on neutral ground to discuss the Scripture.

Following the dictates of the Jurisdictional Conference and in collaboration with the bishops, the SEJ Leaders in Evangelism designed a jurisdiction-wide program for a study of the gospel of Mark in small neighbor groups. Mark was chosen because it is a rapid-paced, straightforward short account of the life and teachings of Jesus.

We negotiated with the American Bible Society to produce three hundred thousand copies of a special United Methodist edition of Today's English Version of the gospel according to Mark plus a twenty-page study guide for six sessions. The cover had a picture of the Memorial Chapel at Lake Junaluska to provide more identification. Each booklet had a picture of the presiding bishop on the inside cover, and a letter from him encouraging the people of his episcopal area to participate. Room was left on the back cover for the name and location of the church and the pastor's phone number to be stamped or printed.

There are five pertinent recommendations for reading the Scripture at the beginning of the study guide. The Reverend James F. Jackson Jr., who was at that time pastor of the St. Mark United Methodist Church in Columbus, Georgia, wrote the study-discussion guide. Dr. Jackson's doctoral project was a design for small groups to study the gospel of Mark experientially over ninety days. The San Francisco Theological Seminary published the dissertation as a book titled *Education for Discipleship*. Jackson prepared the six-session study guide so that there are twenty-five contemporary questions raised in each session from a modern context with an appropriate Scripture verse as reference in finding the answer. Seldom was it possible to complete the discussion of the questions in a session. Many groups continued the study for months with great profit.

Widespread distribution of the gospel portion to the homes of the church community provided a United Methodist presence in these homes whether the families participated in the neighborhood study or not. These copies of Mark were made available at seventeen cents each or seventeen dollars a hundred. Few copies of the three hundred thousand are still available, and they are keepsakes. Think of it. Participating churches distributed hundreds of the books through the neighborhoods where the home studies were held. And it was all done in the name of the United Methodist Church with a letter from the bishop of the area encouraging them to join in the Southwide study of the Bible. Some churches left booklets in nursing homes, hospitals and other places where the people could have them free of charge. They provided an inexpensive public relations piece for the local church.

A *Local Church Guide* was prepared and distributed widely to the pastors and officials of each conference. It explained the program, urged that the effort be undergirded with prayer, and provided instructions to order the material. Suggestions

Dreaming for the Future

were offered for selecting the homes where the six sessions would be held, assigning teams to visit each home of the neighborhood, and training the leaders of the groups.

There are reasons why some churches have found neighborhood Bible study groups the best contemporary method of evangelistic outreach.

KEEPING UP WITH THE DETAILS

Forty-two programs were approved by the Jurisdictional Conference for the Council on Ministries to implement in the 1980–84 quadrennium. It would be easy for some of them to be lost. Our method of tracking them was to assign each one to a responsible unit of the Council. Plans and details were audited by the Committee on Program and Leadership Development (COPALD). Participating in this process were twenty-four Associations of Annual Conference Leaders, each with a life and purpose of its own, who designed the inspirational and training events. Events planned by Gulfside Assembly, Hinton Rural Life Center, and the Junaluska Intentional Growth Center are also coordinated by COPALD.

As a result there were 121 Jurisdictional events planned by units of the SEJ Council. They registered a total of 36,552 persons.

All of this leadership training and ministry was accomplished for less than one dime per member per year.

Our budget has always been stringent. Even so churches of the Southeast, in four years, gave $1,031,663. This was enough for salaries, office expense, and travel. Because the SEJ Council existed, however, units of the council generated funds to pour $2,263,646 worth of program and ministry back into United Methodism in the Southeast.

CHAPTER TWELVE

Making the Story Public

One of Ira Progoff's techniques in intensive journaling is to instruct his patients, or seminar participants, to look back over the junctions of their lives and to imagine what might have happened if they had taken the other fork in the road. In my view, this would serve no useful purpose. But as I stood before a joint session of the Executive Committee and the Nominations and Personnel Committee of my friends in the Southeastern Jurisdictional Council on Ministries February 27, 1986, to announce my resignation, I did wonder.

What if I had not turned from my youthful dream of a career in country music? What if I had not given up sign painting and commercial art? What if I had not left my boyhood business with its promise as a merchant? What if I had not agreed to leave my leadership in the rural church movement and accept the position in academic administration which Dean Cannon offered me? What if I had accepted any of the other offers to change directions? What if I had not left Emory after fifteen very happy and fruitful years and returned to South Georgia as a pastor? What if I had ignored the invitation from Bishop Finger to appear before the Personnel Committee for an interview just as I was completing an exhilarating term as district superintendent? What if I had not allowed my name to be put forward as editor of the *Wesleyan Christian Advocate*? Who knows what might have happened if I had chosen any of the other forks in the road. . . .

THE WESLEYAN CHRISTIAN ADVOCATE

Now I stood on the threshold of another career change. Ten years traveling the nine southern states, primarily by car, had taken its toll. During this time I had heavy responsibilities at the denominational level which kept me in airports and racing to incessant meetings.

My friend, Dr. William M. Holt, was retiring after fourteen years as editor of the *Wesleyan Christian Advocate*. His office was one floor above mine in the United Methodist Center in Atlanta. He recommended that the board ask me to consider replacing him. At first I refused. The work was going well in the jurisdiction. Finances of the council were in good order. We had accumulated some up-front money for starting new ministries. I enjoyed what I was doing through the Southeast and expected to stay in the jurisdictional office until I retired. Still some Georgia friends urged me to take a closer look at the situation of the *Advocate*.

I was completing forty-five years of service to the church as a minister. Even though I was only sixty-three, I could have retired; but I was not ready to quit. The mandatory retirement age was seventy; I had seven more years before I had to step aside. In a moment of weakness and exhaustion, I succumbed to the weariness of traveling and attending national meetings where the atmosphere was sometimes tense. I agreed for the search committee to put my name forward. The change, I thought, would at least allow me to spend most nights in my own bed.

The *Wesleyan Christian Advocate* was first published June 4, 1878, with Atticus G. Haygood, president of Emory College in Oxford, Georgia, as editor. One job was never enough for the vigorous and expansive mind of Dr. Haygood, so holding these two positions was not unusual for him. From 1878 to 1986, fourteen editors had guided the weekly newspaper. Two of them

Making the Story Public

served two years, one three years, three four years, one five years, one for seven, one for eight, one for nine, one for twelve, one for thirteen, one for fourteen, and one for twenty. I was the fifteenth in this line and could serve for seven—if I succeeded.

Only three Methodist newspapers were started in this country before the *Wesleyan Christian Advocate* and its antecedent, *The Southern Christian Advocate*, began publication June 24, 1837, in Charleston, South Carolina. It served the church in South Carolina, Georgia, and Florida.

The *Christian Advocate* was started by Nathan Bangs in 1826 for the Methodist Episcopal Church; it was authorized retroactively two years later in 1828. *The Wesleyan Journal*, a publication for the southern region, also began in 1826. But *Zion's Herald*, a regional Methodist publication for New England, was started three years earlier in 1823 and is still operating.

Seven years after the *Southern Christian Advocate* was launched in Charleston, *The Southern Christian Advocate for the Southern Church* began publication in Nashville in 1844.

When the Civil War broke out, officials were afraid that Charleston would fall to the Union forces, and with it, the destruction of the *Southern Christian Advocate*. The decision was reached in 1861 to remove the presses and offices to Augusta, Georgia, where they might be safer. By the time the move was completed, Union soldiers were already in Augusta. Subscription lists were maintained, but publication was sporadic. The war interfered with obtaining supplies and in distributing the paper. Operations in Augusta became ever more difficult. After four years of struggle, 1861–65, a move was made to Macon, Georgia. For twenty-six years, 1865–91, Macon continued as the center for publication and distribution.

Arrangements were made with the John W. Burke Company to print the paper. The Burkes were staunch Methodists. One member of the family served as a missionary to China. Another was a preacher. For a time John W. Burke was appointed associate pastor to the Mulberry Street Methodist Church, just across the street from the Burke Company, and assigned responsibility for printing the paper.

This was a good arrangement. The John W. Burke Company printed Sunday school literature, hymnals and several editions of the Discipline for the Methodist Episcopal Church, South. Printing and distributing the newspaper for South Carolina, Georgia, and Florida was a natural for them.

The *Southern Christian Advocate* continued to serve the conferences of the three states until 1878 when South Carolina leaders voted to establish a separate publication to be called *The South Carolina Advocate*. At that point, Methodists in Georgia and Florida decided that a name change was in order. That year *The Wesleyan Christian Advocate* was born. Eight years later, in 1886, the Florida Conference withdrew to establish is own *Florida Advocate*. Since then *The Wesleyan Christian Advocate* has been the official newsweekly for Georgia Methodists.

Look at the giants who served as editors in the early years. Atticus G. Haygood was first. The second editor was Weyman H. Potter who served eight and a half years.

John W. Burke, for fifteen years, was publisher and assistant editor with several editors to both the *Southern Christian Advocate* and the *Wesleyan Christian Advocate*. He resigned December 24, 1890, after twenty-five years. His health failed three years earlier. The following year, in 1891, the editorial offices were moved to Atlanta where they remained forty-five years.

The third editor was Wilbur Fisk Glenn (for whom Glenn Memorial on the campus of Emory University was named). He served a decade.

The fourth editor was William C. Lovett. He loved it and served twenty years, longer than any other person.

The fifth was William Peter King, editor for three years. He left to become book editor of the Methodist Episcopal Church, South, and editor of the *Christian Advocate*, Southern Methodism's weekly news journal based in Nashville. That publication continued until it was merged with three others at the time of Methodist Union in 1939 to form the churchwide *Christian Advocate*.

Alfred Mann Pierce was the sixth editor; for the first of his seven-year tenure, he received no salary.

Making the Story Public

Elam Franklin Dempsey served only two years because of the depression; he had to do the work of two. When he submitted his resignation, the North Georgia Conference voted to discontinue publication of the *Advocate*. William T. Watkins, professor of Church history at the Candler School of Theology, volunteered to assume the responsibility without salary just to continue the paper. He used students to help with the work. Even without paying the editor a salary, the indebtedness grew from $2,500 in 1932 to $6,135 in 1936. Dr. Watkins, later elected a bishop, felt that he had given enough.

A Fresh Approach

The editorial offices and printing operation were moved back to Macon in 1936. There it remained thirty-five years (1936–68).

A new plan of administration and operation was adopted by the conferences. The plan called for the *Advocate* to employ an experienced newspaper person as business manager. It was hoped that he could save the publication. Other policies adopted by the conferences at the time were: to make the *Advocate* a "real church newspaper," to operate without going into further debt, to reduce the subscription rate to $1 per year, to have an editorial staff of six pastors—three from North Georgia and three from South Georgia—who would write and supervise the contents of the paper, to contract with the Masonic Children's Home in Macon to print the paper. In order to pay the indebtedness of $6,135, each conference agreed to give $2,500 the first year and $600 the second.

Charles A. Britton Jr. was chosen business manager to direct the new thrust. He brought seventeen years experience in Atlanta and Moultrie daily papers and an energetic passion and vision to serve the church. The formula was a success. In four years time, circulation had increased from 6,500 in 1936 to 21,600 in 1940. No further subsidy was needed after the second year, and in 1939 the trustees reported to the Annual Conferences that they were giving six scholarships to Methodist students in six Methodist colleges. They also eliminated all patent medicine advertisements from the *Advocate*.

Then Charlie Britton was chosen in 1941 to move to Chicago and consolidate seven publications into the *Christian Advocate* for the general church.

Subscription rates remained constant at one dollar per year for twenty-five years with circulation increasing each year. Those were years of expansion and growing influence. By 1961 the number of subscribers hit a peak of fifty-six thousand.

Those were the glory years. After Britton, Frank Q. Echols (1940–45) was named the first general manager and the tenth person to be in charge of the *Wesleyan Christian Advocate*. The arrangement of six pastor-editors continued. Echols introduced the system of assigning quotas to each local church with the pastor having responsibility for reaching the quota. Circulation grew from 21,600 to 34,498 during his five-year administration.

In the nine years since 1936 when the *Advocate* was flat on its back, subscriptions had increased 900 percent. Good management enabled the paper to operate in the black financially.

Florence M. Gaines (1945–58) followed Frank Echols. The subscription rate remained at one dollar. Circulation continued to climb. The twelve years and seven months of his leadership was a period of expansion and financial stability. Under his administration, the trustees bought property, erected a building, and purchased a state-of-the-art printing press.

The building was dedicated debt free June 15, 1951, an achievement of considerable magnitude in six years without a drive for funds or grants from the annual conferences. Gaines brought Bruce Yandle Jr., a devoted layman, on board to serve as production manager for twenty years (1948–68) through the editorship of C. Hoke Sewell and Dan H. Williams.

Dan Williams reported fifty-six thousand subscribers in 1961, the twenty-fifth consecutive year with an increase. Rising paper and labor costs forced the trustees to raise the $1.00 subscription rate to $1.50. Subscriptions dropped to fifty thousand, still by far the largest circulation of any Methodist publication in the Southeast.

The printing press was now obsolete. Repairs were time consuming and costly. The land on which the building was located had become very valuable. The trustees decided to sell the property in Macon, negotiate a printing contract, and move again to Atlanta. Sale for the property, completely paid for, provided a two-hundred-thousand-dollar permanent reserve fund or endowment to assure the continuation of the *Advocate*. By 1971, the entire operation, with four staff people, was located in the new United Methodist Center to be near the bishop's office in Atlanta. Another rate increase became necessary in 1971. Circulation dropped to forty-four thousand.

Bill Holt

When William M. Holt became editor (1972–86) spiraling costs in postage and paper forced the subscription rate from $2.50 to $3 per year. Circulation dropped again in 1973 to 41,350.

Dr. Holt was popular in both conferences. He came to the position with an academic and practical background in journalism, a worldview shaped by a distinguished career as a missionary, and a succession of outstanding pastorates in the North Georgia Conference. His fiscal toughness, fairness, and unquestioned integrity guided the paper through one of the most difficult periods in modern times.

Bill Holt had long been one of my heroes. In spite of unbelievable budgetary problems, he brought an international flavor and an editorial flair to the *Advocate* for fourteen years, as he says, without "missing a deadline." After graduating from the Candler School of Theology in 1946 followed by a two-year pastorate, he was sent to Bolivia as a missionary by the Board of Missions (the General Board of Global Ministries since 1972). From there he was assigned to Argentina where he edited the Buenos Aires *Christian Advocate* as well as other South American church papers. When he returned to the North Georgia Conference in 1955, he served Dahlonega, Trinity Atlanta, Carrollton First, and LaGrange First before becoming editor of the *Wesleyan Christian Advocate* in 1972. He was always a missionary at heart and continued to teach in the regional, conference, and local church Schools of Missions. Completely unselfish with a deep commitment to journalism, Bill Holt was

A Journey Beyond

Former editor of the Wesleyan Christian Advocate, Bill Holt, welcomes me to the "Retired Editors" ranks at the retirement party, June 3, 1993.

the embodiment and soul of the paper. His career as editor was the second longest in the history of the *Advocate*. It was no small assignment for the board to replace the legendary Bill Holt.

During his tenure, a new phenomenon emerged to threaten the life of the religious press. Staggering jumps in postage forced many church papers to stop publication. Others became bimonthly instead of weekly. Several became monthlies. For fourteen years, Bill Holt and the trustees struggled with capricious postage rate increases (one year without previous warning, the Post Office raised the rate a total of $60,000; that kind of increase continued to come in surprising moves from 20 to 45 percent each year). Such runaway inflation multiplied costs in every area of the budget. Had it not been for the wise and careful management of the editor and trustees, the *Advocate* could not have survived. The only way to meet these unanticipated increases in the middle of the year was to draw from the permanent funds. *Advocate* reserves dwindled to less than $117,000.

When he retired Bill Holt left a superb staff. There were two associate editors, Jan Glass and JoAnn Campbell, well-trained, loyal, and committed. Martha Berry, meticulous and careful with a background in teaching math, was the bookkeeper whom I later promoted to treasurer. Circulation was in the competent hands of Princella Davis, assisted during campaign months by Martha Freeman. Dan Williams brought Princella to the staff as a young woman. She remained the key to an accurate subscription list for almost twenty years until her very untimely death. All of them agreed to stay with me during a "trial period" to see if they could work with me.

A New Career

It was not an easy decision for me. After ten years of being on center stage, planning and promoting and influencing the life of the jurisdiction, I would no longer be at the heart of what was happening. It was not easy to change my role to being an observer and a reporter rather than an active participant.

This career change brought a major shift in the way I looked at things. As editor, I observed and reported rather than created; I functioned as a business executive rather than a programmer; I reflected the decisions of others rather than participate in making them.

On the other hand I had a chance to record what was important, interpret what was happening, chronicle United Methodist history and serve as a press agent for the church.

As with every career move, I had much to learn. I went about it methodically and called upon friends across the church to teach me. I wanted to be a good editor, a worthy successor of those who had gone before. I set about to prepare myself.

A Journey Beyond

Dr. Holt was patient and untiring in the transition. In addition to hours spent with him, between March and June I registered for two seminars, traveled thousands of miles to visit every conference publication in the Southeast and about a dozen outside the jurisdiction to see what I could learn about design and publishing a newspaper. Then I went to Nashville—the fount of all wisdom—and spent days with friends at the United Methodist Commission on Communications, the United Methodist News staff and the staff of *Newscope* and *Circuit Rider*. Some pointed me to books and other resources, but those who helped me the most just told me how they did their jobs.

I discovered quickly that the editor of a weekly publication does more than write. He or she must develop the skills of a reporter, a photographer, a journalist, an advertising specialist, and a graphic layout artist. He or she must be able to rewrite material written by others so that it reads well, and conveys the essence of the story without making the author feel that it was mutilated.

More than that, an editor has to be a businessman or woman finding ways to increase and manage income, a financier learning to make dollars work when they are not immediately needed, and a promoter striving to keep the *Advocate* on the minds of pastors and leaders of the conference. At the same time the editor has to maintain good public relations with clergy and laity and officials of the two conferences. Tact has to be exercised in dealing with angry subscribers who do not like what was written, who did not get their paper on time, or wondered why we did not cover a particular story that seemed important to them. All the time the editor must use discretion in selecting stories of importance and interest to readers—and above all, maintain personal integrity and a sense of fairness.

In June of 1986, the *Advocate* anticipated a deficit of twenty-five thousand dollars by December, had a wornout label-addressing machine which sometime caught fire, antiquated typewriters, and very little else but a patient staff operating in cramped quarters and a board who wanted to do better. At one meeting, the board instructed me to buy an electric pencil sharpener and a trash can in response to a complaint from one of the staff.

Making the Story Public

It was a tough time for newspapers generally, especially church publications. People were not reading. The old sense of denominational loyalty and pride in what we were doing was gone. Other conference papers were reducing pages and publishing schedules. Some within the jurisdiction were submerging their historical identities in the Dallas based *United Methodist Reporter* family.

The board convinced me that it wanted to maintain a weekly newspaper, to continue the *Advocate* traditions, to make the publication attractive, readable and packed with information for United Methodists of Georgia. I had come to believe in the mission of the church paper, wanted it to continue as a newspaper of force, worthy of Methodism in the state. Though the *Advocate* could pay me far less than my successor received from the jurisdiction, I followed my policy never to allow salary to determine my career decision.

Slowly over the years, through careful management and the efforts of a committed staff, we began to change the climate. We moved into larger quarters in the United Methodist Center; installed our own telephone system with incoming and outgoing watts lines and fax capabilities; installed a modern postage weighing and metering system; and invested in a state-of-the-art copier which proved invaluable in our editorial work as well as other aspects of the operation; updated and computerized the maintenance of subscription lists.

By studying postal regulations, we learned of ways to obtain reductions and instituted changes to qualify for them. The computer technology also enabled us to generate letters and/or invoices to subscribers to alert them when it was time to renew.

There was an even more radical revolution in setting type and preparing the paper for printing. Desktop publishing was becoming practical and economically feasible. Before then our method was to mark copy which came in, estimate space requirements, draw up a rough layout sheet to guide the typesetters, and trust in luck that the finished product would be close to what we intended. Sometimes we would have an attractive paper. Sometimes we wouldn't. Much of the final result was beyond our control. We worked as hard as we could all week, often late at night, to meet Friday night deadlines.

The board authorized me to investigate the possibility of setting our own type, using computers and the new desktop publishing technology, and furnishing camera-ready pages to the printer. Our study concluded that there would be three advantages to making the change: (1) we could control the quality and content right up to printing time; (2) we could reduce preparation time—we actually were able to move the deadline from Friday night back to Tuesday afternoon at 3 o'clock enabling us to have much fresher news faster; and (3) we could save money in production costs.

We took the plunge, with some reluctance on the part of the staff. They quickly adjusted and became proud of what we were accomplishing. Every news item was rewritten—even those from Nashville—in keeping with our style to make the stories more uniform and focused for our readers.

We upgraded the computers and printers to produce sharper, clearer, more reproducible copy. In cooperation with Walton Press we learned to add color. Almost $60,000 worth of high-tech equipment was added and paid for without borrowing money or purchasing anything on credit. And we did it while providing increases for the staff, absorbing rising costs in postage and production, and living within our income—thanks to Martha Berry. Slowly we stopped the drain on the permanent fund and started putting money back into it. We arranged to build the corpus back to $190,000 with my recommendation that $10,000 more be added from the year-end balance of $104,862, which was $21,000 more than Martha Berry had projected in October 1992.

Editor

My time as editor was sinfully gratifying—even when angry letters and phone calls kept me depressed for days. It seems that all my life I had been involved in communications as a marginal activity preparing for a full-time job as editor of the historic and prestigious *Wesleyan Christian Advocate*.

Making the Story Public

It helped me to be informed as news releases came from United Methodist News Service, all the denominational agencies, the ecumenical Religious News Service, and the secular press. In addition I received copies of all the other area and conference publications. We didn't have internet connections in the early years, but we did have access to weekly electronic releases via telephone computer hookups. Since superintendents, pastors, and others sent their bulletins and newsletters directly to me with information about the districts and charges and institutions in Georgia, I probably knew as much about what was happening in the church as anyone. I had opportunity, and made it a point, to keep informed.

My philosophy as editor was to seek news aggressively. I was unwilling to wait two or three weeks for someone to submit an important story. So we stayed in touch with sources, used the telephone and traveled to where newsworthy events were taking place. The mails were too slow.

Major elements each week were news, opinions, and features of interest to Georgia readers. My priorities for news to be included were conference, district, and local news in that order with stories from the general church being given less space. We used few full-length stories from United Methodist News Service (UMNS), Religious News Service (RNS) or any other news service. Our subscribers, we found, were interested in general church news, but not enough to read long full-page articles. We didn't ignore what was coming from the general church. We simply condensed, rewrote, and gave the stories a Georgia point of view. My watchwords were fairness, objectivity, and balance.

Weekly editorials gave me an outlet for speaking to the state. Some were humorous and whimsical. Others promoted conference programs. Occasionally they were pointed and provocative enough to generate "letters to the editor." I relished these. It was my policy never to answer critical attacks or to defend myself in the *Advocate*. After I had written a controversial story or editorial, I let it stand on its merit. The next week I moved on to another topic or emphasis. But I was careful to give space to anyone who wanted to write in disagreement. I thought it would be unfair to use pages and space I controlled to debate those who took a different view.

Sometimes the chairman or other members of the board took heat. Occasionally the bishops got blistering letters protesting something I had written. Once Bishop Ernest Fitzgerald defended me from an attack by a prominent bishop from the Northeastern Jurisdiction because of an editorial I had written in protest of the way a General Agency filled a vacancy. We had a brilliantly qualified, highly-respected candidate for the position from North Georgia. He followed the procedures outlined for applying, but his application was never even acknowledged. No person from the Southeast was even considered. I charged the search committee with bias against the Southeastern Jurisdiction and made a forceful case. It stung the chairman of the committee. The offended bishop wrote Bishop Fitzgerald demanding that I be reprimanded if not fired for daring to write such an article criticizing him. Bishop Fitzgerald fired a letter back—I learned months later about the correspondence—not only defending my right as an editor to voice what many people of the Southeast felt in attacking the work of the search committee but stating that he agreed with my assessment.

I was never afraid to express an opinion or to state a case even though I knew it would be controversial. It was not my intention to stir up opposition. I did feel obligated, however, to be faithful to my convictions as a Christian and as a United Methodist.

The Georgia Lottery

Probably the longest running fight I had during my years as editor was my opposition to bringing the lottery to Georgia. An analysis of the role the media played in the campaign has been released by Dyan Roth Cohen in a thesis written as a part of the requirements for a master's degree in the College of Journalism and Mass Communications, University of South Carolina, 2000. Newspaper coverage of the 1992 Georgia lottery campaign became the focal point of her study. Her analysis is based on approximately five hundred newspaper articles, editorials, and published letters to the editors. These came primarily from Georgia's largest circulation newspapers. Additional preparation included six in-depth interviews, three from professional leaders in the pro-lottery forces, and three volunteers from the anti-lottery forces. Ms. Cohen interviewed me about the role the United Methodists and the *Wesleyan Christian Advocate* played.

Pro-lottery forces were found to have superiority over their opponents in garnering news coverage, including photos, on the front pages of newspaper sections. Ms. Cohen attributed this to the unequal power and financial relationship between the media and high-ranking government officials with the governor as the dominant figure. She found, however, that extensive grass roots anti-lottery activity generated news coverage and large volumes of letters to the editor and facilitated editorial support. Front-page coverage represented the influence of the governor's clout in promoting his program. Editorials, op-ed columns, and letters to the editor, on the other hand, reflected the growing opposition among people around the state. In her review of the newspaper clippings she found that the voices opposing the lottery were heard much more loudly than those supporting it. Few in positions of leadership came forward in public to support the lottery.

The governor's pro-lottery efforts centered in paid advertising, primarily television, radio and newspaper ads. Intensive effort was made, Ms. Cohen reported, to influence newspapers editors.

Anti-lottery activities centered in the churches. Methodists and Baptists took the lead. We were quarterbacked by Dr. Emmett Henderson and the Georgia Council on Moral and Civic Concerns. A review of the *Advocate* stories on the issue revealed factual analysis from other states, rallies and efforts to get out the vote by churches around the state.

The campaign was heated and intense. Voter turnout was 72.7 percent of those registered to vote, the highest in modern Georgia election history, according to the Federal Election Commission' records. Except in metropolitan counties with large concentrations of population where the church has little influence, results show that the lottery lost in most counties. Counties with large cities swung the tide.

The anti-lottery forces were defeated by fewer than one hundred thousand votes out of the two million cast. This means that more than a million Georgians voted against it. Actually the "no" vote retained the lead throughout the day and into the late evening hours. Early the next day, lottery proponents achieved a slim lead due to late returns from the heavy metro precincts. They favored the lottery. One of the pastors of a large metropolitan church lamented the morning after, "If churches in the cities had known how close the lottery came to being defeated, perhaps we would have exerted a little more effort."

Few urban pastors took a stand from the pulpit or publicly against the lottery.

GEORGIA COMMUNICATION COUNCIL

In addition to charting the course as editor of the historic journal, I coordinated the comprehensive electronic and print media communication system as Executive Director of the Georgia United Methodist Communication Council.

Bishop Joel McDavid decided to take a look at the communications enterprise of Georgia. He appointed a task force to analyze what was being done and to make proposals for a comprehensive and coordinated communications network for the future. He wanted all of our efforts to be under one umbrella. He insisted that the Communications Committees of the two Annual Conferences Councils on Ministries, Good News Television, the *Wesleyan Christian Advocate*, and the Office of News and Media Relations be working in the same direction.

After naming the task force, he asked me to chair it.

I had been a member of the Protestant Radio and Television Center board of trustees for sixteen years. In that capacity I helped make decisions for its international radio program, the Protestant Hour, and launched it in television. Their resources and equipment made possible the communications workshops for seminary students and continuing education programs for pastors while I was at the Candler School of Theology. A part of my responsibility during the fifteen years at Emory was to write and edit publications and booklets and reports for the school and the workshops under the scrutiny of the Dean and Faculty and University Office of Publications.

We started Good News TV in Macon while I was district superintendent and published a Macon District edition of the *Wesleyan Christian Advocate*. While I was executive director of the SEJ Council on Ministries, our staff edited and published the first Jurisdictional newspaper, the *SEJ United Methodist* and worked with Don Wood to create a SEJ network of cable TV systems for Methodist programs.

In addition to serving on the General Commission of Communications as a representative of the General Council on Ministries, I worked four years on the task force to establish a United Methodist presence on network television.

When Bishop McDavid asked me to chair the task force to create a comprehensive and coordinated Georgia United Methodist Communications Council, I was delighted.

The task force began its work with three basic concepts: (1) that a statewide effort would be better than a conference emphasis because media markets cross conference lines; (2) a comprehensive program is better than splintered, overlapping approaches so there will be consistency; (3) a multiple utilization of material, which the GUMCC would make possible, would result in less wasted energy and more complete coverage.

Membership of the GUMCC was made up of representatives and staff from both Conference Councils on Ministries, both Conference Committees on Communication, the *Advocate* board and editor, and the Good News Television board and director.

Little did I know that within four years I would be asked to assume those duties along with being editor of the *Advocate*. Bill Holt was named Executive Director and put the program into action. What a fortunate day when he persuaded Alice Smith to accept the position in the Office of News and Media Relations. Her husband Walt worked with CNN news. Both of them were graduates of the University of Tennessee College of Journalism. They were staunch Methodists. She worked as religion editor for the Knoxville papers before coming to this position. Her work brought a professionalism and class that quickly won her respect from the church and media. Her writing for the *Advocate* and the secular press brought quick acclaim.

A Journey Beyond

Her report to the Annual Conferences one year indicated that she had written and released 108 stories to 143 newspapers over the state. There are 160 newsweeklies in Georgia plus the dailies. Almost a hundred of them requested that they be mailed regular releases about United Methodist events and developments. Every story went automatically to the AP and UP wire services in addition to United Methodist News Service for wider distribution. Our clipping service indicates wide use of these stories in local papers around the state.

Religion editors and other reporters rely upon Alice Smith for background briefing for stories they are covering.

A year before I retired from the *Advocate*, I resigned as Executive Director of the Georgia United Methodist Communications Council, though I was still a member as editor and director of print media. Alice Smith was chosen to succeed me. After my retirement in 1993, I offered to work two years with Don Wood and GNTV without pay in an effort to build support for the television ministry and promote GUMCC.

After I retired, the Rev. Mark Westmoreland, a member of the North Georgia Conference, was elected by the board to succeed me. He served four years, and was followed by the Rev. Mike Morgan who resigned after two years. Alice Smith, executive director of the Georgia United Methodist Communications Council, was named editor January 1, 2001. The board had requested her to serve four months as interim editor. The two conferences opted to discontinue the statewide communications council and to move in another direction.

Epilogue: Beyond the Party

When we got up the next morning after driving the new van home from the retirement party in Macon June 3, 1993, the euphoria of the night before lingered. Notwithstanding all the accolades, we still had work to do. Report on Annual Conferences proceedings had to be written for *Advocate* readers. Official retirement ceremonies were still ahead. There was no time for relaxing in memories.

It has been customary in South Georgia for retiring clergy and their spouses to parade across the platform, make some appropriate comments, shake hands with the Bishop to polite applause of the crowd, and leave. I prepared to speak briefly about my debt to the conference when my name was called. But I never got to speak.

As Bess and I approached the podium, instead of standing meekly aside, she stepped ahead of me and reached for the microphone.

She started speaking, with no expression on her face, and confided, "I have been coming to this Annual Conference for fifty years. I've never spoken on the floor. I've never voted. No Bishop, or delegate, has ever asked my advice, though at times they could have used my wisdom. But I've always wanted to say something profound to this conference. Today I decided to take advantage of this occasion to do it."

She paused, leaned into the microphone and said loudly, with a smile wreathing her face, "Something profound!"

The place exploded. The conference gave her a standing ovation. I never got to speak at my official retirement.

On the closing day of conference, June 17, 1993, I sat for a long while in the emptying auditorium of Wesleyan College. Suddenly, I was overwhelmed with the awareness that when Bishop Richard C. Looney had read the pastoral assignments for the coming year, my name was not included.

For the first time in fifty-two years, my name was not read out for an appointment in the South Georgia Conference.

Another had been named editor of the *Advocate*. I didn't have a place. I felt lost. When they finally turned the lights out and I had to leave, I didn't know what to do.

A few days later, I cleared my personal belongings from the office in the United Methodist Center, surrendered my keys to the new editor, Reverend Mark Westmoreland, just as the telephone rang demanding his attention.

Everybody was busy. I walked slowly down the hall to the elevator. It occurred to me that for the first time in seventeen years, I did not have keys to the United Methodist Center. This is what retirement is, I thought. No job. No keys. The telephone rings for somebody else.

THIS DAY MINISTRIES

In the report of the retirement dinner given me by the board of the *Wesleyan Christian Advocate* and the Georgia United Methodist Communications Council with over two hundred of our friends and family members in attendance, I recounted the generosity of Eddie Ray and Gwen Upchurch in shocking us with a gift of a new van. Their friendship and thoughtfulness for us embraces more than half a century.

They sensed how much I hated the thought of no longer having an official position where I could be useful in ministry and communications. So while we were vacationing with

Epilogue: Beyond the Party

them at Daytona Beach in August that summer, they suggested that we join them in shaping a religious component for the new television station they built in Baxley. The idea appealed to us, indeed, fascinated us. By the end of the year, we loaded half our furniture from our home in Conyers, and moved to Baxley again in January of 1994. We moved there first in November of 1947.

We got excited. Dreams multiplied. I had visions of centering my energy in retirement back among people whom I had served early in my ministry. The studio provided me an office and a staff. I went to work to learn some of the finer points of television production, like the proper use of lights, production of pure undistorted sound, using camera angles to create interesting pictures, and how to think visually and graphically. Television communication required a different mind-set from print.

We wanted to establish different types of religious programs, featuring sound Biblical and theological positions, with imaginative formats for contemporary viewers. We wanted to provide alternative opportunities in the Savannah television market area. We wanted to build a team committed to Christian television that could incorporate high-quality video production for use in teaching, and conduct revivals and seminars for local churches in the TV market area. We wanted to create an impressive library of religious music by local artists of the region, a collection of Christian witnesses and interviews, and a sizable resource of completed and edited programs. Most of this was done.

Our dreams were coming true for a television ministry.

We were on the way.

WUBI-TV is a full-powered, commercial television station licensed by the Federal Communication Commission. Our coverage in the Savannah television market area reached eighteen counties in southeast Georgia and all the way to Beaufort, South Carolina, through towers and relay transformers. Over a hundred thousand households had access to our programs through twenty-four cable-TV systems in addition to those who could receive us directly over their television sets from the towers.

A JOURNEY BEYOND

We scheduled daily devotions with pastors from surrounding counties. The list represented a broad spectrum of denominational and theological leaders reflective of the region. We broadcast two and a half hours of programs on Sunday plus a number of services from churches who bought airtime from the station. We originated, produced, edited, and telecast programs an hour and a half each day, Monday through Friday.

When I stopped to give an account of my stewardship from January 1, 1994, through August of 1998, the figures amazed me. They may not be totally accurate, but the overall picture indicates the scope of this ministry.

- There were 1,560 Morning Devotions by local pastors.
- There was a weekly Bible Study program in which we developed and produced 260 programs.
- Dr. Ralph Bailey, senior pastor of Trinity United Methodist Church in Savannah, produced 353 daily programs called *Downtown* which was broadcast at 9:30 A.M. and 11:00 P.M. Monday through Friday.
- Dr. Tab Smith, an educator and scholar, produced 190 weekly programs on *The Bible Speaks* for broadcasting twice a week.
- Reverend Charles Dennis, General Evangelist of the United Methodist Church from Columbus, Georgia, originated 158 weekly programs of *Music and The Word* in our studios.
- Dr. William H. Hinson, First United Methodist Church, Houston, Texas, preached for 312 Sunday worship services.
- Diane Highsmith, Monique Cothern and Reverend Curtis Tillman prepared weekly programs for many months to enrich our offering.
- Dr. Donald R. Wood furnished us 234 of the weekly editions of *Quest*, a thirty-minute program of United Methodist personalities and events produced by Good News TV in Macon and distributed by the Georgia United Methodist Communications Council.

Epilogue: Beyond the Party

- During this time, I produced 176 weekly programs of *Direction Check*, and several Bible Study series of 13 weeks each.

In addition, there were numerous mission programs and special features from the *Susanna Wesley Sacred Art Series* on location from the Trinity United Methodist Church in Savannah.

We were on the way to making the dreams come true.

Then came my "brain attack."

Things were not the same for me after November 1, 1995. Our wonderful staff and team carried my load as well as theirs during the months of my recuperation and therapy. Even after I returned, it was hard to concentrate more than a few minutes at a time.

I tried. The Lord knows I tried.

My disrupted brain circuits had not completely re-routed and would not always connect. My vocal cords were damaged. My voice wouldn't behave. My eyes were not dependable. Sagging energy levels prevented my following through on projects that needed my attention. I was unable to focus on the thinking and planning and creativity necessary to further the dreams. My inability to function and my embarrassing performance kept me depressed.

I finally had to admit that my days before the cameras were over. My ability to keep up with the fast-paced television world would not be recovered. I could no longer be an effective part of the dream.

I wept. With deep sadness over the loss, in August of 1998, Bess and I packed up our furniture and memories. Donnie Morris, a dear friend whose father J. P. Morris had moved us from Baxley to Woodstock in June of 1951, sent his truck and crew to take us back to our home in Conyers and another chapter.

COMMUNICATORS HALL OF FAME

While I was struggling in the summer of 1996, word came from Alice Smith that I had been elected to the United Methodist

Communicators Hall of Fame by the United Methodist Association of Communicators. The induction of three of us was scheduled for Washington, D.C., November 22, 1996. She and the Georgia United Methodist Communication Council had submitted the nomination, and she wondered if I would be able to come. Nothing except a funeral—my own—could have kept me away. What a surprise! What an honor! What a friend!

The nomination was endorsed by Bishop J. Lloyd Knox, Bishop Richard C. Looney, Bishop Mack B. Stokes, Dr. Donald R. Wood, and others.

"Ross is a consummate communicator with an interest in every possible communication tool that can help spread the gospel message. He has personally utilized these tools in his work for the kingdom throughout his active ministry and now in retirement," Alice Smith wrote.

The Nomination

The following is the entire text of the nomination document submitted to the Communicators Hall of Fame.

> The Georgia United Methodist Communication Council instituted a statewide communications award program in 1995 by presenting the Pioneer Award for Excellence in Communications to the Reverend G. Ross Freeman, whose imprint has been on every communications endeavor in the state and who has been a leader in other communications effort in the Southeastern Jurisdiction and the denomination.
>
> Now the council is nominating Dr. Freeman for the United Methodist Communications Hall of Fame in recognition of his long-term and wide-ranging communications ministry that has transcended many mediums—preaching, teaching, writing, editing, radio, newspapers, and television.
>
> He retired in 1993 but still remains active in the communications field and is responsible for several religious programs aired over WUBI-TV in Baxley, Ga. He is a man of extraordinary talent, commitment and drive, who is known throughout the church for his leadership in such areas as empowerment of the laity, United Methodist Men, and small

Epilogue: Beyond the Party

membership churches. This document focuses only on his contribution in the field of communications.

In only one position—editor of Georgia's weekly newspaper, the *Wesleyan Christian Advocate* (1986-93)—was his pastoral appointment implicitly in the field of communications. Yet he has made communications a priority whatever the appointment—whether serving as a local church pastor or district superintendent in the South Georgia Conference; as an academic administrator at Emory University's Candler School of Theology; or the executive secretary of the Southeastern Jurisdiction Council on Ministries.

During his fifteen years at Emory University (1954-69) he directed the first and succeeding communications workshop at the Candler School of Theology.

Perhaps his most visionary leadership came in moving the church into the use of television during a time when almost everything else in the church was print-oriented. But he has always embraced any option to communicate the gospel message. He has long been a lover of the printed word and is a prolific writer.

During his tenure as superintendent of the Macon District (1971-76) he learned that cable television was coming to the middle Georgia city. He realized what a wonderful evangelism tool it would be for the Macon District to operate one of the cable channels, and subsequently worked out the arrangements—providing funding through district resources and personal fund-raising efforts; arranging staff; borrowing equipment; and beginning operation in a house owned by the Inner City Ministry of the district. Today GNTV/WGNM-TV is a video production house utilized by the entire denomination and the only full-time broadcast television station related to the United Methodist Church.

During his years as district superintendent, however, his efforts were not restricted to television. He also started the Macon District edition of the *Wesleyan Christian Advocate* and developed a weekly radio program called "Spotlight," featuring United Methodist News over middle Georgia's most popular radio station every Sunday morning following the 9:00 CBS news. Also during these years in South Georgia he wrote weekly columns and book reviews for three daily newspapers.

When Dr. Freeman left the Macon District to become executive director of the Southeastern Jurisdiction Council on Ministries (January 1, 1977–86), he continued his leadership in communications, including such endeavors as:

- Developing the SEJ Television Network, which provided five thirty-minute United Methodist programs to a network of cable channels across the jurisdiction;
- Spearheading the "Proclaim the Word" campaign across the jurisdiction, a highly successful media campaign that included television and radio spots, billboards and newspaper slicks;
- Inaugurating and editing a jurisdictional newspaper;
- Serving on the Protestant Radio and Television Board of Trustees for sixteen years and providing oversight for the "Protestant Hour" radio program.

It was during this time that he was called by Bishop Joel McDavid to chair a blue-ribbon task force to study communications in his home state and design a statewide communications ministry. As a result of that work, the Georgia United Methodist Communications Council was established in 1983 to provide overall coordination to communication programs in the state. During his years as editor of the *Advocate*, he also served as executive director of GUMCC.

Dr. Freeman's genius has not been limited to spinning great dreams since he also has the practicality and tenacity to turn dreams into reality. These attributes were dramatically seen during his seven years as editor of the *Wesleyan Christian Advocate*, his last appointment in an illustrious career.

In the words of the Reverend Don Kea, chairman of the *Advocate* board at the time of the retirement party, "He came to the post at a crucial time in its history. The times demanded change. Rising postal and printing costs were causing many problems; there was an erosion of

Epilogue: Beyond the Party

subscribers; financial support was shrinking. The age of the computer had arrived, and it was time to do something in that area."

Soon after his arrival, he led the newspaper into computerization. He taught himself the skills of desktop publishing so that the newspaper could be produced in-house, with the exception of printing and mailing, at dramatic savings in cost and time. Along with hands-on involvement in the publication of the newspaper, he also fiercely maintained the *Advocate*'s independent editorial status and took an aggressive stand on many controversial issues. Sometimes that raised the ire of readers, but it also "caused us to think."

In addition to improving the layout and content of the newspaper, he also made it financially stable.

In addition to his leadership in television and newspaper communications, he designed and wrote a number of program publications that were widely utilized in the church, such as the Lenten series, *Forty Days of Prayer for Five Persons*. Always a strong supporter of United Methodist Men, he is the author of several programs published by *The Upper Room* for men such as *A Spiritual Journey for Men* and more recently *A Transforming Journey for Men*. A series of biblical statements he did in 1993 to set the tone and theme for the International Congress of United Methodist Men at Purdue University was printed and made into a video guide for use in local churches with men.

When Dr. Freeman retired in 1993, he continued his work in communications, now overseeing religious programs for WUBI-TV, a Savannah DMA commercial station with studios located in Baxley, Ga. He suffered a stroke in late 1995, and has undergone some surgery and therapy, but he is now back at work in Baxley.

My Response in Washington

On November 22, 1996, I was officially inducted into the Communicators Hall of Fame. The text of my acceptance speech follows.

A Journey Beyond

Thank you, Alice Smith, my colleagues in the United Methodist Association of Communicators, members of my family and others who have gathered for this occasion. Please know how moved I am tonight.

Looking back, it hardly seems that seventy-three years have been enough time to do all that you have recounted. The journey has been wonderful to be sure, and swift, but this year has been difficult and slow. My moods have swung wildly between gratitude and discouragement; between elation that I am alive and grieving that some of my capacities are diminished. These swift mood changes, I have learned, are one of the residual results of a stroke.

October has been especially rough. As the first of November approached, the anniversary of my "brain attack" (as some are now calling strokes), I was struggling with depression and doubt.

In one of these down times, Alice Smith called.

She called to say that you had voted me the highest distinction in United Methodist Communications.

I am grateful to the Georgia United Methodist Communications Council, though a bit embarrassed, for the extravagant language of my nomination.

I have always known the importance of communication in the church whether I was a pastor of small churches, a pastor with resources, a district superintendent, academic administrator at the Candler School of Theology, the executive director of the Southeastern Jurisdictional Council, and even as an editor.

In every assignment I have been able to find some resources, bring people together and open doors for communications. In several instances we started projects without authorization, budget or personnel. It has been my role to function as an enabler, to open doors, to give access, to empower so that others could develop. I am here tonight, not because of my own achievements, but because I have been in a position sometimes to help others achieve.

Epilogue: Beyond the Party

Under any circumstances, I would have been thrilled by this recognition. But at this particular time, you can not begin to imagine what the honor means to me.

Believe me, I shall hug your generosity close to my heart and cherish it forever.

To brighten the memory even more, you linked me with two giants, Bruno Caliandro and Nelson Price, in the UMAC Hall of Fame class of 1996.

All of you who work professionally in church communications are heroes to me. For the most part your work is underfunded and underappreciated.

One of my astute friends from the opulence of commercial television observed, "In an industry that is intolerant of pinching pennies, the church is trying to pinch pennies."

I've seen creative visions for a brighter future in communications shattered by budgetary restraints at every level.

In spite of such disappointments, you work, uncomplainingly and competently, to "tell the church's story" with integrity. You do a good job. That makes you a hero in my book.

Among my personal heroes whom I want to thank publicly tonight is my wife Bess, whose habit of happiness and light-hearted humor have filled my life with unexpected delights for more than fifty-four years. It's never dull at our house. Her tolerance of my clutter, with notes scratched on napkins and scraps of paper, scattered over every table in the house, especially during creative periods, mark her patience.

And this year her gentle nursing and cheerful spirit during my recuperation has been a special benediction from God. I want to acknowledge her presence tonight along with members of our family who could come.

Alice mentioned my work at present with WUBI-TV in the Savannah DMA. It is not national or even regional in scope, but it reaches eighteen counties over the air in southeast Georgia (plus several in South Carolina) and a network of twenty-four CATV systems. We have put together a talented and committed team that we call This Day Ministries.

At present we broadcast twenty programs a week, all but two of which we produce in our studios. Among them are a weekly series for youth, missions, Christian music and commentary, systematic Bible study on *Mighty Acts* and *The Bible Speaks*, *Direction Check* for people who don't go to church, our Georgia United Methodist program *Quest*, a South Georgia favorite Bill Hinson from First Methodist Houston, *Downtown* with Ralph Bailey from Trinity UMC in downtown Savannah, *Scripture Alive* and *Why We Care*, two thirty-minute programs from UMCom, and many specials.

We are experimenting with sixty-second "Gospo-mercials" and "Scenic Spots with Quiet Music" during commercial breaks through the day. We use all the UMCom and GUMCC spots as they become available.

At least in one tiny corner of this vast nation, we are trying to fulfill the dream of having "A United Methodist Presence" on television, proclaiming a positive word of hope . . . and influence.

Thanks for tonight, for countless words of encouragement, and for the pleasure of walking among you.

MY NEW ROLE

Can you imagine? A boy from the wrong side of the tracks in Tennille, growing up on the edges, receiving such attention?

When I reached the three-quarters of a century mark five years into retirement, I realize that I am now the oldest person in my parents' family. That exalted age, though still young by contemporary measures, should have some prerogatives. It had been some years since our extended family was together. We had not had such an occasion since mother died. So as the patriarch of the family, I claimed my responsibility and called a reunion. To my surprise, they came.

Epilogue: Beyond the Party

Our three children presenting us to guests at the beginning of festivities for our Golden Wedding Anniversary, June 15, 1992. Left to right: Rev. George R. Freeman Jr., master of ceremonies, Merrie Freeman Posey, and Joye Freeman Hancock.

It occurred to me that a patriarch has some responsibility for preserving the family memories, keeping alive the family stories, maintaining family traditions, transmitting family values to the young and in-laws marrying into to the clan. With so much in modern society working against the family, somebody needs to provide for the continuation of the heritage lest we lose our roots.

When I retired I was the active member of the South Georgia Conference with the longest record of service. It had not occurred to me until I was reminded by Reverend Alvis A. Waite Jr. that I had inherited the honor from him the year he retired. It was a sobering thought.

After my stroke I was no longer able to do many of the things I had done. It was depressing not to be able to preach with fluency and clarity. Nor was I able to participate in the counsels of the church with any degree of satisfaction. My mental functions are slowed down. Crowds and confusion

Bess and I celebrating fifty years of marriage.

still bother me. I can still work with small groups, and if people will be patient, I can carry on a spirited one-on-one conversation. But I am limited. I had to be reminded in one of my down times that, "God is not limited, just because I am!"

Then came the revelation. The focus of my ministry has shifted. We moved from Baxley back to our home in Conyers. We have identified with the Briarcliff United

Epilogue: Beyond the Party

Methodist Church where our son George is pastor. Members have been welcoming and gracious. They have even accepted me as volunteer staff person to direct the Prayer Ministry. It is very fulfilling, sitting under the ministry of my son and living within easy reach of my children, grandchildren, and great-grandchildren.

Since I can no longer do what I had done, a new assignment has been given. Now I have the ministry of affirmation, of encouragement, and of intercession. That I can still do—in anticipation of a journey beyond.

About the Author

Dr. G. Ross Freeman has championed the ministry of the laity and given strong support to the work of United Methodist Men throughout his career. He researched and wrote the programs *A Spiritual Journey for Men*, *A Transforming Journey for Men*, and *A Ministry Journey for Men*.

For thirteen of the fifty-two years he was under appointment, Dr. Freeman served as a pastor and for five years as superintendent of the Macon District in the South Georgia Conference.

For two years, he directed the thirteen-state interdenominational and interracial Church Development Program sponsored by Emory University and the Sears-Roebuck Foundation.

In addition, he was associate dean and director of Supervised Ministry at Emory University's Candler School of Theology for fifteen years, executive director of the nine-state Southeastern Jurisdictional Council on Ministries for ten years, and editor of the *Wesleyan Christian Advocate* for seven years. He retired in 1993.